Management
and
Gender

Management
and
Gender

ISSUES AND ATTITUDES

Margaret Foegen Karsten

 PRAEGER

Westport, Connecticut
London

Library of Congress Cataloging-in-Publication Data

Karsten, Margaret Foegen.
   Management and gender : issues and attitudes / Margaret Foegen
Karsten.
    p. cm.
   Includes bibliographical references and index.
   ISBN 0–275–94501–4 (pbk. : alk. paper)
    1. Women executives—United States. 2. Sex role in the work
environment—United States.
   HD6054.4.U6K37   1994
   658.4'0082—dc20   93–17666

British Library Cataloguing in Publication Data is available.

A hardcover edition of *Management and Gender* is available from the
Quorum Books imprint of Greenwood Publishing Group, Inc.
(ISBN 0–89930–812–0)

Library of Congress Catalog Card Number: 93–17666
ISBN: 0–275–94501–4

First published in 1994

Praeger Publishers, 88 Post Road West, Westport, CT 06881
An imprint of Greenwood Publishing Group, Inc.

Printed in the United States of America

The paper used in this book complies with the
Permanent Paper Standard issued by the National
Information Standards Organization (Z39.48–1984).

10 9 8 7 6 5

To R. J. K.
M. C. F. & J. H. F.
with gratitude

Contents

Figures and Tables

Preface

Examining issues pertinent to women and racial minorities in management is not just a good idea; it is imperative for business. Subtle or blatant put-downs or mindsets that view any group as inferior are inconsistent with the goal of maintaining global competitiveness by producing high-quality goods and services.

Such behaviors and attitudes may contribute to the underutilization of people's talents. They also may lead to costly human resource problems such as turnover, absenteeism, and reduced morale.

On the positive side, greater diversity within management may yield benefits in terms of innovation and creativity. Due to varying perspectives, people with different backgrounds might be more likely than a homogeneous group to generate new ideas or novel solutions to problems.

All managers must become familiar with perspectives other than their own to lead an increasingly diverse workforce. Executives of both sexes must work together as equals for the good of their organization.

When women and men are regarded as equals in all occupations and when organizations' actions support their realization that equal opportunity makes good business sense, special emphasis on gender issues no longer will be needed. Until then, special attention to such issues is vital during a possibly lengthy transition to that new reality.

Management
and
Gender

1 The Management Process and a Feminist Approach to Management

OBJECTIVES

After studying this chapter you should be able to:

1. Define management in two different ways.
2. Summarize what is involved in the management functions of planning, organizing, directing, and controlling.
3. Explain Mintzberg's managerial roles.
4. Explain ways in which the nature of managerial work is changing.
5. Explain three feminist ideologies.
6. Compare and contrast a hypothetical organization designed according to feminist principles and an entity with an organic structure.
7. Explain two features common to all feminist ideologies.

Before gender issues in management can be discussed, a basic understanding of the management process is needed. Theorists have not agreed on one definition of management. Mary Parker Follett described it as the art of getting things done through people, while others have called it a process of planning, organizing, directing, and controlling an organization's activities to achieve its goals. A manager's job has been compared to that of a symphony orchestra conductor. The manager

tries to maintain a melodious performance in which the contributions of the various instruments are coordinated and sequenced, patterned and paced, while the orchestra members are having various personal difficulties, stage hands are moving music stands, alternating excessive heat and cold are creating audience and instrument problems, and the sponsor or the concert is insisting on irrational changes in the program. (Sayles, 1964)

MANAGEMENT FUNCTIONS

Since the early 1900s, planning, organizing, directing, and controlling have been recognized management functions. Each will be described briefly in turn, though managers actually perform some of these functions simultaneously.

Planning involves setting goals and developing strategies and programs to achieve them. Planning may be long-term or short-term, strategic or tactical. Decision making, though necessary in all phases of management, is usually studied as part of the planning function.

Organizing means structuring resources to achieve goals. Resources available to the company include equipment, money, and employees. Departmentalization and centralization or decentralization of authority are issues of concern, as is job design. Staffing, which includes human resource planning, job analysis, recruitment, selection, orientation, and training, is often considered part of the organizing function.

Directing, or leading, means getting employees to work willingly toward organizational goals. It includes communication, motivation, and an ability to deal with formal and informal groups.

Controlling means ensuring that plans are achieved by taking corrective action, if necessary. Ratio analysis and budgets are financial control tools, and performance appraisal is used in human resource control. The word control sometimes has negative connotations because people associate it with overly strict external control rather than self-control, which is preferable.

MANAGERIAL ROLES

The division of management into basic functions for study purposes was largely accepted until the 1970s. At that time, Henry Mintzberg (1975) criticized the functional approach. He claimed that it did not adequately describe what managers do and preferred to examine three administrative roles—interpersonal, informational, and decisional.

Each of those roles can be subdivided. Figurehead, leader, and liaison duties are associated with the *interpersonal role*. The figurehead role is symbolic and might involve attending an employee's wedding or greeting visitors to the organization. The leader role is similar to the management function called directing, described earlier. One who acts as a liaison coordinates activities of different internal units or makes contacts with external constituency groups.

Informational roles include monitor, disseminator, and spokesperson.

Monitoring means environmental scanning, and disseminating information is distributing it to employees who otherwise would not have access. Serving as spokesperson means presenting the organization's position on an issue to outside groups.

Disturbance handler, resource allocator, negotiator, and entrepreneur are the four *decisional roles*. Despite the best planning, crisis situations occur. When managers respond to them or to other events beyond their control, they are disturbance handlers. As resource allocators, managers decide who gets what. Negotiators resolve differences, and the entrepreneurial role involves developing innovative projects to improve one's unit or respond to changing conditions. When the entrepreneurial role is carried out within an existing organization, it has been called "intrapreneuring" (Pinchot, 1985).

Just as Mintzberg had criticized the traditional management functions because they did not describe what managers do, others in turn derided his approach. They accused him of recording individual activities instead of grouping them according to their purpose. Mintzberg supposedly viewed activities as if they were pieces of a jigsaw puzzle. He was advised to view them, not as individual pieces, but as interconnected (Snyder and Glueck, 1980).

Rosabeth Moss Kanter, an important theorist whose contributions will be discussed in chapter 3, is one of many who believe that managerial work is changing dramatically. Because of restructuring during the 1980s, the organizational hierarchy has been flattened. In the future, hierarchical position will be a less important measure of success in most firms than expertise and connections (Kanter, 1989). Kanter envisions organizations in which the distinctions between managers and employees will diminish, due to a more professional, better educated workforce. Though she does not label specific roles as Mintzberg did, Kanter describes the content of all except figurehead and spokesperson. She most likely would expect the importance of Mintzberg's roles to shift. For example, her statement that horizontal ties will replace vertical suggests that one interpersonal role, namely liaison, will become more crucial.

Leadership, another interpersonal role, will remain important, but motivational methods may change. Fewer traditional rewards will be available, so executives will have to be more innovative. They might motivate employees by allowing them to choose their own projects or by providing training and development at company expense. As leaders, effective managers will operate more as coaches (Harari and Mukai, 1990).

Environmental scanning, or monitoring, will become more vital at every level. Another informational role, disseminator, will be less important because employees will not depend on managers for all their data. They will be more likely to have direct access.

Two of Mintzberg's decisional roles will become indispensable, while two might decline in importance. Entrepreneurial activity, which seeks out and develops opportunities, will be essential as will the art of negotiation. The role of the disturbance handler will change from that of cop to facilitator. Because the manager will not be the sole resource allocator, that role may be less vital (Kanter, 1989).

DEFINITIONS OF FEMINISM

Just as there is no one definition of management, there is no universally appealing definition of feminism. The term has negative connotations to some, evoking images of leftover 1960s demonstrators. To others feminism is a belief that each individual is a valuable human being in his or her own right. Individuals are to be valued as ends in themselves not solely because of what they can produce. According to feminism, women's lives have intrinsic worth. Women are to be valued simply because they exist, not because of status derived through associations with men.

All feminist ideologies question the status quo regarding society and women's roles. Past practices and modes of thinking are not accepted automatically but are subject to scrutiny. As Sheila Ruth (1980) states, "Feminism may be a perspective, a world view, a political theory, a spiritual focus, or a kind of activism." It does not esteem so-called masculine behaviors, such as dominance, at the expense of supposedly feminine behaviors, such as compassion. Feminism rejects negative cultural images of women as weak or incompetent, but affirms their ability to be strong, intelligent, and ethical. Both sexes can be feminists; the term refers to a belief system rather than to traits that have been labelled as feminine.

FEMINIST IDEOLOGIES

Marxist, socialist, radical, and women's rights feminism are separate ideologies. Diverse views exist within these categories. *Marxist feminists* believe that ownership of private property oppresses certain classes. The hierarchical nature of the nuclear family is harmful to women, according to Marxists. To the extent that men are still considered heads of the households, Marxists would see them as the bourgeoisie and women as the working class, or proletariat. Marxists inaccurately predicted that sexism would end when women left the home and joined the workforce (Davis, 1984).

Socialist feminists argue that historically, women were kept out of the labor force due to childbirth. Like Marxists, socialists feel that both gender role and class oppress women. Some socialist feminists believe those working in the home should be paid a living wage for raising a future generation of workers and for enabling others to be employed for pay (Davis, 1984).

Radical feminists think it is insufficient to integrate women into existing organizations that are inherently hierarchical and bureaucratic. They consider such institutions fundamentally flawed (Ferguson, 1984) and favor transforming them into more equalitarian arrangements.

Some radical feminists, such as Shulamith Firestone (Deckard, 1983), believe it is necessary to separate reproduction from sex to liberate women. They feel childbearing limits women's opportunity and that women should "either stop bearing children altogether or be separate from men . . . to move away from basically oppressive institutions" (Davis, 1984).

Women's rights feminists start with the premise that all people are created equal. Advocates of women's rights feminism want women to have equal opportunity. They do not think sex-based division of labor is relevant now, though it once may have served a purpose. Women's rights feminists do not wish to abolish the family but feel the nuclear family may oppress women. In their view, "when women are free to be full, equal human beings, the family will no longer be oppressive" (Deckard, 1983). A nonsexist society can be achieved by working within the present system, according to these moderates.

A HYPOTHETICAL "FEMINIST" ORGANIZATION

An ideal organization, according to feminists, would have much in common with an *organic structure*. Participative decision making, few rules, and lateral communications characterize organic organizations (Burns and Stalker, 1961). Interaction is the preferred method of resolving conflict, and messages communicated are more likely to be advice and counsel than orders. In an organic structure, power is based on expertise and is not concentrated at the top. Feminists try to eliminate position-based power distinctions and refer to leaders as facilitators or coordinators. To them, a leader is at the center of a network, not at the top of a pyramid (Ferguson, 1984).

All these features would appeal to feminists, but the bottom-line goal of profitability might not. Abandoning profit as the ultimate criterion against which success is measured might seem like blasphemy to the business community, but the idea should not be dismissed automatically. A firm that produces goods or services for which there is a real need, and that creates an excellent work environment in which employees are respected and treated equally, may very well be profitable. Profit making would be a by-product under this scheme, but financial results might equal or surpass results of firms pursuing profit directly. The difference would be in the underlying philosophy.

In addition to equal treatment, the hypothetical feminist organization would allow people to balance work and family or personal life by offering flexible schedules, flexible benefits, and family leave. Cooperation and teamwork would be emphasized, yet each individual would be treated as an unique human being.

Dysfunctional win-lose competition, in which co-workers vie for a limited number of rewards, would be discouraged. Instead, competition with oneself would be encouraged. There would be less need for external controls under a system of genuine worker self-management (Ferguson, 1984). If discipline were necessary as part of the control function, it would be corrective, not punitive.

Ferguson (1984) discusses the importance of moving toward a vertical division of labor in which each person is responsible for both the creative and the mundane. She says, "A feminist restructuring of work entails rejection of the hierarchical division of labor ... and a reintegration of planning and performance of tasks." This restructuring resembles *job enrichment*, which gives workers more responsibility for both preparatory and decision-making activities. It adds tasks at different responsibility levels as compared to *job enlargement*, which adds activities requiring similar types of skills. Enrichment is a vertical division of labor, while enlargement is horizontal. Both techniques are used by many organizations to increase employee satisfaction, but feminists would prefer enrichment.

Feminists might be receptive to skill-based compensation, in which employees are paid for what they know instead of for what they do. This encourages workers to learn more about their own job, co-workers' jobs, and the total process involved in providing a good or service. Employers who have tried skill-based pay say that it gives them a more flexible workforce (Kanter, 1987).

Many feminists abhor bureaucratic, or *mechanistic organizational structures*. At the extreme, mechanistic organizations are the opposite of organic. Authority is concentrated at the top, there are many rules, and downward communication is used to give directions or orders. External controls are imposed, and work is highly specialized. Table 1.1 summarizes features of the organic, mechanistic, and proposed feminist structures.

Ferguson (1984) criticizes the notion that bureaucratic, or mechanistic, organizations are philosophically neutral. She says they view workers as objects and are perverted in the sense that rules that were supposed to be means to an end become ends in themselves. To her, bureaucracies produce a fragmented work process, isolated workers, and depersonalization of remaining communication channels. Individual deficiencies, rather than factors inherent in the structure of the institution, are thought to cause employee problems.

The feminist bent in favor of organic structures already has been explained. If feminists advocated these structures in all situations, they would contradict contingency principles, which state that the best organizational structure, or leadership style, depends on the situation. Organic structures are considered more effective in dynamic, turbulent environments. Mechanistic or bureaucratic structures might be preferable in stable, predictable environments.

Table 1.1
Features of Mechanistic, Organic, and Proposed Feminist Organizational Structures

Features	Mechanistic	Organic	Feminist
Specialization of tasks	Highly specialized	Low specialization	Low specialization
Power	At the top	Based on skill wherever competence exists	Based on expertise, not position
Conflict resolution	By superior	By interaction	By interaction
Rules	Many	Few	Few
Type of communication	Downward lateral	Upward, downward, lateral	Upward, downward lateral
Content of communication	Directions orders	Advice, counsel	Advice, counsel
Decision making	Unilateral At the top	Participative	Participative
Control*	External	Internal	Internal, self
Role of profit*	Ultimate goal	Ultimate goal	By-product
Loyalty	To organizational system	To work group	To work group
Appropriate environment	Stable	Dynamic	Any environment

*These features were not mentioned in the original work by Bums and Stalker.

The feminist approach assumes that most employees are motivated by needs such as esteem or self-actualization. Further, it presumes that employees subscribe to McGregor's Theory Y, meaning that they like to work and want to do their best. This perspective may not address problems of motivating employees who view work as a necessary evil and whose main concern is to earn enough money to satisfy basic survival and security needs.

SUMMARY

Management is "the art of getting things done through people." It is a process of planning, organizing, directing, and controlling to achieve an organization's goals. Mintzberg believes it is more accurate to describe management in terms of informational, interpersonal, and decisional roles. His critics say Mintzberg lost sight of the management functions because he examined isolated activities.

The nature of executive work is changing. Distinctions between managers and workers are blurring. Future administrators may have to be more concerned with leader, liaison, entrepreneurial, and negotiator roles.

There are many different types of feminism, some of which are Marxist, socialist, radical, and moderate. All these ideologies question the status quo and value women in and of themselves. Males or females may espouse feminist beliefs.

Management approaches consistent with feminism would have many features of organic structures. Feminist organizations would view profit as a natural by-product of attempts to produce high-quality goods or services for which a real need exists. The work environment in a feminist organization would value each individual's unique contribution and would have a culture and employee benefits enabling workers to balance careers and family or personal life.

DISCUSSION QUESTIONS

1. Which do you think better describes the nature of management, the functional approach, involving planning, organizing, directing, and controlling, or the roles identified by Mintzberg? Why?

2. Interview both a female and male management professor at a college or university or a male and female manager above the supervisory level in an organization with fifty or more employees. Ask them how they think the nature of managerial work and the race and sex composition of managers as a group are changing. Write a one-page summary of the interview.

3. Are the concepts of feminism and business management incompatible, or is there some common ground? Explain.

4. Is a feminist approach to management feasible in existing businesses? If so, explain. If not, what, if anything, could be done to make it feasible?

2 Managerial Women: Yesterday and Today

OBJECTIVES

After studying this chapter you should be able to:

1. Give examples of women who performed management functions in the United States before 1920.
2. Explain the impact of World War II on women who wished to become managers.
3. State two possible reasons why more women have not advanced to higher management levels.
4. Explain the importance of Hennig and Jardim's study reported in *The Managerial Woman* (1977).
5. Explain why women but not men were accused of bailing out of corporations in the mid-1980s.
6. Explain criticisms of the two-track system proposed by Felice Schwartz in the late 1980s.
7. List four major groups considered "people of color" and explain the diversity that exists within each group.
8. Explain the "pipeline theory," the myth of the double advantage, and biculturalism.

It is fitting to recall women's administrative experience throughout history. The purpose is not only to impart previously unknown information, but also to instill a sense of pride regarding accomplishments of women and people of color. Many succeeded despite tremendous odds, and they may be appropriate role models for those struggling with management careers today.

It is beyond the scope of this book to recount fully the history of women in management. This account will begin, arbitrarily, at 1900. Those who wish to begin their study near the beginning of civilization may wish to consult Colwill's (1982) description of possible origins of sex-based division of labor.

This historical perspective on women managers is sketchy because no comprehensive source on the topic is available. Books about the history of women at work have been written. Those interested in women's managerial roles, however, must extract information from many publications.

Incorporating the experience of women of color in management remains a challenge. Hispanics, Asians, Native- and African-Americans typically are considered people of color. Within each of these groups, there is more diversity than similarity. Despite recent emphasis on integrating experiences of people of color in college courses, information is not readily available. Expanding the definition of managers to include the entrepreneur-turned-executive and government and academic leaders is more fruitful. Even using this approach, however, background on women of color can be gleaned only by reading dissertations or tracking biographical data.

The fact that women of color hold less than 5% of management positions in U.S. firms with over 100 employees (Nkomo, 1988), suggests a need to explore conditions that have hindered their progress. Some will be discussed in this chapter.

MANAGERIAL WOMEN 1900 TO PRESENT

The accomplishments of Madam C. J. Walker were remarkable. Born Sarah Breedlove, a child of former slaves, Walker literally made a fortune on hair care products targeted to African-Americans. From humble beginnings as a laundress who mixed hair conditioners (which were really straighteners, but were never called that) on a back burner (Nelson, 1987), Walker became proprietor of a major Indianapolis cosmetics manufacturing firm. At peak production in 1917 it employed 3,000 and had annual sales of $500,000 (Doyle, 1989). An entrepreneur-turned-manager, Madam Walker was the first American black woman to become a millionaire through her own efforts.

Madam C. J. Walker provided career opportunities for black women in sales and as beauty culturists. She said, "I have made it possible for many colored women to abandon the washtub for a more pleasant and profitable occupation." Her recommendation was that "the girls and women of our race must not be afraid to take hold of business enterprise" (Doyle, 1989).

Sarah Bagley and Margaret Dreier Robbins performed management functions within labor organizations during the 1800s and early 1900s. A factory worker, Bagley was president of the Female Labor Reform Association, which advocated the 10-hour work day during a time when the 12-hour work day was the norm. She was called an agitator, public speaker, political activist, and labor organizer. Though never referred to as a manager, Bagley skillfully implemented management functions.

Setting a goal is the first step in planning, and Sarah Bagley's was to establish a 10-hour work day. Her strategy was to petition the legislature. Bagley deployed human resources, the only type at her disposal, to achieve the objective. This is part of the organizing function.

Margaret Dreier Robbins was president of the National Women's Trade Union League of America (NWTUL), established in 1903. The NWTUL wanted an 8-hour work day and was also the only national organization urging working women to join trade unions. During Dreier Robbins' term, the NWTUL set up a training program for women desiring to become union leaders.

Very few women assumed leadership positions in politics in the early 1900s, mainly because universal women's suffrage was not obtained until 1920. Despite this, Jeanette Rankin, elected in 1916, was the first female member of the U.S. House of Representatives. She was from Montana, which granted women the right to vote in 1914. Other early congresswomen included Edith Nourse Rogers, Mary Norton, and Florence Kahn.

The percentage of employed women who were professionals was small in the early 1900s. Most professional women were nurses or teachers. This did not change until World War II, though the total number of employed women jumped in the 1930s. Women took jobs because of economic necessity brought on by the Depression.

Because many employable males were at war, there was a labor shortage during World War II. Women were actively recruited for occupations from which they had been excluded previously. One such occupation was management. Women began as first-line supervisors, and in 1947, 5% of all employed women were managers.

During the 1940s and 1950s, the number of women in high-ranking business positions was small. A *Fortune* article (Hamill, 1956) named the famous seven, only four of whom could be classified as managers. One of those was Dorothy Shaver, president of Lord & Taylor, who earned $110,000 in 1945. This was the highest recorded salary for any American woman until that time, but only one-fourth of what a male executive would have earned. Oveta Culp Hobby, publisher of the *Houston Post* and former colonel and cabinet member, Bernice Fitz-Gibbon, advertising executive at Macy's and Gimbel's, and Elsie Murphy, president of S. Stroock & Company, a textile firm, were the other three managers included in the named seven.

In the 1950s, some have the mistaken impression that all women who had entered the labor force during World War II retreated to the home. Many did, but others had been changed forever. They enjoyed the new work

Table 2.1

Percentage of All Employed Who Are Managers by Sex and Women as a Percent of All Managers, 1970–1991

	1970	1978	1983	1991
of all employed females who were managers	4.5	6.0	9.7	13.8
of all employed males who were managers	14.2	15.0	12.6	13.4
of all managers who were women	22.0	28.0	32.4	40.6

(1984 Statistical Abstract of the United States, Tables 692 and 693, U.S. Bureau of Labor Statistics, Employment and Earnings, 1986; Statistical Abstract of the United States, Tables 629 and 654, 1992.)

they had learned and were reluctant to leave. Also, even during the height of the postwar baby boom, women had begun to realize that they would live an average of 40 years after their youngest child started school. According to Kaledin (1984), "seeing themselves as childbearers who would live long, active lives, women [of the 1950s] began to understand that they had special needs, that society might do much more to make good use of their talents. To underestimate their power was to underestimate their capacity for change."

1959 was a milestone year for women aspiring to be managers. That was when females were first admitted to a Harvard-Radcliffe business program, but their diplomas were still issued by Radcliffe. Women were not admitted to the Harvard Master of Business Administration (MBA) program on an equal basis with men until 1963 (Billard, 1990). An MBA from Harvard or another Ivy League school generally has provided entry to careers in the nation's most prestigious firms.

Many factors led to the passage of laws making employment discrimination based on sex and race illegal in the 1960s. These included technological advances, demographic and attitude shifts, rising education levels, and changes in the social environment.

Because of these changes, more women decided to pursue nontraditional careers, including management. Table 2.1 shows changes in the percentage of all employed women who were managers in selected years from 1970 to 1991, and the percentage of all managers during the same time frame who were women. Percentages of all employed men who were managers are provided for comparison.

Though percentages have improved, numbers alone may be misleading. This is because women classified as managers/administrators tend to be relatively low-level managers such as retail store buyers and restaurant, cafeteria, and bar managers.

As women advanced in management, more were asked to be members of corporate boards of directors. About 6% of newly elected board members were women in the 1970s. One problem female board members faced in that decade was tokenism. Joan Ganz Cooney, who headed a nonprofit organization in the 1970s, said that, though others seemed to value her contributions, she never would have been asked to serve on corporate boards if she had been a man.

In the mid-1980s, only 4% of corporate board members of major U.S. firms were female (Hellwig, 1985). However, by the end of the decade, "the corporation that [didn't] have at least one woman on its board [was] sending out a clear, if inadvertent statement: Women are not wanted at top management levels" (Dusky and Zeitz, 1988). By 1992, 60% of all boards had at least one female member (Hellwig, 1992), and 133 of the top 1,000 U.S. firms had two or more women on its board ("Women on Boards," 1992).

During the 1970s and 1980s, women progressed in management—to a point. They gained business experience, earned MBAs in record numbers, planned their careers, found mentors, formed networks, and learned to be assertive. Strategies involving such individual, behavioral change may have helped women begin management careers, but were insufficient to propel them to the executive suite. The title of a 1980 article, "Profiles of the 801 Men and One Woman at the Top," (Boone and Johnson, 1980), illustrated the problem. The lone woman, Katharine Graham of the *Washington Post*, freely admitted that family connections helped her obtain her position.

During the 1980s the number of women in the highest corporate posts grew slowly. From 1982 to 1987, the number of women with the title of president of U.S. firms rose only 1%, but there was a 6% increase in the number of females who were executive vice presidents and a 10% rise in the number of women vice presidents. At the vice presidential level, 22% of the women were in administration, personnel, or public relations, which are not considered direct paths to the top (Forbes, Piercy, and Hays, 1988).

A *Fortune* study (Fierman, 1990) of 799 public companies among the 1,000 largest U.S. industrial and service firms was less hopeful. Of more than 4,000 of the highest paid officers and directors, there were only 19 women as compared to 10 in 1978. Still, by 1990, Katharine Graham had been joined by two other female chief executives of Fortune 1,000 firms, namely Linda Wachner of Warnaco and Marion Sandler of Golden West Financial Corporation (Billard, 1990). Regardless of how the percentages are calculated, less than 5% of senior managers of major U.S. firms are women (Samon, 1991).

Why Aren't More Women in Charge of Major Companies?

Morrison and Von Glinow (1990) summarize three sets of theories that try to explain why so few women hold top positions in major U.S. firms.

The first theory focuses on differences between male and female managers; the second on overt or subtle discrimination; and the third on systemic or structural barriers to women's advancement.

When matched by age, education level, and experience, female and male executives are more alike than different (Donnell and Hall, 1980). In fact, executive women are more similar to their male peers than to females in occupations historically dominated by women, such as nursing (Moore and Rickel, 1980).

Hatcher (1991) cautions, however, that gender differences may be produced by variation in corporate experiences, which may result from systemic barriers. In a national study of newly unemployed mid-level managers, Hatcher found gender similarities in factors such as aggressiveness and nurturance. In that study, women were more independent, visible, and nonconforming than male counterparts. A possible explanation is that "the females who aspire to and embark on a corporate management career may be more independent and willing to take risks than their male peers at the time of entry into the organization. It may be these very traits that facilitate what is still, for women, an unconventional career decision" (Hatcher, 1991).

Results of a Canadian study show that male and female middle managers differ on *managerial momentum*, defined as sustained career progress that is caused by an interaction of high performance, ambition, and organizational rewards (Cannings and Montmarquette, 1991). The researchers found that despite lower performance ratings than women, men receive more promotions. Supposedly, this is because men depend more on informal networks to get promoted. Women are more likely to rely on formal methods, such as job bidding, which are less effective. Also, for women, but not men, "success in gaining offers of promotion leads to a decline in promotions demanded" (Cannings and Montmarquette, 1991). At some point, women feel they no longer will be promoted due to the *glass ceiling*, a transparent but impermeable structural barrier that prevents women (and minorities) from reaching senior ranks. Therefore, they quit striving for promotion. "Their very success leads them to become less ambitious" (Cannings and Montmarquette, 1991), and they lose career momentum.

Behaviors and characteristics of managerial women are not the most important factors excluding them from the executive suite. Only 8% of 201 chief executive officers (CEOs) of America's largest firms, most of whom were male, said that women lacked the aggressiveness needed to be top managers, and only 5% said women needed to be more willing to relocate to progress in their careers (Fisher, 1992).

Twenty-nine percent of the CEOs cited strains associated with balancing personal lives and family obligations as factors making advancement to upper echelons more challenging. The perceptions of these CEOs are consistent with socialization practices that expect women to have primary responsibility for maintaining family relationships. That may be realistic for some people, but others share home and family responsibilities.

Mid-management women aspiring to top levels of Fortune 500 firms echoed the CEOs' beliefs, however. Thirty who worked in midwestern firms

reported that the pressure of managing outside demands often becomes debilitating. They mentioned being torn between working and fulfilling family obligations. They wanted to have children, spend more time with their husbands and children, support their parents, and do other things they postponed to reach the executive level. (Wentling, 1992)

Another reason proposed to explain why so few women run Fortune 500 firms is that many differ from men in length and type of business experience. The *pipeline theory*, consistent with this explanation, says it takes 20 to 25 years for anyone to gain the experience required to become a CEO. Because the number of women in management began to increase in the early 1970s, this theory would predict that there would be more senior executive women in the 1990s—certainly by the year 2000.

The pipeline theory has adherents, including management guru Peter Drucker. In *Meeting the Challenge* (Hilton/Sucherman Productions and The Leigh Bureau, 1990), Drucker predicts that women will lead major financial institutions within the decade. That is a specific prediction, but not all prognosticators are as optimistic generally. Only 16% of 201 CEOs thought the next CEO at their firm would be a woman, and only 18% believed a female leader would be very likely within 20 years (Fisher, 1992). Jill Barad, who became CEO of Mattel in 1992, thought the CEOs' predictions were unduly pessimistic, however. Barad seemed to agree with the idea that the old guard soon will be replaced by younger men who will be more enlightened about women's roles (Fisher, 1992). Hellwig (1985) expresses the same view when she says, "A new generation of male executives who have climbed the corporate ladder side by side with female peers will help break [the] comfort barrier." Ellen Galinsky, co-president of the Family and Work Institute, also concurs:

These men are almost all in dual career households, and they have a totally different perspective from their fathers' generation. . . . They empathize far more with conflicts between family and work responsibility, since they know firsthand what it's like to have no full-time help tending the home fires. (Fisher, 1992)

It may be incorrect, however, to assume automatically that a younger generation will be more open-minded than their elders. Some younger men have worked productively with women as peers, but others may have viewed them as competitors for scarce mid-management jobs.

The 201 CEOs in the previously mentioned study blamed women's stalled careers primarily on discrimination (Fisher, 1992). Stereotypes are a root cause and reinforcer of discrimination. Their effects on women and minorities in management will be discussed in chapter 7.

Some managerial women see evidence of discrimination in the fact that their male bosses withhold guidance and encouragement. Others cite a lack of performance-based feedback, which is crucial to career progress (Wentling, 1992).

A U.S. Department of Labor initiative to break the glass ceiling concludes that top managers assess male and female candidates differently. Men are evaluated on perceived potential, but women are judged on past accomplishments ("Labor Agency Sees," 1992). Unconsciously, men are assumed capable of a higher level assignment unless they have performed poorly in their current position. Women are not automatically presumed capable; their past track record is scrutinized to determine whether or not they can handle a promotion.

Differential treatment is not necessarily intentional; it sometimes is based on male chief executives' lack of comfort working with women as peers. Many corporate leaders still relate to women as wives or mothers, not as business colleagues. At top levels, competence is assumed; what matters is the fit between a new executive and the corporate elite. An acronym for the process of deciding who will be selected as senior managers that addresses the importance of fitting in with one's peers is BOGSAT (Jacobs and Hardesty, 1987), meaning a "bunch of guys sitting around a table." According to this notion, a group of men pick the people who will join their elite group as leaders of major U.S. firms. They may not purposely discriminate when they choose people with whom they feel comfortable; they are just following the psychological principle that small groups tend toward homogeneity. In other words, top executives, like the general public, feel more at ease with those who are similar to themselves in terms of variables like socioeconomic class, race, and sex. Subconsciously, they may try to select clones. Unfortunately, this has negative consequences for women and minorities striving to excel in business. Since most corporate presidents are white males in their 50s or 60s, they may feel more camaraderie with other white males.

A third possible reason why executive females' careers plateau prematurely is because of structural, or systemic, barriers. These are obstacles inherent in organizations that make it hard even for women who adopt all the "right" behaviors to be promoted above a certain level. Structural barriers are subtle, making them difficult to identify and eradicate.

The glass ceiling is a systemic barrier. Through it, women see top posts but cannot quite reach them.

The existence of dual labor markets represents another structural obstacle to women and minorities in management (Morrison and Von Glinow, 1990). A *primary labor market* offers better jobs with higher pay rates. More males than females have jobs in this market. The *secondary labor market* is statistically dominated by females. Jobs in this market are less prestigious and have comparatively low pay rates. There is relatively little movement between the two markets.

Tokenism is another systemic deterrent to career progress of executive women and minorities. Briefly, the term refers to excess visibility and other problems minorities experience when there is a marked numeric imbalance between them and majority groups. Considering gender, when the percentage of female managers reaches a *critical mass*, defined as 35 to 40% of an occupational group, supposedly the females no longer will be treated as tokens. As will be explained in chapter 11, tokenism may not vanish just because numbers of men and women in an occupation equalize.

What Can Firms Do to Help Women and Minorities Reach Top Posts in Major U.S. Corporations?

Although counseling women and minorities about skills and behaviors needed to advance to top posts is one option, William Ruckelshaus, the chairperson of Browning-Ferris Industries, believes the focus should be elsewhere. With respect to females, he says, "It really isn't a question of what else women should be doing. It's a question of what companies should be doing to ensure that women are getting the opportunities men get" (Fisher, 1992).

There are several actions firms can take to equalize high-level career advancement possibilities. According to the 50 highest ranking female line managers in the United States, "the attention of the CEO is the single most helpful factor in eliminating a company's glass ceiling for women and minorities" (Hellwig, 1992).

Beyond CEO support, organizations need to make sure aspiring top managers of both sexes and all races get the appropriate kinds and amounts of challenge, accompanied by recognition and support (Morrison, 1992).

Women and minorities are deprived of the challenge they need in terms of troubleshooting or start-up opportunities, international assignments, or exposure to many facets of the organization. They face additional challenges when given assignments that seem to be the same as those of male peers. Besides doing the work, they may face isolation or excess scrutiny. On top of that are "pressures to represent their demographic group" (Morrison, 1992) on various committees or in the community.

CEOs must make sure potential female or minority successors receive the right kind of challenge, and must recognize that "the 'same' assignment given to a traditional and nontraditional manager is not the same at all" (Morrison, 1992).

All would-be CEOs need recognition and support. Besides money and benefits, other appropriate rewards are adequate resources and autonomy.

Support includes collegiality, advocacy, and permission to view failure as a change to learn from one's mistakes (Morrison, 1992).

Companies also can create situations that require women, men, and people of varying cultural heritages to work together and discuss ideas. Such experience and exposure may reduce the discomfort some feel when working in a heterogeneous group.

Firms also must pay more attention to career planning. According to a psychologist who implemented a diversity program at Arthur Andersen, "more companies need to ask both women and men what their long-term goals are, what kinds of jobs would interest them most. . . . And then [they should] use that laundry list—which is a kind of blueprint of a person's ambitions—and develop everyone accordingly" (Fisher, 1992).

RESEARCH ON MODERN EXECUTIVE WOMEN

Topics connected to women's strides in management became popular to research beginning in the 1970s. Literature reviews burgeoned, but most dealt almost exclusively with white women.

The first widely read profile of executive women was Hennig and Jardim's *The Managerial Woman* (1977). The authors interviewed 25 white women in line positions at eastern seaboard firms in industries not usually considered feminine. The study was not generalizable, but it was important as the first of its kind. The authors explored subjects' personal backgrounds, trying to identify commonalities in their lives. Partly a reflection of the generation in which they grew up, most of the mothers of these women were full-time homemakers. A disproportionate number of managerial women were first-born or oldest surviving children. They reported feelings of being considered special in their families of origin and of having had close relationships with their fathers, who were executives or professionals (Hennig and Jardim, 1977). Growing up, they were encouraged to achieve, even in activities not necessarily considered appropriate for girls. Many went to college and reported putting their personal lives on hold so they could pursue careers. Few married until later in life, if at all, and few had children. Interestingly, women who advanced beyond mid-management were those who successfully integrated their femininity with their professional selves. Those who were perceived to be imitating men were more likely to have careers that stalled at middle levels.

Hennig and Jardim (1977) proposed reasons why women's careers had not kept pace with men's, some of which may no longer be relevant. Their managerial women grew up in an era when females were not expected to have careers. If they worked, they had jobs and did not view them as anything more until they had been employed for about 10 years. By that time, they were a decade behind male counterparts in career planning. Also these women had little experience working together on teams. Though there may have been other opportunities to learn similar lessons, they did not automatically pick up the tips that transfer to business that boys learned on the playing field. Hennig and Jardim also thought the women they studied viewed risk negatively, whereas men were more likely to see both pros and cons.

The Managerial Woman was followed by many similar books and articles. Most reported findings based on larger samples of younger women. Background variables differed markedly. Some studies (Lemkau, 1979) showed that mothers of executive women were more likely to have been employed. Others concluded that maternal employment was less important than maternal role satisfaction. Daughters of mothers who stayed at home reluctantly were more likely to have careers and to strive for greater achievement than those whose mothers chose to be full-time homemakers. A close relationship with one's mother was crucial to a woman's satisfaction. Gilson and Kane (1987) said that a female's belief that she was her mother's favorite child correlated more highly with that woman's happiness with her career and salary as an adult than any other factor on a 20-page survey.

Who are the women who have reached the top tier at American corporations? Do biographical characteristics set them apart from others? The answer to that question remains no. Lemkau's (1979) conclusion that no single constellation of personality and background factors consistently characterizes the woman who pursues a male-dominated occupation is still true.

It is increasingly important for women—or men—who expect to succeed in business to have an appropriate education. As Forbes and Piercy stated (1983), "A female may make it to the top with a little formal education in smaller firms, [but] higher education becomes almost mandatory in the largest firms; 89% have at least an undergraduate degree in the billion dollar firms."

There is conflicting evidence about whether or not a significant education gap exists between white females and women of color. Using aggregate statistics, women of color have completed a median 12.2 years of school, which is not much less than the 12.7 years white women have finished (U.S. Bureau of the Census, 1992). Overall statistics can mask differences in educational achievement of various ethnic groups, however. Asian-American women are said to have "an impressive educational attainment record" (Hurtado, 1989), but only 6% of Native-American and Hispanic women and 8% of African-American females are college graduates. Thirteen percent of white women have finished at least four years of college (Hurtado, 1989). Though educational disparities do not fully explain obstacles women of color experience getting into management, their importance cannot be ignored.

Senior management women are heeding the advice to get more education. The percentage of females in those posts without an undergraduate degree dropped from 48% to 19% from 1982 to 1987. In the same five years, the proportion of female senior managers with graduate degrees jumped from

18% to nearly one-third (Forbes, Piercy, and Hayes, 1988). Prospective executive females tend to be more highly educated too, as evidenced by the fact that 30% of students enrolled in graduate schools of business were women in 1990 (Roman, 1990).

Executive women are more likely to be married and have children than they once were, but are still less likely to be spouses or parents than their male counterparts. In the 1980s, 48% to 59% of the nation's top executive women were married (Hellwig, 1985; Karsten and Kleisath, 1986). Two-thirds of those who were married had children. In contrast, 95% of 1,700 male vice presidents of Fortune 500 firms were married, and 92% had children (Larkin, 1984).

Supposedly, high-ranking managerial women are motivated risk takers who exploit opportunities. They are intelligent, have well-developed inter-personal skills, and demonstrate brilliant performance that is visible to the top brass. They also adopt lifestyles reducing barriers to advancement by obtaining respectable academic credentials, deferring marriage, choosing supportive spouses, and maintaining uninterrupted work histories (Vaudrin, 1984).

Women tend to thrive in small to mid-sized high-tech or service firms (Fisher, 1992) or in companies that are so new, so troubled, or growing so rapidly that gender is not an issue (Insel, 1987). To move up, they seem to have to perform much better than male counterparts. Those who are top managers demonstrate such extraordinary expertise that their peers defer to them automatically (Insel, 1987).

To what factors do successful business women attribute their achievement? Besides intelligence, they listed hard work, communication skills, and knowledge gained through experience (Karsten and Kleisath, 1987). Thirty women in mid-management positions in Fortune 500 firms attributed their success to hard work, interpersonal skills, demonstrated competence, educational credentials, and willingness to take risks (Wentling, 1992).

As a success strategy, hard work appeals to rugged individualism. Communication, or interpersonal, skills are almost universally recognized as necessary tools for any professional and it is sensible to assume that years of business experience would have taught managers something about what it takes to get ahead. As mentioned earlier, job competence is a given. The importance of educational qualifications and of risk-taking behavior also have been discussed.

Regarding career paths, there is no identifiable route that guarantees success. All managers must be willing to accept several different positions to gain a strategic perspective of the organization and to get exposure to various areas.

Women who wish to become top managers should avoid beginning their careers—or staying too long—in certain staff areas. Otherwise, *glass walls*, see-through but solid barriers to moves from staff to line positions, may appear. Purchasing and public relations are fields to avoid because they can become velvet ghettos that are difficult to leave.

Human resource management, formerly called personnel, was considered an area to avoid until recently. Emphasis on strategic human resource management has upgraded that field's image and status, but historically few chief executives have moved up through personnel. That may change, however, because "human resource executives are realizing that heading the HR function doesn't mean they've reached the pinnacle of their careers. And when upper management is grooming the next president or CEO, they have just as good a chance of being selected as does the director of finance or marketing" (Filipowski, 1991).

Certain behaviors have been expected of female executives that were not expected of males. Morrison et al. (1987) referred to these sometimes conflicting behaviors as hoops that women had to jump through. In their words:

women had to show their toughness and independence and at the same time count on others. It was essential that they contradict the stereotypes that their male executives and coworkers had about women ... but they couldn't go too far, to forfeit all traces of femininity, because that would make them too alien to their superiors and colleagues. In essence, their mission was to do what wasn't expected of them, while doing enough of what was expected of them to gain acceptance. The capacity to combine the two consistently, to stay within the narrow band of acceptable behavior, is the real key to success.

In the mid-1980s, a *Fortune* article (Taylor, 1986) charged that women were dropping out of corporations to become entrepreneurs, to take a break from the fast track, or to achieve more balance in their lives. The author cited family demands as reasons why women were leaving the workplace, but by 1990 two surveys countered that notion. According to the surveys, executive women quit due to "frustration with career progress—not the call of home and child" (Garland, 1991).

Catalyst, a national group that helps firms develop women's careers and leadership potential, rejected the idea that women were "bailing out" of corporations to start businesses. Rather, they were exercising one of many positive options (Abarbanel, 1987) as their male peers had done. Actually, the rate of females leaving corporations was only a fraction higher than the comparable rate for males (Raynolds, 1987).

The accusation that women were bailing out of corporations sparked debate. Another controversial idea, proposed by Felice Schwartz (1989), president of Catalyst, was that women should classify themselves as career-primary or as career-and-family-oriented (the "mommy track"). Despite protests about the inequality of the arrangement, Schwartz contended that females still have greater responsibilities than males for child rearing and household tasks.

Schwartz (1989) urged business to acknowledge that it costs more to employ women than men. Companies would bear the extra expense of hiring women gladly because of the predicted future labor shortage. If it materializes, firms will need to develop talent regardless of race or gender to compete successfully in the 21st century.

Schwartz's proposals provoked criticism from women's groups. They disliked the creation of a group of second-class citizens in the workplace and found a forced tradeoff of promotion opportunities for flexibility unacceptable. Another criticism was that it would be difficult for new employees to decide whether they wanted to be on the career-primary or career-and-family track. Procedures allowing employees to switch tracks would have to be developed. Those who were pegged as mommy-trackers might experience problems due to others' perceptions when they wanted to shift to the career-primary track.

Finally, implementing a two-track system only for females would discriminate against males. More men want to be actively involved in raising their children. Hammonds and Symonds (1991) wrote profiles of several fathers who had taken lengthy parental leaves despite negative peer pressure and warnings that they were committing career suicide.

WORKFORCE DIVERSITY AND MANAGERIAL WOMEN

In the late 1980s, women starting careers wanted to know which organization would encourage them to get ahead and be receptive to their needs. *The Best Companies for Women* by Dusky and Zeitz (1988) partially filled that need. By the early 1990s, *Business Week* had labelled several firms as women friendly, meaning that they tried to help women advance, had females in key executive posts, and were sensitive to work and family issues. In the early 1990s, such firms included US West, CBS, Gannett, Dayton Hudson, and Kelly Services (Konrad, 1990).

As the 1990s began, workforce diversity became a buzzword. More than 80% of the entrants to the labor force were expected to be minorities or women during the last decade of the 20th century. American firms could no longer afford to keep these groups on the sidelines. Businesses had not only to accommodate women and minorities but also to welcome them into inner circles. Specifics regarding the management of workforce diversity will be discussed in chapter 6. The goal of diversity management, as Avon executive Phyllis Davis said, is to "consciously create an environment where everyone has an equal shot at contributing, participating, and most of all, advancing" (Konrad, 1990).

Programs geared toward valuing workforce diversity may go a long way toward integrating women of color into management. Because race has been assumed subordinate to gender (Nkomo, 1988), women of color have remained invisible in business literature. Many articles have been written

Figure 2.1
Percentages of Management Jobs[1] Held by African-American and Hispanic Women versus Others, 1988 Data

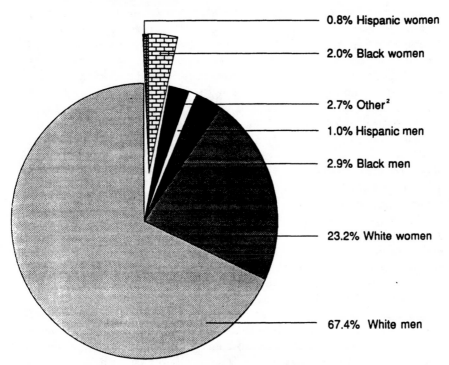

0.8% Hispanic women

2.0% Black women

2.7% Other[2]

1.0% Hispanic men

2.9% Black men

23.2% White women

67.4% White men

Source: U.S. Equal Employment Opportunity Commission

[1]At companies with 100 or more employees.
[2]Includes Asian-American and Native-American men and women.

about executive women, and some studies about minority managers have been done. Most such studies incorrectly assumed that conclusions drawn from samples of white females or black males would generalize to women of color.

Very few women of color have administrative positions. As stated earlier and as Figure 2.1 shows, less than 5% of managers in firms with 100 or more employees are women of color. However, according to Gordus and Oshiro (1986):

Ethnic minority women have improved their representation in managerial and administrative positions during the past 10 years [1976 to 1986]. These gains have been concentrated in a few industries (health care, hospitals, social services) where legislation has worked effectively because of sanctions or where representation may have fit in with a changing customer group. Many are industries where men tra-

ditionally have not wished to be employed because of low wage rates and poor
benefit packages.

The phrase "women of color" is intended to promote unity (Van Horne,
1986). The government categorizes women of color as Native-Americans,
blacks, Asian-Americans, and Hispanics. (Though government studies still
use the word *black*, some prefer African-American because it is more specific.) This classification scheme masks variations among people within each
group. For example, each of the tribes grouped together as Native-Americans has its own heritage. Those of Chinese and Japanese ancestry make
up the largest percentage of Asian-Americans, but Koreans, Vietnamese,
Filipinos, Hawaiians, and Pacific Islanders also are included. Mexican-
Americans represent the greatest proportion of Hispanics, but that group
also is comprised of Cubans, South and Central Americans, Puerto Ricans,
and other Spanish people.

Why are there so few minority female executives? Some explanations are
specific to particular ethnic groups, but there are a few general reasons.
These include lack of role models, difficulty obtaining mentors, stereotypes,
and biculturalism. White women experience most such problems too, but
they tend to be more extreme for women of color. For example, while white
women confront sex-based stereotypes, women of color must deal with
myths based on both race and sex.

Specific sex- and race-based stereotypes will be debunked in chapter 7,
but one general preconception to be addressed here is the *double advantage
myth*. Because of affirmative action goals, some assumed that women of
color had an unfair advantage. The "twofer" theory claimed that hiring or
promoting a woman of color would allow an organization to score two
points in terms of affirmative action compliance, one point because of her
sex and the other for her race. Besides being false, such a notion insults
anyone who wants to be judged on competence, not on skin color or gender.
It encourages others to view women of color as tokens, and in doing so,
makes it more difficult for them to advance. In reality, women of color face
a double disadvantage. If white women see a glass ceiling that halts career
progress, women of color deal with a concrete ceiling (Ray, 1988).

Biculturalism has been discussed as an issue of concern to African-American women, but other women of color deal with it too. A bicultural life
structure means an awareness of two cultural contexts. In their careers,
females of color operate in the white world, but in their personal lives, they
remain part of an ethnic community (Bell, 1990).

Trying to hold on to ethnic roots while feeling forced to adopt another
culture's style to advance professionally can cause stress. It also may lead
to *marginality* or to *identity conflict*. Bell (1990) explains that "a marginal
person is one who lives on the boundaries of two distinct cultures, one being
more powerful than the other, but who does not have the ancestry, belief

system, or social skills to be fully a member of the dominant cultural group." Marginalization creates added pressure as does identity conflict, caused by "a strong personal and emotional commitment to two distinct components of one's life that are incompatible" (Baumeister, 1986).

Some executive women who are black felt that they had to compromise their cultural identity to succeed in predominantly white organizations. According to Sheryl George, a small business consultant, "You now have to go to the opera...to be a part of the [group] and deny everything... relative to your culture. You can't mention things that [whites] don't understand because then you're different, and they don't want to talk to you anymore" (Ray, 1988).

SUMMARY

The number of women in professional and managerial positions remained low in the early 1900s. More entered the workforce during the Depression of the 1930s, but World War II was the turning point. During the war, supervisory positions opened to women because men were not available. Not all women retreated to the home in the 1950s. Some were determined to have business careers, but there were many obstacles. By the 1960s, discrimination was illegal, women were admitted to Ivy League business programs, and many social changes occurred. These and other factors set the stage for the influx of women into management.

In the 1970s and 1980s, scholars began to study women's progress as business executives. With limited success, they tried to determine skills, educational background, and other demographics linked with advancement.

In the 1980s, white women felt they had hit a glass ceiling preventing further upward movement, but to minority women, it seemed more like a concrete barrier. White women could see upper levels, which remained closed to them, but most women of color still had no view. Some hypothesized that women had not been in the pipeline long enough to achieve high levels and that a "critical mass" of managers had to be women before all positions would be open to them. The prescription was patience; time alone would solve the problem. Others questioned this approach. They believed underlying structural and attitudinal obstacles hindered women's progress. The lack of comfort some senior male executives experienced working with females as colleagues was not the least of the attitudinal difficulties.

In the 1990s, a diverse labor force gives new hope to those who think women and men of various races should have an equal chance at all executive positions, including top posts. A workforce increasingly composed of women and minorities, coupled with a predicted labor shortage, will make it mandatory for business to use all available human talent effectively, regardless of race or sex.

DISCUSSION QUESTIONS

1. Since Sarah Bagley was a union member, not an executive, why should her activities be discussed in a course on gender issues in management?
2. List and explain five factors you believe have contributed to an increase in the percentage of female managers in the past twenty years.
3. Explain the relevance of the psychological principle, "small groups tend toward homogeneity," for women or minorities who wish to become top executives in major U.S. firms.

3 Women's Contributions to the Evolution of Management Thought

OBJECTIVES

After studying this chapter you should be able to:

1. Define technology, unit, mass, and continuous production, organic and mechanistic forms of organizational structure, the managerial grid, flextime, and the compressed workweek.
2. Explain Lillian Gilbreth's contributions to scientific management.
3. Explain why Mary Parker Follett could be considered a prominent general management theorist and founder of human resource management.
4. Explain why important contemporary management theories have not been attributed to Mary Parker Follett though some were based on her ideas.
5. Explain Joan Woodward's contributions to the behavioral school of management thought.
6. Explain Rosabeth Moss Kanter's ideas about power and successful adaptation to change.

Women's contributions to the classical, behavioral, and management science schools of thought are presented in this chapter. Table 3.1 lists those whose work advanced each major school.

Women discussed in this chapter are all Caucasian, and most had at least middle-class backgrounds. So far no women of color who advanced management theory have been identified.

Table 3.1
Women Who Contributed to the Major Schools of Management Thought

Classical	Behavioral	Management Science
Scientific Management	Follett	Hopper
Gilbreth	Mouton	Woodward
	Kammerer	
Administrative Theory	Poor	
None identified		

MAJOR SCHOOLS OF MANAGEMENT THOUGHT

The three major schools of management thought were classical, behavioral, and management science. Scientific management and administrative theory were two branches of the classical school. According to the behavioral school, efficiency, stressed by classical theorists, did not guarantee high productivity. People's social needs also had to be considered. A quantitative approach to management emerged when mathematical techniques used by the military during World War II were applied to business. Such applications began what is known as management science or quantitative management theory.

Scientific management was concerned with improving individual workers' productivity, whereas administrative theory dealt with issues affecting the total organization. To date, no prominent women connected with administrative theory have been identified.

Frederick Taylor, founder of scientific management, often is depicted as treating workers as machines. Actually Taylor was concerned with employees' well-being. He believed he could help them by offering financial incentives for improved performance. He advocated scientific training and selection of workers. Though against labor unions, Taylor thought worker-management cooperation was indispensable. In practice, scientific management was not always consistent with Taylor's ideas, however.

PIONEERS IN MANAGEMENT THEORY: GILBRETH, FOLLETT, WOODWARD

Lillian Moller Gilbreth

Lillian Moller Gilbreth (1878–1971), in collaboration with her husband, Frank, advanced scientific management through motion and fatigue study. In the early 1900s some believed that a poison entering the bloodstream after exertion caused fatigue. The Gilbreths thought that eliminating needless movement could reduce exhaustion. They used cameras to determine the most efficient motions for each task, believing that economical motions would increase productivity and morale. Morale would rise, not only because employees had more energy, but also because motion study would indicate management's concern.

The Gilbreths also developed the *three position plan of promotion*, in which workers would do their own jobs, train successors, and prepare themselves for promotion. Doing these things simultaneously would keep them interested in their work.

Frank and Lillian opened a management consulting and engineering firm during World War I. Reflecting the times in which they lived, the company was named Frank B. Gilbreth, Inc., with no official mention of Lillian's role. After World War I ended, the Gilbreths applied time and motion study to the problem of rehabilitating returning soldiers with disabilities.

Before Frank's sudden death in 1924, he and Lillian co-authored five books on motion study and scientific management. After Frank died, Lillian presented the paper he was scheduled to deliver at a management conference in Prague, Czechoslovakia.

Lillian Gilbreth continued the family consulting firm, but faced initial resistance from clients unsure about whether a woman could run it. One woman, whose husband contributed to scientific management, knew of Gilbreth's predicament. She telephoned the president of AT&T and explained Gilbreth's situation. He made sure her next workshop was filled. Clients attending were so impressed with Gilbreth's expertise that opposition to her consulting firm nearly vanished (Greenwood, 1985).

Gilbreth applied motion study to the home and developed equipment facilitating greater independence for the handicapped. She was a consultant to the Institute of Rehabilitative Medicine at the New York University Medical Center. Her application of efficiency techniques in the home was discussed in *The Homemaker and Her Job* (1972) and *Management in the Home* (1954). She also co-authored *Normal Lives for the Disabled* (1944).

Gilbreth was the oldest of eight surviving children. Her parents, the Mollers, owned a hardware store in Oakland, California, and were fairly prosperous. As the eldest, young Lillian helped care for her siblings because her mother was often ill.

The first woman commencement speaker at Berkeley, she earned a bachelor's and a master's degree in English literature there in 1900 and 1902, respectively. She had begun work on a doctorate in industrial psychology when she interrupted her studies to travel to Boston in 1904. There she met and later married Frank Gilbreth.

Together they had 12 children in 17 years. Besides the children, the family had a live-in housekeeper and cook, and Frank's mother lived with them for several years. The Gilbreths managed their family as they ran a business and applied motion study to methods in the home. For example, they taught the children the most efficient bathing technique. The children also had to listen to foreign language records while bathing so they would not waste time.

Lillian Gilbreth submitted *The Psychology of Management*, her doctoral dissertation, to the University of California–Berkeley in 1912. The dissertation was accepted, but Berkeley refused to award the degree because she had not met a residency requirement, which she had thought would be waived. So *The Psychology of Management* was published in installments in *Industrial Engineering* and was later published in its entirety under the condition that the author's name be stated as L. M. Gilbreth, with no mention of her gender. In 1915, Gilbreth received a doctorate in applied management from Brown University. To get the degree, she had to write a new dissertation entitled *Waste in Teaching* (Yost, 1949).

Gilbreth's teaching career spanned three decades. While a professor at Purdue, she was a consultant on women's careers. She stressed the importance of the human factor in management and the role of women in industry.

Lillian Gilbreth received many awards, including the American Woman's Association Award for Eminent Achievement. In 1931, she was the first recipient of the Society for the Advancement of Management's Gilbreth Medal for motion, skill, and fatigue study, established to recognize the Gilbreths' accomplishments. She was named one of ten outstanding women of the year in 1936. Gilbreth was the first woman to be elected to the National Academy of Engineering and to receive the Hoover Medal. She wrote and lectured past age 80 and lived to be 93.

Mary Parker Follett

Mary Parker Follett (1868–1933) usually receives credit for advancing the behavioral school of thought, but her contributions are more far-reaching. The seeds of management theories popular today can be found in her work.

There are at least three reasons why important contemporary theories have not been attributed to Follett. First, male researchers may have developed similar ideas. For example, both Mary Parker Follett and Henri Fayol stressed the need for direct, lateral interdepartmental communication. This link between departments, which Follett called *cross-functioning* (see Figure 3.1), is referred to as Fayol's gangplank in most management texts. Because the book in which Fayol explained this concept was not translated from French to English until 1948, the two researchers may have thought of the same idea simultaneously.

Second, other theorists refined Follett's ideas years after she had explained them. For example, in the 1920s, Follett discussed concepts that were forerunners of contingency leadership theory. Her law of the situation, described in *Creative Experience* (1924), claimed that each set of circumstances constantly evolves. A current theorist may have considered that law when

Figure 3.1
Cross-Functioning Between Departments

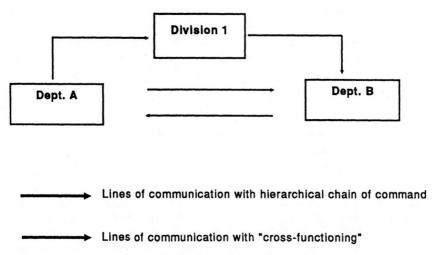

developing the contingency approach to leadership, which states that there is no one best way to manage (Fiedler, 1967).

A third reason why Follett's work did not attract more attention during her lifetime might have been because she was so unpretentious. She studied management, not for self-aggrandizement, but because she enjoyed interacting with business leaders who were willing to apply her ideas in their firms. Follett was unassuming to a fault. For example, an unfulfilled last wish was that all her business papers be burned after her death.

Mary Parker Follett was a founder of human resource management. Her ideas were revolutionary at a time when scientific management taught that trained workers performing specialized tasks would be motivated mainly by money. She created an awareness of employees' social needs and developed innovative ways to deal with people problems in business.

Follett also was a prominent general management theorist. She believed administration was a profession that included a body of knowledge that should be taught.

Her process-oriented definition of management as the art of getting things done through people is still used today. Follett advocated coordination and cooperation in an enterprise, a systems approach to management, positive labor-management relations, shared power, and a holistic view of life.

Cooperation and coordination were common themes in Follett's writing. She felt those involved in a situation should strive for coordination early in a project. Furthermore, this process should be reciprocal and ongoing. Follett was impatient with false cooperation. She criticized a business leader for saying, "Let's cooperate," when he later admitted that he really meant, "Do what I say, and do it damned quick" ("Famous Firsts," 1964).

Follett's view that the value of every fact depends on its position in the whole world process (1924) typified an often-stated belief about interconnectedness. That theme reflects a systems approach taught in most management principles courses. According to the systems approach, each unit has an impact on every other unit and on the total organization.

Follett (1924) espoused positive labor-management relations. She was impatient with an adversarial approach but favored confrontation that allowed integration to be used to resolve conflict.

Follett questioned traditional power concepts. She disliked power over another based on hierarchical position but favored shared power. Like Rosabeth Moss Kanter, whose contributions will be explained later in this chapter, Follett believed that empowering others creates more power. In Follett's words (1924):

There is an idea prevalent, which I think very harmful, that we give up individual power...to get joint activity. But first, by pooling power we are not giving it up; and secondly, the power produced by relationship is a qualitative, not a quantitative thing.... If we look at power as the power to do something, we shall understand this.

From *Creative Experience* (1924), one can conclude that an integrated, holistic lifestyle would have appealed to Follett. She probably would have opposed as unworkable attempts to separate completely one's job from one's personal life. Professionals, by their nature, might be unable to leave their work at the office entirely. On the other hand, they might find it difficult to concentrate fully on workplace tasks if plagued by unresolved personal problems.

Follett was the oldest child of a family that owned a granite quarry in Quincy, Massachusetts. As a child, she had little time to play because she had to help care for her younger brother and invalid mother. She was said to be close to her father. She had a proper upbringing and graduated from Thayer Academy in Braintree, Massachusetts, in 1884.

Though not wealthy, inheritances allowed Follett to attend college in the 1880s and 1890s, when fewer than 19% of undergraduate degrees were awarded to women (Deckard, 1983). She enrolled at the Harvard Annex in 1888, where prominent professors befriended her. Today those professors, who supported Follett's ideas and gave her credibility in Boston and beyond, would be called mentors.

Follett attended college sporadically in England and at the Annex in the late 1880s and 1890s. Once she was called home to care for her ill mother, and she took a break to write her first book, *The Speaker of the House of Representatives*, published in 1896.

In 1898, Mary Parker Follett graduated summa cum laude from Radcliffe (formerly the Harvard Annex) in economics, government, and philosophy.

She began a career in social work and established the Boston Placement Bureau, which later became the Department of Vocational Guidance. Through this work, and through her service on a Massachusetts minimum wage board, Follett met well-known area business leaders like E. A. Filene and H. S. Dennison. Thus, networking helped her discover an interest in applying her knowledge of social work, politics, public administration, and psychology to management.

Follett also became acquainted with Henry Metcalf, head of the Bureau of Personnel Administration in New York City. He invited Follett and other prestigious speakers to address the bureau. Follett spoke to bureau members several times from 1925 to 1932, seemingly the only woman invited during those years (Fox, 1968).

After the death of a lifelong friend in 1926, Follett left for England, where she lectured at Oxford. She went to Geneva, Switzerland, to study the League of Nations and later moved to London, where she lived until her death.

Follett's accomplishments were even more notable, considering the general treatment of women during her lifetime. There were exceptions, but women in the late 1880s generally were perceived as having "limited mental and physical capabilities as compared to men" (Schlagenhaft, 1988). Economically, they depended on husbands or fathers unless they were widowed or unwed, orphaned daughters, as was Follett.

The fact that Follett never married helped her career. She lived during an era when women's employment was tolerated, grudgingly, if they were single or married with no children. In the 1880s, when she began college, women made up 15% of the labor force. By 1930, toward the end of her career, they had increased to 22% (Deckard, 1983), which reflected steady, if slow, progress.

As a professional, Follett probably was considered a different breed. Professional women in her time were thought to have independent spirits and the desire for definite work. They were so in love with their jobs that they labored without fatigue. Preoccupation with work reduced their desire to please, which explained why many remained single ("The Professional Woman," 1906).

A scholar rather than a competitor, Follett was nonthreatening to the business community. Her style was not to tell business leaders what they should do, but to make suggestions. The relationship between Follett and Boston business people was one of mutual admiration. Bird (1976) describes it best:

Mary liked to talk to business people because they spoke out of their own concrete experience instead of in generalities and were more willing, she found, than scholars and politicians to try experiments.... If Mary loved business people because they were practical, the repressed philosophers among them loved Mary because she provided a rationale for their most puzzling experiences.

Follett's concern for human needs and her interpersonal skills also may have helped her gain business leaders' acceptance. Her interests were consistent with stereotypes about women that still persist. She has been described as "just the kind of sympathetic listener to whom a hard-boiled man of large affairs didn't mind expressing his half-formed thoughts and feelings" (Bird, 1976).

Joan Woodward

Joan Woodward (1917–71) also made important contributions to management. Her studies of the relationship between organizational structure and technology led to the development of organizational behavior as a field of knowledge.

Woodward first planned to study organizational size and technology, but did not find any link. She then examined organizational structure.

To appreciate her work, it is necessary to define technology and structure. *Technology* is a process of converting inputs to outputs. Woodward looked at three types of technology—unit, mass, and continuous production. A system with *unit production* features custom-made, one-of-a-kind products, while the assembly line would be an example of *mass production. Continuous production* is used when units of a product are indistinguishable from each other. An oil refinery uses continuous production.

Organizational structure ranges from organic to mechanistic. Few firms can be neatly categorized at one extreme or the other. As mentioned in chapter 1, companies that are more *organic* feature few rules, lateral as well as vertical communication, participative decision making, and internal control. An organic structure is more appropriate for firms operating in a dynamic, turbulent environment. Large bureaucracies are more *mechanistic* and have many rules, downward communication, centralized decision making, and external control. Mechanistic structures are appropriate in stable environments.

Woodward's team of researchers gathered data from 100 firms in southern England. They found that successful manufacturers using unit or continuous production technology were more likely to have an organic structure. A mechanistic structure was more prevalent among successful firms relying on mass production. Success was measured according to financial performance.

Though Woodward acknowledged limitations, her research was criticized because she studied only small and medium-sized manufacturing firms, because her classification of firms in terms of success seemed imprecise, and because she did not use enough statistical tests to analyze data.

Woodward's main critics were British researchers conducting the Aston studies. Their conclusions were similar to Woodward's, but she completed her studies first.

An industrial sociologist, Woodward studied at Oxford. Her master's degree was in medieval philosophy and her doctorate in social and public administration. She was the second woman professor at Imperial College in Great Britain and became head of its Industrial Sociology Department. Woodward was a manager of a branch of British government for seven years and served as a consultant to British firms.

OTHER WOMEN PIONEERS

Another contributor to management thought, Jane Srygley Mouton, is best known for the Managerial Grid, later renamed the Leadership Grid, which she developed with Robert Blake. The grid deals with leadership style. It measures concern for production on the horizontal axis and concern for people on the vertical axis. Values on both axes range from 1 to 9.

Five points on the grid describe particular management styles. One extreme style, called authoritarian, stresses production and efficiency at the expense of sensitivity to people. At the opposite extreme is a style characterized by high concern for people and low concern for production. A point in the center of the grid represents a manager who tries to balance the need to get work done with the need to maintain satisfactory morale. A point near the origin depicts a manager who exerts minimal effort to get work done and shows little concern for people.

Blake and Mouton advocate a style in which managers express high concern for both people and production. They believe this is the best style and that, if necessary, the situation should be changed to make it amenable to this type of management.

Mouton and Blake's work has been criticized by contingency theorists, who argue, for example, that in certain situations a style typified by a low concern for production and a high concern for people might be effective. In other circumstances the opposite management style might be appropriate.

Jane Mouton earned her Ph.D. at the University of Texas. She taught there before becoming vice president of Scientific Methods, Inc., a consulting firm doing projects using the managerial grid in 25 countries.

Christel Kammerer and Riva Poor promoted alternative work schedules. Kammerer, a German woman, developed *flextime*. The basic plan features core time, flexible starting and quitting times, and a fixed number of hours worked per week or month. During core time, which corresponds to the organization's busiest time, all employees must be present. Within a predetermined range, employees may start and end the workday when they wish. Flextime gives workers greater autonomy. It also eases scheduling of appointments that must be made during normal working hours. Disadvantages include scheduling problems and possible customer or supplier ill-will.

Though initially interested in the *compressed workweek*, in which employees work four ten-hour days, Riva Poor would rather be known as a change agent or decision-making expert. Married at 19, Poor had two children by age 23. She tired of the homemaker role and attended graduate school at the Massachusetts Institute of Technology in her late twenties. While completing master's degrees in city and regional planning and in management, she edited *4 Days, 40 Hours*. Managers who thought they were interested in the schedule described in that book called Poor to discuss this. Usually Poor could help them identify underlying problems that were unrelated to alternate work schedules.

Captain Grace Hopper of the U.S. Navy has been associated with management science models. A highly skilled mathematician, she was a developer of COBOL, a computer language for business.

Rosabeth Moss Kanter, a current contributor to management thought, has studied many topics, including power and its impact on relationships between male and female executives, shifts in the nature of managerial work, and the change process in U.S. corporations. Her approach to management seems humanistic, and she probably would favor an organic structure, which is appropriate in the turbulent environment facing many organizations.

To Kanter, the quantity of power is not fixed. Giving away power actually increases it in her view, expressed in *Men and Women of the Corporation* (1977). Kanter believes power should be linked to personal skills or expertise rather than to hierarchical position (1989). Chapter 11 expands on Kanter's ideas about power.

In her book, *The Change Masters* (1983), Kanter deals with successful adaptation to change. She defines change masters as people and organizations adept at anticipating the need for productive change and leading the process. These individuals or corporations tune into the environment and are capable of kaleidoscope thinking, in which ordinary ideas are recombined into new patterns. Masters of change also work through teams, persevere, develop coalitions, and make everyone a hero.

Kanter urges corporations to cut excess layers and abandon cumbersome rules or structures in *When Giants Learn to Dance* (1989). Postentrepreneurial organizations, which apply entrepreneurial skills to existing firms, can become more agile by developing synergies and alliances. Specifically, they should maintain high ethical standards, develop a process focus, learn to do without the crutch of a hierarchy, remain humble, be multifaceted, compete in a way consistent with cooperation, and gain satisfaction from results.

Kanter and co-authors Stein and Jick expand on a favorite theme in *The Challenge of Organizational Change: How Companies Experience It and Leaders Guide It* (1992). The book's main premise is that 1990s firms should determine how to become "competitive world organizations" instead of simply trying to describe what such organizations would look like.

In the 1970s Kanter co-founded Goodmeasure, Inc., a management consulting firm specializing in quality-of-worklife and diversity issues. One of

Kanter's projects at Goodmeasure was to write *Tale of O: On Being Different in Organizations,* which dealt with tokenism in a unique way. The book, later made into a film, used Xs as majority group members and Os as the minority. When a group consisted of 70% or more Xs, the Os experienced overload and overexposure (Goodmeasure, Inc., 1979).

Kanter has taught at Harvard, Yale, and at the Massachusetts Institute of Technology. While at Harvard, she edited the *Harvard Business Review.* She was a founder of a group of top executive women, called the Committee of 200, which tries to make changes in the U.S. economy and create more visibility for female business leaders.

SUMMARY

Lillian Moller Gilbreth advanced the classical school by using motion and fatigue study in industry and in the home. Mary Parker Follett was associated with the human relations movement but should be considered a founder of human resource management. Her ideas about management often were ahead of their time. Joan Woodward's study of relationships between technology and organizational structure led to the development of organizational behavior as a field of knowledge. Besides Woodward, other female contributors to the behavioral school were Jane S. Mouton, Riva Poor, and Christel Kammerer.

Rosabeth Moss Kanter is a contemporary management theorist. She has studied power issues, the relationship between women and men in organizations, the future of U.S. business, and the changing nature of managerial work. Her ideas have not been linked to any existing school of thought.

DISCUSSION QUESTIONS

1. Because of the shortage of executive women to serve as role models, some have suggested that historical figures can serve that purpose. Which, if any, of the women discussed in this chapter would be good role models for women aspiring to be managers? Explain your answer.

2. Do you think the ideas of any of the women discussed in this chapter reflect a feminist approach to management or not? Explain.

4 Equal Employment Opportunity

OBJECTIVES

After studying this chapter you should be able to:

1. Define comparable worth, reverse discrimination, and bona fide occupational qualifications (BFOQs).
2. List two reasons why managers should be knowledgeable about equal employment opportunity (EEO) laws and regulations.
3. Restate arguments for and against comparable worth.
4. List steps involved in establishing an affirmative action plan.
5. Explain procedures for filing discrimination charges with the Equal Employment Opportunity Commission (EEOC).
6. Restate provisions of the Equal Pay Act.
7. Explain the Pregnancy Disability Amendment to Title VII of the Civil Rights Act of 1964.
8. Compare and contrast provisions, coverage, and penalties of Title VII of the Civil Rights Act of 1964 and Executive Order 11246.
9. Explain the provisions of the Civil Rights Act of 1991.

There are at least two reasons to become familiar with equal employment opportunity laws. First, prospective managers must understand firms' legal obligations, assuming that it is their responsibility to make sure their organizations comply. Second, all employees should be aware of their EEO rights and know how to deal with job discrimination.

This chapter will focus on provisions of federal EEO laws that prohibit sex discrimination. Laws concerned with unfairness in employment based on factors other than gender will be mentioned only as related to sex discrimination.

TITLE VII OF THE CIVIL RIGHTS ACT OF 1964

Title VII of the Civil Rights Act is a comprehensive federal employment discrimination law. It prohibits job unfairness based on a person's race, color, sex, national origin, or religion. Discrimination is banned not only in hiring and firing, but also in recruitment, selection for training, pay and benefits, or any other condition of employment. Groups that must comply with Title VII include private employers with at least 15 employees, labor unions with 15 or more members, public and private educational institutions, and state and local governments.

As originally worded, Title VII did not prohibit sex discrimination. Opponents of Title VII added sex as a protected class to ensure its defeat. They thought few legislators who favored barring race discrimination would vote to outlaw bias against women. When votes were counted, the joke was on Title VII's foes. The law, including a ban on sex discrimination, had passed (Deckard, 1983).

Firms violating Title VII may be penalized in several ways. Courts may issue an injunction against them, which halts discriminatory practices. Companies may be ordered to reinstate workers fired or denied promotion because of discrimination. These employees are entitled to *back pay*, or compensation they would have received had they not been discriminated against, for up to two years. At their discretion, courts also may design more creative penalties, an example of which is a court-ordered affirmative action plan. Title VII does not require a company to develop a plan automatically, but a court may order a firm found guilty of discrimination to do so.

The *bona fide occupational qualification* exception to Title VII permits discrimination based on sex, religion, or national origin under certain conditions. A BFOQ is a quality reasonably necessary to a firm's normal operation. For example, a company could legally refuse to hire males for actresses' roles for authenticity reasons. A firm's refusal to hire females as men's restroom attendants also could be justified under this exception. BFOQs usually have been interpreted narrowly, because there are very few jobs that one sex is physically unable to perform.

Refusal to hire women based on sex-related stereotypes or real or assumed negative co-worker preferences is not a BFOQ exception, but violates Title VII. Likewise, having to provide separate facilities does not justify denying employment to women unless the cost would be excessive.

The Equal Employment Opportunity Commission enforces Title VII. Its five members are approved by the President and confirmed by the Senate.

Figure 4.1 shows EEOC procedures from the time a charge is filed until it is settled or pursued in federal district court. A discrimination charge must be filed either in person or by mail within a certain time after the alleged illegal act occurred. Employers are not legally required to attend a fact-finding conference, but many do to resolve the issue quickly, thereby avoiding publicity and cost. If the EEOC cannot establish "probable cause" that discrimination occurred, it gives charging parties a "right to sue letter," allowing them to file suit in federal district court. The EEOC only litigates precedent-setting cases, which represent a small percentage of the total. Charging parties are notified of the EEOC's intentions and decide whether or not to let the commission pursue the case. If they do not want the EEOC to pursue the case, charging parties still may sue in federal district court.

The EEOC has negotiated large voluntary settlements involving firms such as AT&T, General Motors, and USX. In the early 1970s, AT&T signed a consent decree for $15 million to be paid to women and minorities denied promotions. General Motors' $42.5 million settlement included $15 million earmarked for scholarships and endowments and $21 million set aside to train minorities and women in high-level positions. In 1991, USX agreed to settle a 15-year-old class action discrimination suit filed by black applicants at a Pennsylvania steel plant for over $40 million (Ansberry and Adler, 1991).

RECENT PRECEDENT-SETTING COURT CASES

A few of the many cases that have been filed under Title VII will be mentioned here. These include *Griggs v. Duke Power, General Electric v. Gilbert*, and three reverse discrimination cases. Also to be discussed are *Price Waterhouse v. Hopkins*, a case involving sex-based stereotypes, *Wards Cove Packing v. Atonio*, which revoked precedents set in *Griggs*, and *Automobile Workers v. Johnson Controls*, dealing with fetal protection.

Griggs v. Duke Power (1971) was the first U.S. Supreme Court case to consider issues raised by Title VII. The case involved racial discrimination but is presented here because it made it easier for employees to prove they had been discriminated against based on sex or any other "protected class" besides race.

Griggs established *disparate impact discrimination* theory. According to this theory, seemingly neutral practices that are not job-related but exclude a disproportionate number of minorities or women from employment are illegal unless the employer can show a "business necessity" reason for maintaining them. For example, requiring all employees including laborers to have a high school education may seem unbiased. However, if only 60% of minorities in the recruiting area have completed high school as compared to 90% of whites, and that education level is not necessary to be a laborer, requiring a high school diploma would exclude a much greater percentage

Figure 4.1
Investigation of an Employment Discrimination Charge: EEOC Procedure

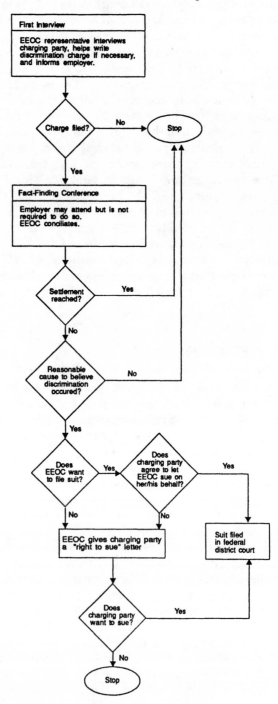

of minorities than whites. Regardless of whether or not the employer intended to discriminate, such a statistical comparison alone could lead to charges of disparate impact discrimination. Before *Griggs*, employees had to prove they were treated differently because of their race, color, religion, sex, or national origin and that the employer intended to discriminate against them. This is called *disparate treatment* discrimination and is more difficult for employees to prove than disparate impact discrimination.

In *General Electric v. Gilbert* (1976), the Supreme Court ruled that firms could omit pregnancy-related disabilities from a temporary disability insurance program. Public outcry after this decision led to the passage of the Pregnancy Disability Amendment to Title VII in 1978. It required pregnancy to be treated as a temporary disability in existing insurance plans. Employers without such programs were not required to offer them just so pregnancy could be covered, however.

Another 1983 Supreme Court case, *Arizona Annuity Plans v. Norris*, made pension plans paying women lower monthly retirement benefits than men illegal. The plans had been previously justified based on actuarial tables showing that women, as a group, live longer than men. Therefore, the average woman's total pension benefits would roughly equal the average man's. In its decision, the high court ruled that contributions to pension plans made after August 1, 1983, had to yield equal monthly benefits to men and women.

The next three high court cases, *University of California v. Bakke, Steelworkers v. Weber*, and *Johnson v. Santa Clara County Transportation Agency*, involved reverse discrimination. The first two dealt with race discrimination but set precedents courts considered when deciding sex discrimination cases.

Before discussing these reverse discrimination cases, it is important to understand different meanings of that term and of related words. *Discrimination* refers either to different treatment of minorities or to neutral practices with dissimilar effects on minorities as compared to the majority. As commonly understood, *reverse discrimination* is unfair treatment of the majority resulting from going "too far" to try to rectify past discrimination against minorities. Proponents of this view contend that fair policies provide no special treatment based on race or sex. They should not consider such factors at all. To consider immutable, non-job-related characteristics insults women and minorities who wish to be evaluated on competence.

Some supporters of this interpretation of reverse discrimination rely on the legislative history of Title VII. Justice Rehnquist, in a dissent to *Steelworkers v. Weber*, a 1979 Supreme Court case, said:

Not once during the 83 days of debate [about Title VII] in the Senate did a speaker, proponent or opponent, suggest that the bill would allow employers voluntarily to prefer racial minorities over white persons. In light of Title VII's flat prohibition on discrimination against any individual... because of such individual's race, such a contention would have been... too preposterous to warrant response. (443 U.S. 193 [1979])

An alternate idea, which views fairness and discrimination as polar extremes, would define reverse discrimination out of existence. According to this notion, if "reverse" means opposite, and if the opposite of discrimination is fairness, then the term "reverse discrimination" is meaningless (Jones, 1980). Not all agree with this logic, however.

Personal opinions aside, managers and co-workers will have to deal with employees who are angry about what they perceive as reverse discrimination. Such individuals should be allowed to express feelings but must understand that they are expected to work together with minorities, women, and those of different lifestyles for the good of the organization.

Because there are so many misconceptions about affirmative action plans, such programs should be explained to workers concerned about reverse discrimination. Though they might disagree with the concept, workers need to understand affirmative action.

Affirmative action gives minorities and women a temporary advantage to make amends for past discrimination. Because of generations of different treatment, minorities and women may begin careers at a disadvantage through no fault of their own. According to this view, they should be given a temporary edge until they reach the same starting point as the majority. When that happens, affirmative action plans will no longer be needed.

Critics point out that majority group members should not be blamed for past societal inequities. If they personally did not discriminate, why should they be penalized for actions of previous generations over which they had no control? Besides that, a few mid- to upper-class minorities have had advantages. Perhaps socioeconomic class, rather than race or sex, would more accurately identify those who need the temporary advantage affirmative action provides.

In *Bakke* (1978), the U.S. Supreme Court said that rigid numerical quotas to achieve racial balance "unnecessarily trammeled" majority rights. As part of voluntary affirmative action plans, race (and by extension, sex) could be considered as one of several factors when hiring people or, in this case, selecting students for admission to medical school. Race or sex could not be the sole deciding criterion, however. In this particular case, 16% of the medical school slots were reserved for blacks. Allan Bakke, a white male, was denied admission despite having higher Medical College Admission Test (MCAT) scores than minorities who were accepted. The Supreme Court said this was reverse discrimination. It ruled in Bakke's favor and ordered the University of California–Davis to admit him to medical school (438 U.S. 265 [1978]).

In *Steelworkers v. Weber* (1979), the high court ruled against Brian Weber, a white male who, despite having greater seniority than a black employee, had been passed over for admission to a training program due to a voluntary affirmative action plan negotiated between Kaiser Aluminum and the United Steelworkers of America. According to the Supreme Court, the question to be decided was narrow. Justice Brennan, in the majority opinion, said that "the adoption of the Kaiser-USWA plan ... falls within the area of discretion left by Title VII to the private sector voluntarily to adopt affirmative action plans designed to eliminate conspicuous racial imbalance in traditionally segregated job categories" (443 U.S. 193 [1979]).

Though the Court did not enumerate guidelines to distinguish between acceptable and impermissible affirmative action plans, Twomey (1990) concluded that such plans must be voluntary, temporary, and must not "unnecessarily trammel" majority interests. Furthermore, plans must be

remedial to open opportunities in occupations closed to protected classes under Title VII or designed to break down old patterns of racial segregation and hierarchy.... [To ensure] that affirmative action is justified, the parties must make a self-analysis to determine if and where conspicuous racial imbalances exist.

Johnson v. Santa Clara County (1987) tested whether or not a voluntary affirmative action plan would be upheld in the public sector. Diane Joyce and Paul Johnson both applied for promotion to a radio dispatcher position in Santa Clara County, California. Both were qualified, but Johnson scored slightly, but not significantly higher, than Joyce on a job-related test. Joyce was promoted to dispatcher. Johnson filed a reverse discrimination suit but lost at the Supreme Court level.

In its decision, the Court noted that the road dispatcher position was part of Santa Clara County's skilled craft job category, and that there were no women in that group. Thus, there was a marked imbalance. Also, the voluntary affirmative action plan the county had adopted forbade quotas. It simply allowed race or sex to be considered as one of several factors to be examined in a hiring or promotion decision. The Supreme Court found no flaw with the plan, described as a "gradual approach ... which establishes realistic guidance for employment decisions, and which visits minimal intrusion on the legislative expectations of other employees" (107 S.Ct. 1442 [1987]).

Price Waterhouse v. Hopkins (1989) concerned not reverse discrimination but sex stereotypes and non-job-related criteria used to deny a woman partnership in a Big Eight accounting firm. Though she brought in more business than any other candidate for partnership, Ann Hopkins initially was not promoted to that level because partners on the selection committee felt she did not wear makeup, was "too macho," and needed to go to "charm school." Hopkins argued that her swearing and strident manner would have been overlooked had she been male, given her outstanding record. The Supreme Court agreed.

As liberal justices retired and were replaced by more conservative nominees in the 1980s and early 1990s, Supreme Court decisions involving equal employment opportunity issues began to shift. This change in the Court's outlook was apparent in several 1989 decisions that reversed 18-year-old precedents dating from *Griggs v. Duke Power*. One such case was *Wards Cove Packing v. Atonio*. *Wards Cove* made it more difficult for employees to prove they had been discriminated against. It involved race discrimination, but precedents it established also apply to sex discrimination suits.

From 1971 until the *Wards Cove* case in 1989, employees filing discrimination suits had to show that an employment practice, though seemingly neutral, had a disproportionately negative effect on women or minorities as compared to whites. Then the burden of proof shifted to employers, who had to demonstrate that maintaining the challenged practice was a "business necessity." Employers unable to do so would lose the case.

Wards Cove said statistical evidence that an employment practice had an adverse impact on women or minorities was insufficient proof of discrimination. Employers no longer had to justify the questionable practice as a business necessity but could defend themselves merely by stating a legitimate reason for it. Then, the burden of proof would shift to employees. They had to show that the practice was not business-related, which was difficult to do.

From 1989 until the Civil Rights Act of 1991 was passed, few employees won discrimination suits. The 1991 law restored burden of proof standards *Griggs v. Duke Power* had established 20 years earlier. Once again, statistical evidence that a neutral practice had disproportionately negative effects on women or minorities created an assumption that discrimination had occurred. To rebut that presumption, employers had to prove that the "neutral" practice was a business necessity. Other provisions of the Civil Rights Act of 1991 will be described later in this chapter.

Over the years, employers have found compliance with equal opportunity laws challenging enough even when those laws do not conflict with other requirements. When they do conflict, employers often feel they have been placed in a "no-win" situation.

Until the Supreme Court decided *Automobile Workers v. Johnson Controls* (1991), employers perceived a conflict between equal employment opportunity and safety. At issue was the legality of protective policies banning women of childbearing age from hazardous but high-paying jobs involving lead exposure at levels harmful to an unborn human. Johnson Controls justified such a policy by citing relatively high rates of unplanned pregnancy coupled with concern about future lawsuits filed by individuals who had been harmed by exposure to lead in utero.

Some women objected to the policy, saying that they should be able to decide whether or not they wanted to trade higher wages for lower lead exposure. They claimed unequal treatment based on sex in violation of Title VII. Also at issue was that reproductive health hazards to women were being singled out with no concern about effects on offspring of male employees exposed to lead.

In this situation, the Supreme Court sided with the women. They should be able to decide whether they want to work in toxic areas. The Court also labelled future lawsuits brought by individuals disabled due to in utero lead exposure a "remote possibility."

By dictating a course of action, the Court tried to simplify decisions of employers who wrestle with conflicting EEO and safety requirements. However, a *Wall Street Journal* editorial ("Justices Adopt," 1991) criticized the Court's decision, saying that it required Americans to walk "north and south at the same time." The *Journal* interpreted *Johnson Controls* as saying "(1) Businesses may not prohibit women from jobs that will result in birth defects, and (2) women and children born deformed can then sue the employer." According to this view, *Johnson Controls* would not insulate companies from future lawsuits.

CIVIL RIGHTS ACT OF 1991

After vetoing a civil rights bill in 1990 and loudly objecting to so-called employment "quotas," George Bush signed the Civil Rights Act of 1991, a compromise drafted by House and Senate leaders. That law made it easier for employees to win discrimination suits and allowed victims of sex, disability, and religious discrimination to collect punitive damages for the first time.

As explained earlier, the 1991 act toughened burden of proof standards employers had to meet in disparate impact discrimination cases, thus making it easier for employees to win. The Civil Rights Act of 1991 replaced standards adopted after *Wards Cove Packing v. Atonio* with those originally stated in *Griggs v. Duke Power* in 1971.

Before the 1991 law, only race discrimination victims could sue for punitive damages. Those experiencing sex discrimination, including sexual harassment, could only collect court costs and back pay. Though race discrimination victims could sue for unlimited punitive damages, the 1991 Civil Rights Act capped the maximum permissible damages awarded to sex, disability, and religious discrimination victims. Exact dollar amounts depended on the number of employees a firm had, and smaller firms were liable for less money. Victims of discrimination suing even the largest firms were limited to $300,000 in damages.

Besides having an impact on burden of proof standards and damages awarded in employment discrimination cases, the 1991 Civil Rights Act set up a Glass Ceiling Commission. Its purpose is to remove invisible barriers

Table 4.1
Steps in the Development of an Affirmative Action Plan

Policy	Develop a policy of commitment to EEO.*
Person	Appoint a high-ranking official to take charge of the program.
Publicize	Publicize the commitment to EEO internally and externally.
Survey Workforce	Survey the current workforce by department and job classification for areas where women and minorities are underutilized.
Set Goals	Where underutilization exists, set goals to correct the problem and timetables for their completion.
Specific Programs	Develop specific programs, or training such as internships, to cultivate minority and female applicants and promotion candidates.
Audit	Monitor the process.

* EEO = Equal Employment Opportunity

that thwart progress of women and minorities who aspire to top positions in major U.S. firms.

EXECUTIVE ORDER 11246 AND AFFIRMATIVE ACTION

Unlike Title VII, Executive Order 11246, as amended, is a presidential edict. It has the same effect as a law but did not have to pass Congress. Executive Order 11246 only applies to firms doing business with the federal government as contractors or subcontractors. There are two levels of compliance. Firms that get $10,000 or more in government contracts must have a written commitment to equal employment opportunity. In addition, firms with $50,000 or more in contracts or at least 50 employees must have a written affirmative action plan.

An *affirmative action plan* is an ongoing, results-oriented process that identifies underutilization of minorities and females in employment and develops specific procedures to remedy the situation. Table 4.1 shows steps required to develop an affirmative action plan. In its plan, a firm must write and disseminate a policy supporting equal employment opportunity.

There should be two-tier accountability for the implementation of affirmative action plans. At one level, a top corporate official who commands employee respect should be in charge of compliance. This individual should not assume the entire responsibility alone, however. Managers throughout the organization must share accountability. Their commitment to affirmative action should be evaluated, along with other factors, during their performance reviews.

The firm must keep records showing the number and percent of women and minorities in each of several job classes. These data are then compared to percentages of women and minorities available in the relevant labor market who are qualified for particular job classes.

The *relevant labor market* is the area from which a firm normally recruits for certain types of jobs. For example, a company may recruit nationally for highly paid professional jobs requiring advanced education. It may limit its search to the local area for less skilled jobs.

Underutilization exists if a firm employs a smaller percent of women and minorities than there are women and minorities qualified for a job category in the relevant labor market. In 1991, 39% of U.S. managers were female. If a firm's relevant labor market for managers were nationwide, about 39% of that company's executives should have been female. If females comprised only 3% of management, they would have been underutilized in that job category. In each category where underutilization occurs, the firm must have written goals to increase percentages of minorities and women and timetables for their accomplishment. Goals must be realistic and achievable.

Firms must notify recruiting sources that they want qualified women and minorities referred for all vacancies. Companies also could establish links with organizations of women and minorities and inform them of job openings.

A company is expected to take specific steps to remedy the situation if underutilization exists. Exactly what will be expected depends on the firm's financial resources and whether it expects to expand or contract employment. One option would be to establish internship programs with colleges enrolling a large proportion of minority students. The firm might then be able to employ some interns after graduation. Another idea would be to start training programs allowing women and minorities to learn skills needed for promotion.

Periodically, a company must audit its affirmative action program. It must monitor hiring and promotion data to make sure minorities and women receive equal consideration with male candidates. If goals are not met, the person in charge of the plan must try to determine the reasons.

If a company covered by Executive Order 11246 is supposed to have an affirmative action plan but does not, the Office of Federal Contract Compliance Programs in the Department of Labor, which enforces the order, may assess penalties. These include cancellation or suspension of government contracts, injunctions, or criminal proceedings for filing false information. Noncomplying contractors or subcontractors can be banned from future government contracts. Their names can be published on a list geared to force compliance through public pressure.

EQUAL PAY ACT AND COMPARABLE WORTH

Besides complying with Title VII and Executive Order 11246, if applicable, a company needs to be concerned with pay fairness. The Equal Pay Act of 1963 is an amendment to the Fair Labor Standards Act of 1938, better known as the minimum wage or overtime law. Men and women must be compensated equally for jobs that are alike in content and that require similar skill, effort, and responsibility, and are performed under similar working conditions, according to the Equal Pay Act. It applies to incentives and employee benefits as well as base wages.

If jobs are generally similar but men exert more physical effort and women have more responsibility, those factors "even out." Men and women in this example would have to be paid equally. If jobs are otherwise similar, but males must lift heavy equipment, lifting does not justify higher pay unless it is done regularly. Differential pay rates are not justified for occasional lifting.

There are four exceptions to provisions of the Equal Pay Act. Women and men may be paid different rates for doing the same work based on a bona fide seniority or merit system. Differential pay is justified based on a production-based system, such as a piece rate incentive, or any other legitimate factor besides the worker's sex.

Whereas the Equal Pay Act applies to jobs similar in content, *comparable worth* applies to dissimilar jobs of equal value to an organization. Proponents of comparable worth argue that these jobs should be equally paid.

In some circles, *pay equity* has replaced comparable worth. The new term sounds positive, but critics claim it is misleading. Technically, the pay equity issue arises when two job categories, both statistically dominated by the same sex, are judged of equal value to an organization. Therefore, they should be paid the same. For example, if 70% of accountants and the same percent of engineers were male, and those occupations were deemed of equal worth, the requirement that they be paid the same would be a pay equity, not a comparable worth, standard.

Is implementing comparable worth like trying to equate apples and oranges? Yes says the head of Ontario, Canada's, Pay Equity Commission, who is adamant that it can be done. "First," she recommends, "assign points for such measurable qualities as fiber content and vitamins. Then, add up the points to find the value of different fruits. The same method applies to workers" (Kilpatrick, 1990).

Not all agree. Some have derided comparable worth as "looney tunes." Others say aggregate pay comparisons, used by proponents, are inappropriate. They examine overall earnings of women and men in the United States rather than pay of samples of males and females within a given occupation, matched by age, education, and experience.

Opponents of comparable worth insist it is at best irrelevant, and at worst, counterproductive. It does not address root causes of sex-based pay differences, such as occupational channeling before labor market entry. According to this idea, women are encouraged to choose relatively low-status, low-paying jobs through socialization.

Malveaux (1985–86) argues that comparable worth would particularly benefit black women, who are overrepresented in low-paying clerical jobs and in state and local governments, where such a policy is more likely to be instituted. Her analysis ignores the fact that, as the price of labor rises, employers may substitute capital for labor. Thus, some with low-paying jobs would lose them. Holleran and Schwarz (1988) conclude that "women most in need of help . . . very likely would be harmed by a comparable worth policy."

Proponents, on the other hand, see comparable worth as an ethical issue transcending economics. They contend that work women do is at least as valuable as work done by men. For example, nursing positions, held mainly by females, require more skill than janitorial jobs, usually dominated by males. Nurses typically have earned less than janitors because the occupation is female-dominated. Comparable worth advocates believe this is unfair.

To implement comparable worth, firms would have to equate jobs with different content. Though not easy, this could be done using job evaluation plans, which have been used to rank jobs by worth since the early 1900s. Job evaluation plans are no panacea, however. All involve subjective judgment. Also, evaluation plans may not be independent of labor market supply and demand forces, as is commonly assumed. Rather, they may incorporate discriminatory features of the market. A full discussion of how this occurs is beyond the scope of this book, but is presented in *Comparable Worth: A Symposium on the Issues and Alternatives* (Equal Employment Advisory Council, 1981).

Even if job evaluation systems were purely objective and independent of the market, firms relying on them to set wages under a comparable worth standard might be less able to select and keep good employees. Employers typically use competitive pay to attract and retain workers. Under comparable worth, if there were a shortage of employees in a certain job category, a firm could not raise the pay for that category without also increasing wages for all equally valued jobs. Thus, one employer adopting comparable worth would be at a disadvantage.

The counterargument would urge employers to compete on a nonwage basis. Perhaps the company could stress its quality-of-worklife, espirit de corps, and benefits package. Additional arguments for and against comparable worth are summarized in Table 4.2.

Table 4.2
Comparable Worth: The Arguments

Pros	Cons
I **Start** American women are systematically underpaid for jobs of equal worth to those men hold.	It is not the employer's fault if women prepare for low-paying jobs.
Women prepare for low paying jobs because of the socialization process, for which they are not totally responsible.	Why should the innocent employer be penalized for societal inequities?
As a part of larger society, the employer is partly responsible. Precedent has been set.	
II **Start** The market, on which the current wage system is partly based, perpetuates past discrimination.	This may be true, but what else would be better? Abandoning supply and demand leads to inefficiency and perhaps government intervention.
III	**Start** Comparable worth leads to (1) inflation, if not accompanied by productivity gains (2) substitution of capital (machines) for labor, which leads to a rise in women's unemployment.
A rise in women's unemployment would cause more women to prepare for nontraditional careers. Retrained women could crash barriers to traditional male occupations. This would not be all bad.	
IV It has been implemented in Canada and Australia.	**Start** Comparable worth will not work.
V That process is too slow.	**Start** Equity can be achieved through existing legislation without comparable worth.
IV If comparable worth is sex discrimination in violation of Title VII, cost should have been dealt with before Title VII was passed.	**Start** Costs of implementing comparable worth are excessive.

*Adapted from arguments presented in Michael Evan Cold, A Dialogue on Comparable Worth (Ithaca, NY: IILB Press, 1983).

Table 4.3
Average Aggregate Pay of Women as a Percent of Men's Pay

Group of Women	1987	1990
All women	65-70%	66-71%
Ages 20-29	83%	
Ages 30-44	72%	
Ages 45 and up	60%	
Black women		61%
Hispanic women		55%

Sources: "Women of Color". Executive Female (May/June 1990), p. 20; "Bridging the Gap" Executive Female (November/December 1987), p. 17.

Beverly Ledbetter, general counsel at Brown University (1985), used the following example to illustrate issues underlying comparable worth:

It was a blustery winter morning in Chicago. Several secretaries (all female) were working in a top story of a huge glass and steel building. Below was a group of construction workers (all male). As a joke, the secretaries hoisted a message down to them with a rope. It read, "It's 72 degrees up here, what's it down there?" The men laughed as they thought about how they should reply. They scrounged to find an old piece of cardboard on which they wrote: "It's $18.00 an hour down here, what's it up there?"

The problem Ledbetter described is *occupational segregation*, defined earlier as a situation that occurs when 70% or more jobholders in an occupation are of one sex. In general, jobs statistically dominated by men tend to pay well. Those in which women are concentrated still have relatively low status and pay.

The well-documented earnings gap between women and men is slowly narrowing. In 1980, women's average pay was 60% of men's. Table 4.3 shows that this had increased 5 to 10% by 1987 and another 1 to 6% by 1991. By 1992, women earned about 74% of men's wages. At this rate, average wages between the sexes are not projected to be equal until 2020.

The pay picture for younger women seems brighter than for older women, according to Table 4.3. Racial comparisons indicate that the pay of women of color lags behind that of white peers.

When men's and women's compensation is compared within an occupation, equal pay, rather than comparable worth, is the relevant issue. Nonetheless, it may be of interest to compare managers' wages by sex. According to 1990 Census Bureau data, female managers and executives employed full time earned 64% of their male counterparts' salaries. For newly minted MBAs from the top twenty business schools who begin management careers, the pay gap by sex is smaller—nearly 14%. At the executive vice president level or above, pay discrepancies are greater, and marked regional differences exist. Women's salaries at this level are only 58% of their male peers' salaries. In 1987, women vice presidents in the South and Southwest earned just $68,000 and $82,000, respectively, compared to male counterparts' $212,000 and $217,000. The pay discrepancy was slightly smaller in the Midwest, where females made $163,000 to males' $202,000.

Why has a sex-based wage differential continued for so long? Education and experience distinctions account for only 7% of the pay gap, so other factors must be involved. Perhaps women's skills have been devalued or their career aspirations have been stifled in the recent past. No definitive explanation of the pay gap has been proposed; it seems to have resulted from a combination of factors.

Court cases regarding comparable worth emerged in the 1980s. Two examples are *County of Washington v. Gunther* (1981) and *AFSCME v. State of Washington* (1985). In the first, the U.S. Supreme Court left the door open for future comparable worth cases in what was really a sex discrimination suit. The *AFSCME* case eventually led Washington State to pay over $400,000 to undercompensated female employees in a settlement. In the 1970s, the state had done a pay study, found wage differences not based on job content between female- and male-dominated jobs, but took no corrective action. Female employees filed suit in the 1980s and won in district court. The ninth circuit appeals court overturned the previous court's decision, but AFSCME promised to take the case to the Supreme Court. Instead of continuing to litigate, the state reached the previously mentioned compromise with the union.

States have been leaders in implementing comparable worth in public sector jobs. Minnesota was the first to adopt it, and several other states also have done so. Many other states are studying the possibility.

There has been less action in the private sector. Once touted as the most important human resource issue, comparable worth has all but fizzled. Employees, who were more concerned about keeping their jobs in the downsizing decade, did not push it, and employers were not enthusiastic.

SUMMARY

This chapter has examined issues arising from Title VII of the Civil Rights Act, the Equal Pay Act, and Executive Order 11246. One of the most controversial issues resulting from civil rights laws and executive orders is affirmative action. A *Business Week* cover story on race in the workplace (Gleckman et al., 1991) said it is "an important symbol of America's commitment to civil rights" and "an effective club" to deal with "a deep vein of prejudice that still runs through U.S. society, despite all the upbeat talk about the increasingly diversified workforce." The authors continued:

in the past 25 years of affirmative action, blacks and other minorities have benefitted socially and economically. Individual businesses and the economy have profited, not lost. Until America comes up with a better idea, it's wise to stick with a policy that, despite its flaws, is both a moral imperative and an economic necessity.

DISCUSSION QUESTIONS

1. Are you for or against affirmative action for minorities and women? Justify your answer.

2. Are you for or against comparable worth? Justify your answer. Try to use more than superficial arguments.

3. To implement an affirmative action plan required by Executive Order 11246, is it sufficient for an employer to state in all advertisements that it is an "equal opportunity employer?" Explain.

4. May a company refuse to hire a woman because she is pregnant? Why or why not?

5. You are a man who wants to be actively involved in raising your children. You and your spouse believe in a balanced lifestyle so you both can fulfill affiliation and achievement needs. You are a mid-level manager at a large, progressive automobile manufacturer. You and your spouse are expecting a second child, and you would like to take one week off work when the baby arrives and an additional three months on a part-time schedule after your wife returns to work as an attorney when her six weeks of temporary disability leave ends. This will make things less hectic for the family and will mean your children will spend fewer hours per week in child care. The firm's policies allow such a leave; the problem is more subtle. Some of the guys at work have been giving you a rough time. More worrisome than that are the rumors that you've been "daddy tracked." In other words, you might not be considered for promotion next year. How will you deal with reactions of some of your male co-workers? With the rumor that you're no longer considered promotable? Explain.

6. A male president of a firm was truly proud to welcome a new member to the board of directors. He began to introduce her to his colleagues by saying, "We'll all have to clean up our jokes," and ended with, "As you can see from her appearance, she'll add a lot to the looks of this board" (Reece and Brandt, 1990). If you were the woman who just joined the board of directors of this firm, what would you do or say now? Later?

7. A female employee has just found out that her annual pay is $4,000 less than that of a male co-worker doing the same job. She is angry and threatens a lawsuit. You have just been promoted to manager of her department and are knowledgeable about EEO laws. You don't want a lawsuit. How will you handle this situation?

8. You are interviewing with a major firm based in Milwaukee, WI, that offers a

good starting salary and excellent benefits. You are a woman who has just completed your college degree in mechanical engineering. When you talk to the human resource manager, she seems enthusiastic about the firm's commitment to EEO. The supervisor of the department where you would work explains that women usually don't last long in his department because they don't like to deal with "dirty" industries. He says you would be the only woman in the department. He also inquired about your marital status and future plans to have children. You really want the job. How should you deal with this situation?

5 Sexual and Racial Harassment and Corporate Romance

OBJECTIVES

After studying this chapter you should be able to:

1. Define sexual, racial, third party, and gender harassment, and the "reasonable woman" standard.
2. Explain the importance of the U.S. Supreme Court case *Meritor v. Vinson*.
3. Explain and debunk three myths regarding sexual harassment.
4. Explain the individual and organizational costs of sexual harassment.
5. Explain features of a preventative program a firm could set up to protect itself from liability for sexual harassment.
6. Explain why women of color may be more likely than white women to be sexually harassed.

Actions of co-workers and bosses directly affect morale and productivity. When those actions include sexual and racial harassment, or at the opposite extreme, corporate romance, the work environment can become hostile. Sexual harassment, the most familiar topic to the public, will be covered first. A few examples of blatant sexual harassment follow.

- Male aviators pinched, grabbed, and ripped clothing off 26 women, including naval officers, by passing them down a gantlet in a Las Vegas hotel hallway at a 1991 Tailhook Association convention.
- A group leader at a Chrysler plant in Beaver Dam, Wisconsin, "set down the telephone during a conversation, walked to the woman as she inspected a door

panel and reached under her arms to squeeze her breasts. He returned to the telephone and said, 'Yup, they're real' " (Chrysler Takes Harassment, 1992).

- Mr. Showalter's boss, Mr. Smith, forced Showalter to engage in sex acts with Smith's female assistant. Showalter was a jewelry store worker who said he complied because he was afraid he would lose his job and health insurance. Showalter was married and had a son with heart problems (Templin, 1991).

SEXUAL HARASSMENT: A DEFINITION

Though the Equal Employment Opportunity Commission (EEOC) has issued guidelines to explain behavior that constitutes illegal sexual harassment, incidents like those in the preceding examples occur too often. EEOC guidelines define sexual harassment as unwelcome sexual advances, requests for sexual favors, and other verbal or physical conduct of a sexual nature when (1) submission to such conduct is explicitly or implicitly a term or condition of an individual's employment, (2) a person's submission to or rejection of such conduct is used as the basis for employment decisions affecting that individual, or (3) the conduct unreasonably interferes with a person's work performance or creates an intimidating, hostile, or offensive work environment.

There is a continuum of behavior that constitutes sexual harassment. Sexually explicit jokes or remarks exemplify the mild forms. Attempted or actual rape represent the other extreme. In between are graphic displays of sexually oriented material or unwelcome pinching or touching, to give a few examples.

Harassment depends on the receiver's perceptions, not on the harasser's intent. If a person finds sexually oriented behavior unwelcome or offensive, it is harassment.

To be legally actionable, verbal sexual harassment either must be pervasive enough to create a hostile work environment or must be linked to employment conditions. In other words, telling a lewd joke at work once, though inappropriate, probably would not meet the legal definition of sexual harassment. On the other hand, a sexual proposition coupled with a promise of job advancement would only have to be made once to be unlawful.

TYPES OF SEXUAL HARASSMENT AND SELECTED HISTORICAL EXAMPLES

The first two parts of the EEOC definition of sexual harassment describe quid pro quo harassment. It refers to an exchange of favors. For example, perhaps the boss promises a pay raise or promotion to employees who perform sexual favors. Or maybe workers who spurn sexual advances later receive less desirable assignments.

The third part of the definition focuses on the environmental form of sexual harassment. A workplace is considered hostile when it is so charged with sexual innuendo or lewd behavior that the atmosphere interferes with employees' ability to work.

The first U.S. Supreme Court case to consider the sexual harassment issue, *Meritor Savings Bank v. Vinson*, dealt with hostile environment. In that case, described as "so steamy it could germinate orchids" (Greene, 1986), Machelle Vinson's supervisor, Robert Taylor, exposed himself to her, chased her into the women's restroom, fondled her in front of other workers, and had intercourse with her. This occurred over several years, but Taylor made no job-related promises or threats to Vinson based on the sexual relationship. Vinson later stated that, though she had not refused Taylor's advances, they had been unwelcome. Vinson won the case. The Supreme Court unanimously ruled that serious, widespread, and unwelcome sexual conduct violates Title VII of the Civil Rights Act regardless of whether or not it has economic impact.

Meritor Savings Bank tried to deny liability because it had a written policy prohibiting discrimination. The bank's defense failed because its policy did not specifically ban sexual harassment and because the only way to voice complaints was for employees to contact their immediate supervisor. Vinson's supervisor was the harasser.

The Supreme Court did not definitively rule on employer liability in *Vinson*, however. According to the Court, employers are absolutely liable for supervisory actions in quid pro quo sexual harassment, but may not be in hostile environment cases.

There are other forms of sexual harassment besides quid pro quo and offensive environment. One variation involves a third party. For example, if a female supervisor annoys a male employee based on his sex and then promotes him instead of a better qualified female worker, that woman may file a harassment claim. A California operating room nurse who was not sexually harassed nevertheless sued her employer because male doctors repeatedly grabbed other nurses in her presence at work. This behavior offended her (Hayes, 1991).

Third party harassment must be distinguished from paramour preference, which is legal. *Paramour preference* occurs when there is a consensual sexual liaison between a boss and employee. The boss then promotes the employee with whom he or she is having an affair. This is favoritism and is associated with many human resource problems, but it does not violate the law. Other employees who are denied the promotion lack a claim "because all of the individuals, whether women or men, are not disadvantaged because of their gender but because of the intimate relationship the manager enjoys with one favored person" (Wagner, 1992).

It is obviously unlawful for a man to harass a woman, or vice versa.

Same-sex harassment also is illegal. Though repugnant, bisexual harassment, in which a person annoys both women and men, is not illegal under Title VII. This is because the victims are not being singled out based on their sex.

Gender harassment is another form of illegal sex discrimination that some classify as sexual harassment. Though not sexual, it denigrates or offends people because of their sex. For example, male college professors who do not call on female students in class because they want to make sure they are not accused of sexual harassment are committing gender harassment. In another example of the same type of illegal activity, male construction workers resorted to extreme tactics to let female peers know they were unwelcome. They knew about, but did not correct, a dangerous condition in a truck the women had to drive, refused to unlock the restroom door at the job site so the women could use it, and urinated in the gas tank of a female co-worker's car (*Hall v. Gus Construction Company*, cited in Wagner, 1992).

Sexual harassment is not a new problem; it has existed for thousands of years. An example of the age-old nature of the issue is the story of an Egyptian pharaoh's wife harassing the biblical figure Joseph. The pharaoh's wife, whose name is unknown, asked Joseph to sleep with her. When Joseph refused, she claimed he had propositioned her, and Joseph was sentenced to prison.

More than 100 years ago, the author Louisa May Alcott experienced sexual harassment, which she called a "personal dilemma." Alcott, a companion to an elderly woman, complained that the woman's brother made unwanted sexual advances toward her (Biles, 1981).

TARGETS OF SEXUAL HARASSMENT

Who are the people who receive unwanted sexual or gender-based attention? From two-thirds to nine-tenths are women (Deutschman, 1991; Templin, 1991). The most typical scenario involves a man over age 35 harassing a woman younger than that age. One survey of 20,000 federal employees conducted in the 1980s showed that women with a college education or graduate degree had a better than average chance of being harassed. Usually the harasser has more power than the person she or he is bothering.

According to an analysis of complaints in Illinois, 51% of the filers held service, clerical, skilled, or semiskilled positions. Eighteen percent had paraprofessional or technical jobs, 12% were in sales, 11% were managers, and 8% were either skilled craft workers or professionals (Deutschman, 1991).

Illinois's profile of complainants differs from the composite *Working Woman* developed based on its 1992 survey of readers and Fortune 500 firms. Results of that survey showed that "the higher a woman is in the corporate hierarchy, the more likely she is to be harassed" (Sandroff, 1992).

This is consistent with an earlier report that claimed that supervisory rank "is no protection" against sexual harassment (Clarke, 1986).

According to the *Working Woman* report, managerial and professional women who earn at least $50,000 and are employed in industries or firms comprised mainly of men are likely targets of sexual harassment. Supposedly this is because these women represent a threat to some men who hold upper management positions.

Harassment is more common in sex-segregated organizations and occupations. Segregation exists when more than 70% of jobholders in a firm or profession are of one sex.

Harassment also is more likely in small businesses because "owners wield so much unchallenged power" ("In Many Small Businesses," 1991). Offensive sexual behavior is less likely in "stable companies where employees feel some loyalty to the corporation and to one another" (Deutschman, 1991).

Though it is possible to generate profiles of people who have been sexually harassed and organizations in which the problem is prevalent, stereotypes should be avoided. Victims vary based on age, occupation, and socioeconomic status, and people may make unwelcome overtures in any workplace.

TYPICAL HARASSERS

Who are the harassers? Why do they continue unwelcome, obnoxious behavior? In a 1988 study of Fortune 500 firms, 36% of harassers were immediate supervisors; 32% were co-workers; and 26% held positions higher than immediate supervisor of the complainant (Fritz, 1989). A previously mentioned survey of federal employees showed that most harassers were co-workers (Deutschman, 1991). Reasons for harassment vary considerably. Some perpetrators attribute it to mixed communication signals. For example, instead of telling co-workers that innuendos are unappreciated, employees may first brush off comments to avoid conflict. Other harassers have been called "office adapters." If the environment subtly encourages unwelcome sexual advances, they follow the crowd. "Power players" may be repeat offenders who do not respond to feedback from the person being harassed or from the organization regarding the offensiveness of their behavior. Their "desire to subjugate others comes ahead of common decency" (*The Power Pinch*, 1981).

NUMBER OF SEXUAL HARASSMENT COMPLAINTS

Since the EEOC issued guidelines on sexual harassment, the number of formal complaints has risen by more than 50%. In 1981, 3,661 complaints were filed, and by 1991, the number had jumped to 5,644. This happened even though many who have been sexually harassed are reluctant to file formal charges. Perceived costs of doing so may outweigh benefits. Harassment victims may not wish to be labelled as troublemakers and may fear that others will not believe them. Before 1991, even those who won sexual harassment cases could not collect damages; they had to settle for court costs and back pay, if appropriate. Many decided it was not worthwhile to initiate a sexual harassment case.

THE "REASONABLE WOMAN" STANDARD

In cases that are pursued, courts have started to use a new standard to judge whether or not illegal harassment occurred. Instead of relying on the "reasonable man" standard, which has been applied to both sexes for over 150 years, some courts have adopted a "reasonable woman" standard to determine whether behavior constitutes illegal sexual harassment.

This is because women's and men's opinions of objectionable workplace behavior differ. For example, when asked how they would view sexual advances at work, 75% of the women surveyed said they would be offended, but 75% of the men polled claimed they would be flattered (Hayes, 1991). This discrepancy led the ninth U.S. circuit court of appeals to adopt a "reasonable woman" standard in sexual harassment cases involving female victims.

THE HILL-THOMAS CONTROVERSY: SENATE INVESTIGATION OF SEXUAL HARASSMENT

The topic of sexual harassment arouses strong emotions. Nowhere was this more evident than in the televised Senate hearings to investigate sexual harassment claims Professor Anita Hill brought against Judge Clarence Thomas in October 1991.

Hill alleged that Thomas had repeatedly made lewd comments and had discussed pornographic films and his own sexual prowess with her while he was chairperson and she was an employee of the EEOC in the early 1980s. Thomas vehemently denied all charges and was ultimately confirmed as a U.S. Supreme Court justice.

Whether one felt that Hill or Thomas was more credible, or that both told the truth as they perceived it, a positive outcome was the increased awareness of sexual harassment as a serious business problem. Offices across the nation were buzzing about the topic. Companies realized it was time to do more than dust off and circulate sexual harassment policies. The state of Maine passed a law requiring employers to educate workers about sexual harassment. As a result of the Hill-Thomas controversy, 90% of Fortune 500 firms are expected to offer training on the issue (Lublin, 1991, Dec. 2).

Another result of the Senate investigation was a surge in the number of complaints filed with the EEOC. Rather than having a chilling effect, as some predicted, the Hill-Thomas episode opened the floodgates. In the last quarter of 1991, the EEOC reported a 71% increase in claims as compared to 1990 (Meyer, 1992).

Terpstra (cited in Moskal, 1991) analyzed harassment claims filed in Illinois over two years and found that most were based on unwanted physical contact, offensive language, or sexual propositions unrelated to employment conditions. Along the continuum of behaviors that constitutes sexual harassment, he characterized these forms as "less severe."

When compared to the same questionnaire administered in 1988, a 1992 Fortune 500 survey showed a rise in certain forms of sexual harassment. For example, 50% of reported cases involved verbal pressure for sexual favors and/or dates in 1992, as compared to 29% in 1988. More than 34% of the incidents involved cornering or touching in 1992, as compared to 26% in the older study (Sandroff, 1992).

PREREQUISITES TO A REDUCTION IN THE AMOUNT OF HARASSMENT

Before heightened awareness of sexual harassment resulting from Hill's charges can reduce the incidence of such behavior in the workplace, three things must happen. First, if they are able, those who feel harassed should clearly state that the behavior in question is unwelcome. Second, those who state that they find certain types of behavior offensive must be respected, not viewed as overly sensitive or prudish. Third, organizations must give potential harassers a loud, clear message that locker room behavior will not be tolerated in the workplace.

Those who believe they have been harassed must become assertive communicators. They need to develop the ability to level with the harasser, look that person in the eye, and say, "I don't like that behavior. Please stop." This may be difficult for people who have been socialized to view passive behavior as the norm. However, assertiveness can be learned and has worked to eliminate sexual harassment. Sixty-one percent of those who used a "just-say-knock-it-off" approach found that it ended unwanted sexual attention (Deutschman, 1991).

People who request that offensive behavior stop should be respected. They should not be caricatured as prudish or easily offended. An organization that wants to stamp out sexual harassment must teach its employees and executives that people have different perceptions of acceptable workplace behavior. If a person finds certain conduct offensive, and says so, that behavior must cease, even if it would not be objectionable to someone else.

Finally, managers and employees must realize that the office is not a locker room. Conduct and speech that might be acceptable there are no longer appropriate in the executive suite, if they ever were.

MISCONCEPTIONS ABOUT SEXUAL HARASSMENT

People develop mindsets about sexual harassment, and until these can be openly confronted, discussions may center more on feelings than fact. There are several misconceptions. For example, some view harassment as solely a women's issue or believe it is not very prevalent. Others think it deals mainly with sexuality, that false accusations are rampant, or that attempts to prevent it stifle office humor. These will be debunked in turn.

Women file more sexual harassment complaints than men, but the number of men reporting harassment has increased. If women are reluctant to report sexually obnoxious behavior, men also are hesitant. Part of the "macho" stereotype is that men enjoy being harassed. To report harassment in some workplace cultures would be to risk being labelled a wimp. Nonetheless, men file at least 1 out of 10 sexual harassment complaints (Templin, 1991), so it is incorrect to assume harassment is only a problem for women.

Sometimes sexual harassment is portrayed as an issue that pits men against women. This is counterproductive. Regarding this issue, the president of DiversiTeam Associates comments, "If you're a man, you were force-fed attitudes that may make you susceptible to perpetrating, discounting, or ignoring sexual harassment." The executive adds that men have a responsibility to abandon such attitudes, though they should not be blamed for adopting beliefs that were instilled in them as youths (Stuart, 1991).

Those who contend that sexual harassment does not exist—at least not in their organizations—probably are misinformed. Surveys done in the 1970s and 1980s estimated that from 57% to 88% of employees had been harassed then (Ford and McLaughlin, 1988). A 1988–89 study of 38,000 military personnel worldwide showed that two-thirds of the women and 17% of the men had experienced harassment (Schmitt, 1990). Fifty-three percent of the 1,300 members of the National Association of Female Executives surveyed in 1991 either were sexually harassed or knew someone who had been (Galen, Weber, and Cuneo, 1991). Finally, 60% of the 9,000 readers who responded to a 1992 *Working Woman* questionnaire had endured sexual harassment.

Sexual harassment is an issue of power and dominance, not of sexuality. Basically, it is an abuse of power at another's expense.

Some tend to fear that false allegations of sexual harassment could ruin their careers. Fraudulent accusations do not occur often. AT&T estimates that about 5% of harassment claims are untrue. Many of these are made by employees trying to get revenge against supervisors who have evaluated their performance unfavorably (Deutschman, 1991). The fact that few spurious claims are made is small consolation to those who are falsely accused, however. Some react by filing defamation charges against the firm, but they seldom win, because "in fighting these retaliatory suits, corporations believe they must pull out all stops...to protect their anti-harassment efforts" (Lublin, 1991, Oct. 18).

Some fear that concern about harassment could stifle office humor, often regarded as a stress reducer. Others say that jokes dealing with the human condition always will be appropriate, but that those told at the expense of any person or to insult someone purposely really are not funny (Ingrassia, 1991).

Perhaps the best solution is to consider one's audience when attempting to be humorous at work. If someone might be offended by a suggestive joke, do not tell it in a business setting. One executive whose position required him to promote his state learned this lesson when he told sexist jokes at a conference. The organization that had sponsored the executive's appearance felt compelled to send notes of apology to all in attendance (Riddle, 1992).

COSTS OF SEXUAL HARASSMENT

Sexual harassment costs individuals and organizations plenty in both economic and noneconomic terms. Employees subjected to it may feel angry, humiliated, or embarrassed. Frequently, their self-esteem drops. They may fear that others will not believe they have been harassed.

Some may feel guilty about the harassment or blame themselves for it. For example, a woman in her 20s blamed herself when her boss repeatedly put his arms around her waist at a community event held on company premises. Not realizing at the time that sexual harassment is a power issue, she attributed her boss's improper behavior to the fact that she had worn a dress with a slit in the back to the event.

Sexual harassment affects victims' careers negatively. Twenty-five percent of respondents to a *Working Woman* survey said they were fired or forced to quit their jobs following harassment (Sandroff, 1992).

Sexual harassment can have harmful effects on victims' health. It leads to dysfunctional stress, which can result in chronic fatigue, headaches, and gastrointestinal problems. Twelve percent of survey respondents who had been sexually harassed reported negative health effects (Sandroff, 1992).

Besides being bad for individuals, sexual harassment hurts the entire organization. It causes morale to drop and contributes to absenteeism and turnover. This has an effect on productivity. Opportunity cost also is associated with sexual harassment. It drains time and energy that could have been used to pursue other goals.

Defending a firm against sexual harassment charges is expensive. Legal fees vary from thousands of dollars to more than $200,000. In 1988, K Mart paid $3.2 million to settle one case (Wagner, 1992). If a firm loses a lawsuit, awards have been as high as $4 million (Wagner, 1992).

It is difficult to quantify the impact of sexual harassment charges on a firm's public image. If a company develops a reputation for overlooking harassment, people may not want to work for the firm.

As mentioned earlier, employers are absolutely liable for quid pro quo sexual harassment by supervisors if they know or should have known that such behavior occurred but do not act promptly to stop it. They also may be liable for sexual harassment by co-workers or even by customers or clients.

PROTECTION AGAINST EMPLOYER LIABILITY

If employers face extensive liability in sexual harassment lawsuits, what can they do to protect themselves? First, they need a policy prohibiting sexual harassment that is written in easily understandable language and is distributed to all employees. Managers must be knowledgeable enough about the policy to be able to discuss it with employees. If the policy is placed in a manual that sits on a shelf, no one will be aware of its existence.

A policy alone is insufficient to protect firms from sexual harassment liability. Companies must conduct training, which should cover the nature of the problem, suggestions for dealing with it as an individual, internal channels for reporting harassment, investigation procedures, and links between harassment and discipline and grievance procedures.

The fact that sexual harassment depends on the receiver's perception makes some people nervous. Some overreact, refusing to go to lunch or to play golf with a co-worker of the opposite sex. Such an extreme reaction detracts from the camaraderie that helps people succeed in business. It could result in the exclusion of one gender from the informal organization.

The legal ban on sexual harassment was not designed to hinder friendly but professional interaction between women and men. On the contrary, the prohibition is intended to build an atmosphere in which each person is comfortable and is therefore free to direct his or her talents toward legitimate business ends.

Theoretically, people may accept this rationale, but practical questions remain. Assuming they do not want to be accused of sexual harassment, what guidelines should people follow? The American Management Association has some useful suggestions. That organization urges people to ask themselves if they would say or do something in front of their parents, spouse, children, or same-sex peers. Furthermore, they should consider whether they would like their statements quoted or actions described in the newspaper or on television. If they can answer affirmatively, it probably is all right to make the statement or take the action. Otherwise, the statement or action should be avoided (Meyer, 1992).

DEALING WITH SEXUAL HARASSMENT
AS AN INDIVIDUAL

The next topic to be covered in sexual harassment training is how the recipient of unwanted attention should deal with it. Contrary to popular belief, ignoring unwanted advances usually does not make them stop. This tactic, used by 46% of survey respondents who had been sexually harassed, was effective in only 25% of the cases. Deutschman (1991) dismisses the idea that unwelcome sexual behavior will cease if ignored. He says this tactic "doesn't work at all."

If a refusal to attend to offensive behavior does not squelch it, what will? As previously mentioned, direct confrontation has been most successful. When confronting a harasser, it is important to be specific and to focus on the behavior, not the person. For example, someone who does not appreciate office back rubs could say, "Chris, it makes me uncomfortable when you try to rub my back in the office. I don't think it's appropriate. Please stop."

If there are mixed signals about whether or not office back rubs are welcome, the direct approach clearly states that they are not. If Chris's behavior persists or escalates, the person being harassed should write Chris a memo again stating that she or he would like the back rubs to stop. The person could indicate that she or he will follow formal company procedure if the undesirable behavior continues. If the company has no procedure, the person could state that she or he is willing to pursue the matter with the EEOC if necessary. Complaining to the EEOC should be a last resort, however.

Throughout the ordeal, a person who is being harassed should document specifically what happened, when it occurred, and identities of any witnesses. This information is valuable if a formal complaint is filed. Also, the documentation process itself gives a victim some control over the situation, thus preserving self-esteem (Sandroff, 1992).

When implementing a harassment policy, there must be multiple channels for reporting complaints. Managers and others to whom individuals with complaints are directed should be knowledgeable about the problem of sexual harassment. They should be good listeners with well-developed interpersonal skills who are able to treat sensitive matters confidentially. Complaint intake personnel should be able to refer individuals to appropriate organizational units for additional assistance. People with concerns about sexual harassment must be able to discuss those matters with others besides their supervisors. Human resource department staff and others with reputations for sensitivity and fairness could be designated referral persons for those with concerns or complaints.

Firms that want to avoid sexual harassment liability must investigate all complaints promptly, thoroughly, and as confidentially as possible. First, they should appoint one or more investigators who are knowledgeable about sexual harassment and who have reputations for sensitivity. Investigators must be sensitive to both the complainant's fear of reprisals and the accused's concern about possible false accusations and resulting career harm.

To ensure objectivity, investigators should not be friends of either the complainant or the accused. Some firms, such as DuPont, appoint a man and a woman to an investigative team (Segal and Schiller, 1991).

The investigator or investigative team first listens to the complainant's version of events. After that person has specifically stated what happened, investigators should paraphrase his or her words to make sure they understand the situation. Then they should probe for details regarding the context of the behavior, its frequency and severity, and the type of relationship between the complainant and accused before the harassment allegation (Wagner, 1992).

Then investigators meet with the person accused of harassment. Again, they listen to that individual's side of the story. If the accused refuses to cooperate, investigators should end the interview and tell the person that the investigation will proceed without his or her input.

Witnesses also must be interviewed. Before making inquiries, investigators may have to define sexual harassment. They should then ask general questions such as whether or not witnesses have observed actions they would consider harassment. Investigators must protect identities of the complainant and alleged harasser until witnesses reveal them.

Investigators develop a "mosaic" of information about the alleged sexual harassment, interpret the facts, and present their findings to line managers. Those decision makers take appropriate actions, which may include discipline.

Judgments regarding credibility of witnesses and involved parties must be made, and facts must be distinguished from hearsay. Otherwise, a company that fires a person for sexual harassment could be sued for wrongful discharge. In 1988, Pennzoil paid $500,000 for wrongfully firing a male supervisor who had been accused of sexually harassing a female employee. The payment could have been avoided had the investigation not been flawed. In that case, investigators did not differentiate rumor from facts (Wagner, 1992).

Indisputable findings that sexual harassment occurred should result in sanctions. Disciplinary measures should depend on the harassment's severity. For example, perhaps verbal harassment that made the environment hostile would be punished by a written warning placed in the perpetrator's personnel file. On the other end of the spectrum, first-degree sexual assault might lead to immediate dismissal. Other penalties could include reduced compensation, suspension, or demotion.

When it is impossible to prove whether or not harassment occurred, both parties should know that the charge was taken seriously. A management consultant recommends assuring the alleged victim that, though there is no reason to doubt her or his sincerity, no action can be taken. Then the complainant should be urged to report any retaliation or additional instances of harassment. The alleged harasser should be told that there is not enough evidence to take further action and, at this point, his or her name is cleared. This person should be warned that future allegations will be taken even more seriously (Segal and Schiller, 1991).

CORPORATE RESPONSES TO SEXUAL HARASSMENT

Large, progressive companies have had sexual harassment policies and have conducted training for 10 to 20 years. Some have recently revamped programs or tried novel approaches. DuPont has a 24-hour telephone hotline that people can call to discuss concerns about harassment or personal security confidentially. That company also has a four-hour training program called "A Matter of Respect," which is led by one female and one male facilitator (Solomon, 1991). Honeywell has an interactive program featuring group exercises in which participants determine whether certain behaviors are harassment or not. Employees are allowed to discuss topics that were previously taboo at work, and that process seems to defuse tension (Meyer, 1992). Other major companies that conduct extensive sexual harassment training include Digital, Corning, Pacific Gas & Electric, and US West.

WOMEN OF COLOR AND SEXUAL HARASSMENT

Women of color are more likely to be sexually harassed than white women, for two reasons. First, minority women are concentrated in low-level, relatively powerless positions. As mentioned earlier, having a high-ranking position does not mean a woman is immune from sexual harassment. However, those who are powerless and perceived as dependent are particularly vulnerable to harassment too. Second, myths that African-American women are more sensuous and less upset about being harassed than white women make them likely targets (*Who's Hurt*, 1986).

According to Catharine MacKinnon, "black women's reports of sexual harassment by white male superiors reflect a sense of impunity that resounds of slavery and colonization" (MacKinnon, 1992). To support this contention, MacKinnon cites a case in which the white, male boss harassed a single-parent, African-American woman with two children to support on her first day of work. Among other things, he asked her whether she would sleep with a white man or slap him if he made a pass at her. She refused his advances and was subsequently fired for "inadequate job knowledge" (*Munford v. James T. Barnes & Co.* 441 F. Supp. 459 [E.D. Mich. 1977]).

RACIAL HARASSMENT

Women of color must contend not only with sexual and gender harassment but also with racial harassment. Verbal put-downs, accusations, or slurs based on one's ethnic origin constitute racial harassment, but it also may include racially motivated assault. To be legally actionable under Title VII, one must demonstrate that the employer did nothing to stop the racial harassment and that it was more than an isolated comment (Denis, 1984–85).

CORPORATE ROMANCE

Unlike harassment, in which power is the issue, corporate romance involves mutual attraction. Romance is an ambiguous term encompassing simple sexual attraction that has not been acted on, active affairs, and "nonsexual love relationships" (Solomon, 1990). Westhoff (1986) thinks supervisors should intervene to defuse tension produced when simple attraction creates self-consciousness or conflict or when others begin to notice it. She advises managers to meet with both employees separately and suggest that attraction may be the basis for these difficulties. Then the supervisor should counsel the couple "on how to mesh this personal development with their business lives to cause the fewest problems or none at all" (Westhoff, 1986).

If a couple is having an active affair, both individuals should first be counseled separately. Instead of judging them, the manager should focus on performance effects. After the parties weigh the consequences of their actions and consider options, the supervisor should meet with both together and let them devise a solution.

If this is ineffective, and discipline is necessary, it should be administered fairly to avoid violating Title VII. If termination is the only choice, both lovers should be fired. In the past, often only the woman lost her job. Now this would be clearly illegal.

A firm that demotes, rather than fires, romantically involved employees must be careful too. Those demoted could claim *constructive discharge*, meaning that their new jobs were so inferior to prior positions that their only real option was to resign.

Intra-office dating should not be ignored if it has a negative impact on performance. As Anderson and Hunsaker (1985) state,

When something other than romance causes productivity losses, lowered morale, poor quality of work, or failure to offer equal employment opportunity, management steps in to remedy the problem. It may be time for organizations that are affected to address this sticky but troublesome issue.

When relationships involving intense loyalty and trust are nonsexual, positive outcomes may outweigh the negative. So say three University of Michigan professors who asked over 1,000 women and men to describe their most psychologically intimate relationship with an opposite-sex peer. Most respondents said the collegiality improved morale and made them more creative and productive at work (Solomon, 1990).

Critics question whether a psychologically intimate relationship can continue without becoming sexual. For mature, self-disciplined individuals, this should be possible, but evidence shows that romantic entanglements often begin as workplace friendships (Anderson and Hunsaker, 1985; Solomon, 1990). When asked why their friendships stayed platonic, those in nonsexual relationships cited either moral principles or fear of repercussions.

Most managers feel uncomfortable confronting employees about interpersonal attraction, even when it has contributed to productivity declines. For example, the president of a New England manufacturer said he turns a blind eye when faced with office romance among workers. "I wouldn't know what to do if I saw something" (Westhoff, 1986).

Three steps could be taken to make managers more at ease in such situations. First, training regarding successful ways to approach sensitive issues could be provided. Second, managers could be given a list of professionals to whom they could refer particularly complex entanglements. Finally, the corporate philosophy on office romance could be discussed more openly.

At issue is worker privacy versus the employer's right to make rules needed to operate a business. Unless performance drops seem attributable to intra-office relationships, noninterference may be the only sensible approach. Otherwise, assuming productivity was not affected, companies that try to ban intra-office romance evenhandedly could be sued by employees claiming a violation of privacy rights.

Because people spend so much time at work, the office has become a natural meeting place. Proximity may lead to friendship and friendship to liking. Shared job successes may add "special excitement" (Anderson and Hunsaker, 1985). For this reason, the prevalence of office romance is not likely to diminish soon. It may be just one more sensitive issue managers must learn to deal with if the organization is affected.

SUMMARY

Quid pro quo and hostile environment sexual harassment are the two major forms of that workplace problem. Other variations are gender and third party harassment. The provision or denial of favorable job conditions, pay raises, or promotions based on acceptance or rejection of requests for sexual favors is quid pro quo harassment. Hostile environment harassment occurs when verbal, physical, or graphic sexual displays are so pervasive that they interfere with job performance or create an offensive or intimidating atmosphere at work.

Sexual harassment is widespread in U.S. firms. Companies have increased the amount of training offered on the issue to alleviate the problem. If left unchecked, harassment has harmful effects on a firm. These include increased absenteeism, turnover, legal fees, decreased morale and productivity, and negative publicity.

Racial harassment also creates a negative atmosphere and constitutes illegal discrimination. Women of color must contend with both sexual and racial harassment.

Some organizations disapprove of intra-office romance, but others take no position unless the relationship interferes with job performance. In that case, a manager should meet with both parties, discuss the situation frankly, and devise a solution. If discipline is necessary, it should be administered in a nondiscriminatory way.

DISCUSSION QUESTIONS

1. What positive steps should you take if you think you are being sexually harassed on the job?

2. You are a new manager at Goldman, Sachs & Company's Boston office. You have been made aware that some male employees in the office cut out nude photographs of women from magazines and pasted them on copies of company newsletters next to brief biographies of new women employees, as if they were photos of the new workers (Pereira, 1988). As the manager, what should you do?

3. How should sexual harassment charges be investigated?

4. Under what circumstances, if any, do you think organizations should try to regulate the practice of employees in the same firm dating each other?

5. Aurelia Jones, an African-American woman, was assistant director of human resource management in a Midwest electronics company. After giving a lengthy seminar on sexual and racial harassment to 20 white male senior managers, one of the men, whose last name was pronounced "coon," asked, "Does this mean the coons can't stick together?" All the men, including Aurelia's boss, began to laugh. What should Aurelia do or say? Now? Later? (adapted from Alexander, 1990)

6 Diversity Management

OBJECTIVES

After studying this chapter you should be able to:

1. Explain the meaning of diversity management.
2. Explain reasons for recent interest in diversity management.
3. Explain advantages of effective diversity management to the organization.
4. Explain the four stages of a prototypical program designed to value workforce diversity.

DIVERSITY MANAGEMENT: A DEFINITION

Diversity management is a process in which each worker's unique contributions are valued and used to achieve an organization's goals. It is not a one-shot program but an ongoing commitment to acknowledge explicitly employees' and the firm's cultural roots. Trust is a prerequisite to the process. Diversity management accepts and celebrates differences in race, gender, and other qualities.

At first, diversity management focused on race and sex. The process tried to integrate divergent races and both sexes in all organizational levels. Later, other characteristics were added to the definition of diversity. To some, the term includes anyone who either is not in the majority or does not conform to top management's expectations (Hanamura, 1989). This broadened definition may embrace single parents, the illiterate, people with disabilities, exempt and nonexempt employees, religious minorities, ethnic and cultural groups, gays and lesbians, and white males. In short, the expanded definition of diversity seeks to include and respect everyone.

Diversity management does not endorse certain lifestyles nor does it expect people to change long-held beliefs. It requires employees and managers to change workplace behaviors to the extent necessary to value each person's distinctive contribution.

If the definition of diversity management stops at inclusion of and respect for all based on legitimate business needs, it should gain widespread acceptance. If, on the other hand, it urges employees and managers to "celebrate" behaviors they find offensive based on religious convictions, for example, some will resist.

Also, some conditions resulting in a mosaic work force, under the expanded definition, are deplorable. Illiteracy is a prime example. According to values many share, it is important to respect the personhood of those who are illiterate or have deficient reading skills. But there seems to be nearly worldwide consensus that intervention to improve reading skills is desirable. Most do not view illiteracy as anything to applaud.

Thomas (1991) distinguishes between valuing diversity and diversity management. He believes that the former aims to improve interpersonal relations, and the latter is geared toward economic competitiveness. Valuing diversity lends itself to programming, but management of a mixture of people who vary on many dimensions is a long-run process. Programs designed to value diversity can be added to current equal employment opportunity efforts, but diversity management requires fundamental change of the system itself. Strict adherence to the distinction between valuing and managing diversity distinction would show that few firms take the managerial approach.

APPROACHES TO EMPLOYEE DIFFERENCE

Since the 1960s, organizations have taken various approaches to employee dissimilarity. At one time, difference and deficiency were equated. Women and minorities whose management styles diverged from methods that had made their white male peers successful received special training. During the 1980s, some thought that the differences women supposedly brought to management, such as more highly cultivated interpersonal skills, made them better managers. In chapter 7, Gary Powell's article addresses problems associated with the presumption that gender determines managerially relevant skills.

Regarding "difference," however, the pendulum has swung from viewing it as deficient to viewing it as better (Fine, Johnson, and Ryan, 1990). In reality, "difference" should have a neutral connotation. As Songer (1991) states, "there is a huge spectrum of useful qualities for people to have." No group has a monopoly on them all. Songer adds that "being aggressive, independent, individualistic, task-oriented, and analytical can make an excellent employee. But so can humility, a sense of collaboration, process-orientation, and intuition."

Overman (1991) explains the paradoxical nature of diversity, or multicultural, management. She says it is "having an acute awareness of characteristics common to a culture, race, gender, age, or sexual preference, while at the same time managing employees with these characteristics as individuals." Overman speaks of the need to weave individual and cultural fibers into the corporate cloth.

REASONS FOR DIVERSITY MANAGEMENT

Diversity management has been in the spotlight lately for several reasons. First, projections about the dwindling workforce and its changing composition have made firms realize the importance of attracting and retaining a future labor supply. This, coupled with the competitiveness of the global marketplace, makes it imperative for organizations to use human talent fully regardless of how it is packaged. Also, mergers and acquisitions have increased the need to integrate corporate cultures. The philosophy behind diversity management translates into ideas about how to create hybrid organizations that respect cultures associated with the merging firms.

Employees are less willing to give up part of themselves to fit the corporate mold than they were in the past. This fact also contributes to the popularity of diversity management. Most employees realize that some assimilation is needed, but they prefer a give-and-take process. They do not wish to compromise their uniqueness to have a career (Thomas, 1991).

Multicultural management represents a positive, new approach to goals that affirmative action programs previously tried to achieve. Capitalizing on difference is, depending on one's view, either an outgrowth of or a reaction to compliance-oriented affirmative action and equal employment opportunity programs.

Mandated affirmative action plans opened doors to minorities, but they alienated many, including some they were intended to help. Distortions of the goal-setting process within affirmative action plans led well-meaning companies to insist on hiring only minorities. This caused some whites to feel resentful and set the stage for subtle or overt conflict. Preferential treatment offended some minorities. It insulted their pride and desire to be hired and promoted based on the quality of their work rather than on immutable traits.

Economic survival, not social responsibility, lies behind new ways of handling the rainbow work force. The slowed growth of the labor force, coupled with its divergence, make new approaches vital. For example, from 1976 to 1988 the labor force grew at a rate of 2% per year. Since 1991, that annual growth rate has dropped to 1.2% and is projected to stay at that low rate through the year 2000 (Piturro and Mahoney, 1991).

In addition, demographics are changing in such a way that white males, who once accounted for 45% of new entrants to the workforce, now comprise only 15%. Immigrant males make up 13% of those joining the American work force in the 1990s, and men of color native to the United States constitute 7%. Sixty-four percent of those joining the labor force in the 1990s are female, 13% of whom are women of color. Another 42% of the new female workers are whites who are native to the United States, and 9% are immigrants (Solomon, 1989).

These statistics show that the work force already is diverse. The question is not whether to accept a medley of employees but, rather, whether to manage the new labor force potpourri effectively or ineffectively.

ADVANTAGES OF DIVERSITY MANAGEMENT

Creating a climate to support diversity has several advantages. It is crucial to recruitment and retention. It also reduces absenteeism, prevents poor morale, and reduces miscommunication. Multicultural management may yield greater creativity and innovation. In addition, heterogeneous workers bring fresh perspectives to problem solving and may have synergistic effects. A diverse labor force gives firms a strategic advantage when marketing to heterogeneous customers. A management style that respects and tries to develop each person fully is socially responsible. Finally, dealing with diversity effectively may result in a more equitable distribution of economic opportunity (Cox, 1991).

The importance of properly managing divergent workers to attract and retain them has been discussed. If predicted labor shortages materialize, employees will gain power. They may leave organizations that have done nothing to identify and accommodate their unique needs or to create a positive atmosphere.

Firms that do not adjust to diverging employee needs may have high absenteeism. In a seller's market for labor, workers who feel alienated in a company that expects them to conform to an outdated, "one size fits all" model may withdraw from the organization. Excess absenteeism is one manifestation of such withdrawal.

Those who go to work though they feel disconnected from groups that do not seem to value their contributions may have poor morale, which is contagious. On the other hand, appreciation of uniqueness may inoculate workers against attitudinal malaise.

Miscommunication can occur among the culturally similar. Its likelihood increases when workers are ethnically diverse. In those circumstances, people tend to project similarity where none exists (Adler, 1991). They falsely assume that those with varying cultural heritages are basically alike. They do not attend to language nuances or culturally determined aspects of socialization, and later wonder why communication breakdowns have occurred.

To avoid miscommunication based on culture, people must recognize the existence of high and low context cultures. Kennedy and Everest (1991) describe most Asian, Hispanic, and African-American cultures as high context because they are more sensitive to surroundings, value nonverbal cues, and communicate to establish and maintain relationships. More new workers now come from groups socialized in high context cultures.

Low context cultures, on the other hand, deemphasize surroundings. Nonverbal cues are less important because words alone convey meaning. Information exchange is presumed to be the purpose of communication.

Until recently, most American managers have been descendents of Northern Europeans, whose cultures were traditionally characterized as low context. Employees reared in high context cultures therefore were predisposed to communications breakdowns with their managers.

One manager, whose culture of origin stressed information exchange, had difficulty communicating with her boss. She was frustrated that the boss seemed to talk around a problem, expecting her to pick up cues about what was really bothering him. At first, the manager attributed this to a personal style difference, but later conceded that the difficulties may have had cultural origins because her boss had emigrated from a country with a high context culture.

Employees in firms that deal with differences effectively have more energy to devote to organizational concerns. For example, companies that are candid about the biculturalism racial minorities experience may be more understanding of the difficulties associated with operating in two cultural spheres simultaneously.

The next two benefits of diversity management are related. The process enhances creativity and innovation and provides new perspectives to organizational problems. If a heterogeneous work force exists in an organization that fosters trust and encourages all employees to express their ideas, novel approaches to problems are likely. Employees will be able to draw on their differing backgrounds to devise innovative solutions. The unique assumptions, values, and views a varied employee group brings to bear on a problem could have synergistic effects.

If an organization's commitment to diversity means that employees of every type are represented at all levels of the organization, their presence may give the firm a marketing edge. Employees, who are individuals first but also members of various groups, might be more sensitive to concerns of customers who belong to those same groups. It might be easier for them to establish rapport with those customers. Though this may be true, firms must guard against excluding certain employees from sales or public relations positions based on consumers' desire to interact with those similar to themselves. Such a rationale constituted unlawful discrimination when used in the 1970s to exclude women from certain jobs based on clients' preference for dealing with men.

Though a diverse work force may provide a strategic marketing advantage, Songer (1991) cautions against selecting new hires solely for that reason. She fears they may be considered tokens in the sense of being valued because of unchangeable features instead of because of their accomplishments.

Managing employees in a way to encourage full use of their talents is socially responsible. Some advocates argue, however, that the process should not be started just for that reason. Songer (1991) claims that starting the diversity management process "because it is the right thing to do" will not generate long-run enthusiasm.

Tapping each employee's full potential will result in a more equitable distribution of economic opportunity (Cox, 1991). An organization that values diversity will make sure all employees have access to the social support and political savvy they need to complement task knowledge. This should help distribute promotions, and hence, higher pay levels, more equitably.

DISADVANTAGES OF DIVERSITY MANAGEMENT

Disadvantages of diversity management stem from misunderstanding of the process or from implementation difficulties. An "affirmative action mentality" can interfere with diversity management. Even when reassured that everyone including white males will be valued, people with this mindset assume an "us versus them" stance. This is counterproductive, but until some employees see tangible evidence that diversity management is not preferential treatment with a new name, they are skeptical.

Pitfalls to implementation of diversity management are related to resistance to change. When organizations consider a major shift in focus, employees deserve an explanation of the need for the change. Educational strategies may help minimize resistance, as may methods that involve employees in the change and allow them control over it.

Top management must be squarely behind the move toward diversity management, and leaders appointed to activate the change must be facilitators, not dictators. They must understand diversity concepts thoroughly and be committed to them in word and deed.

Since diversity management is situational and is philosophically rather than technique oriented, it is inappropriate to discuss specific steps for its implementation. So the focus now will shift to a description of some programs that have been developed to value diversity.

PROGRAMS TO VALUE DIVERSITY

One prototype involves assessment, skills training, improvement of organizational life, and evaluation (Mandell and Kohler-Gray, 1990). During Phase I, assessment, the organization reviews its commitment to each employee's career growth. Bias-free recruitment, selection, and training procedures give evidence of this commitment, which must be more than a written policy.

Phase II, skills development, involves evaluating training materials to remove bias and to ensure that women, men, and minorities serve as role models. Ongoing skill-building workshops should be integrated, with special training provided for minorities or women only if they request it.

Phase III, improvement of organizational life, is the part of diversity programs that has captured most attention. It features awareness training and may use workshops or role playing to build understanding among different groups and a feeling that each employee is unique and valued.

Awareness of one's culture must precede appreciation of the ethnic heritage of others. Consultant Lewis Griggs urges training participants to "start with themselves, recognizing first that they have a cultural identity which determines the style of eye contact, body language, and communication." He says, "we need to understand what our own culture is, our own style and ... set of values before we can possibly recognize that somebody else has an equally justifiable, culturally-determined set of behaviors and values" (Leonard, 1991).

Security Pacific Bank uses an exercise in which employees describe themselves in terms of four factors that define their identity, such as race, sex, class, occupation, or citizenship. Workers then divide into small groups to explain how these qualities have affected their lives. When the large group reassembles, employees are surprised to discover the extent of diversity within the firm (Cohen, 1991).

Still another Phase III option involves switching gender or cultural roles. If gender roles are the focus, men play the part of women in management and discuss positive and negative aspects of men's professional conduct in the workplace. Then participants exchange roles. The ensuing discussion may be intense but usually leads to greater understanding of gender issues.

Some companies begin diversity programs with awareness training, usually considered part of Phase III. Honeywell cautions against such an approach. In that firm, opening with education about other cultures led to stereotyping. Managers with one Hispanic woman in their department wanted to know how to deal with Hispanic women. Instead of treating that person as an individual, she was categorized. Lumping people into ethnic groups in this way would defeat the purpose of programs intended to value people as individuals (Overman, 1991).

During Phase IV, the organization should evaluate whether more minorities and women are represented at all management levels, not just in the lowest ranks. In the final phase, it is important to assure accountability. Hughes Aircraft does this by tying each operational unit's eligibility for a bonus pool to achievement of diversity objectives (Overman, 1991). Amtrak links pay and promotion to attainment of affirmative action goals. Exxon requires division managers to submit, as part of their performance appraisal, a summary of career development plans they have set up for at least 10 female and minority male employees (Cox, 1991).

Many Fortune 500 corporations have begun diversity training. Those listed as the 12 most proactive are Digital, Avon, Corning, DuPont, Hewlett-Packard, Honeywell, Pacific Bell, Procter & Gamble, US West, Apple Computer, and Security Pacific Bank (Livingston, 1991).

SUMMARY

Most new entrants to the workforce in the 1990s will be minorities and women. Businesses must actively welcome these groups. They must develop programs that capitalize on differences and simultaneously minimize race or gender-based tensions.

An organizational climate that supports diversity has several advantages. It aids recruitment and retention, improves morale, and helps cut absenteeism and turnover. In addition, a workforce in which divergent groups bring their perspectives to problem solving may have synergistic effects and may result in increased creativity and innovation.

Implementation of diversity management involves change and can, therefore, be difficult. Employees may resist. They deserve an explanation of the need for change. Top management support of the transformation will facilitate its acceptance.

Some distinguish between diversity management, which is a long-term process, and valuing diversity, which lends itself to programming. One program designed to value diversity has four phases, namely assessment, skills training, improvement of organizational life, and evaluation. Several Fortune 500 firms offer sophisticated diversity training.

DISCUSSION QUESTIONS

1. Do you think a program to manage workforce diversity should be considered an outgrowth of affirmative action or a business necessity? Explain.

2. Why is "managing diversity" such a challenge to business?

3. Why can't we assume "that everything will simply work properly for the women and other minorities who make it into the pipeline of business"? (Songer, 1991)

4. How can people avoid culturally based miscommunication?

5. How can people determine whether miscommunication is an interpersonal matter or whether it has been influenced by cultural or ethnic differences?

7 Stereotypes and Their Effects on Leadership Perceptions

OBJECTIVES

After studying this chapter you should be able to:

1. Define the term stereotype.
2. Explain and debunk three general stereotypes about females and males.
3. Explain stereotypes that are applied to women of color.
4. Explain whether or not research supports stereotypical differences between male and female managers.
5. Explain how subordinates of both sexes react to managerial women.
6. Explain whether or not leadership theories favor behaviors linked with the stereotypical sex role of either women or men.
7. Explain what is meant by androgynous management.

Stereotypes are consistent patterns describing most remembered qualities of a group. They can be based on people's sex, race, ethnic group, religion, or the geographical region where they live. A categorization process that simplifies people's thinking, stereotyping occurs because people are bombarded with more stimuli than they can handle. Generalizing frees them from concern about mind-boggling details.

SEXUAL STEREOTYPING

When applied to individuals, stereotypes may be inaccurate. They prevent people from knowing each other as individuals. For example, when students know a professor belongs to the women's studies department, some assume they know several other beliefs of that faculty member. Such assumptions, when applied to an individual professor, may be incorrect. In reality, people and their beliefs are more complex than stereotypes would indicate. Attributing an entire set of characteristics to a person based on one known affiliation or behavior is risky. At best, it causes misunderstanding, and at worst, it can stifle development and limit options.

The following statements will be discussed in turn. Some are obviously false, while others contain a grain of truth.

1. Women experience greater mood swings than men and are thus unsuited for top management positions.

2. Girls lack achievement motivation; boys have this motivation.

3. Women have lower self-esteem than men.

4. Females have better verbal skills; males have better mathematical skills.

5. Males are more aggressive than females.

6. Men must always appear to be in control of their emotions, jobs, and lives.

7. Men who do not climb the career ladder to the topmost rung are wimps.

Regarding the first stereotype, a common belief is that women experience drastic mood shifts due to the menstrual cycle. In both sexes, hormones and moods are related, but the connection is complex and is not fully understood. Studies done in the 1970s showed that men have recurring patterns of hormonal and associated mood changes (Doering et al., 1974). On this point, Maccoby and Jacklin (1975) concluded:

Male and female hormonal cycles may differ only in that (1) there is a greater variability in male cycle length and (2) there are external signs of the female cycle. Both of these differences for girls and women may actually be an advantage. A woman can more easily take her cycle into account in understanding her own mood swings. One could then argue that the male hormone mood cycle is more dangerous, since a man cannot as readily take it into account and deal accordingly with his hostile feelings.

Mature adults are not slaves to their hormonal systems. Most cope with mood swings effectively both at work and in their personal lives. Typically, men do not have physical fights with co-workers, nor do women cry at the office for several days each month (Powell, 1988).

Regarding the second stereotype, in early studies, girls' achievement motivation was higher than that of boys. Boys had to be challenged by appeals to their ego or sense of competition to bring their achievement motivation up to the same level as the girls (Maccoby and Jacklin, 1975).

Until recently, inter-sex self-esteem differences were thought to affect only those attending college. For unexplained reasons, college men had a greater sense of control and confidence in task performance (Powell, 1988). Otherwise, self-esteem between adult women and men differed little.

Perhaps sex-based distinctions in self-regard are related to the university environment. Before the late 1980s, when many colleges tried to increase campus diversity, universities were not particularly hospitable to women. In *Out of the Classroom: A Chilly Campus Climate for Women?* (1984), Hall and Sandler pointed out subtle differences in the ways professors treat male and female students. For example, faculty of both sexes tend to call on male students more frequently in class and give them more eye contact. Outside the classroom, women students have fewer interactions with faculty and receive less informal feedback. Added together, all such "micro-inequities" may have contributed to lower self-esteem of female college students.

Sex-based self-esteem variations may occur among adolescent females as well as among college women. In a recent study, a Bucknell University psychologist concluded that adolescent girls ages 11 to 13 seemed to be "more down on themselves" than male adolescents. He attributed their reduced self-image to body changes that made the girls feel less attractive (Wade et al., 1989). Other studies on girls' self-esteem showed it to equal that of boys during childhood and adolescence (Powell, 1988).

Sex differences in mathematical and verbal skills are small and may depend on research design. Hyde and Linn (1988) claim such distinctions in verbal abilities have diminished over the past decades and are nearly gone. One reason for the decline could be an attempt to make test items gender-neutral. Jacklin (1989) says the only remaining sex differences in intellectual abilities are at the high end of the math skills continuum, where boys have been overrepresented for years. Andersen (1988) attributes this to cultural role expectations.

Males traditionally have been considered more aggressive than females in many cultures from the age of two on. Hormonal variations do not explain boys' increased dominance adequately, however. According to Andersen (1988), "if high levels of testosterone were needed to produce aggression, then we would expect to see little difference in aggressive behavior between prepubescent boys and girls. However, much research shows that boys are more aggressive at an early age."

Powell (1988) claims that sex differences in dominance among adults are situational. Though men are more likely to initiate aggression, both sexes are equally aggressive when provoked and during marital conflict.

RACIAL STEREOTYPING

Dealing with sex-based stereotypes is difficult enough, but women of color must deal with myths based on both sex and race. For example, Asian women are portrayed as either docile and submissive or are assigned erotic labels such as "geisha girl." Asian women who wish to succeed in business must overcome obstacles these stereotypes create.

Another problem Asians of both sexes experience is that others consider them a "superminority." They are expected to do well and are viewed as "shy, brainy nerds who are especially good at math" (Rigdon, 1991). All Asians, whether they come from rural or urban countries, are lumped together.

How could success expectations harm those who wish to excel in management? They could create undue stress, contributing to nervous breakdowns and even suicide. Though absolute numbers are small, suicide rates among Asian-American teens have tripled in the past two decades, largely because of pressure from society and family (Rigdon, 1991).

While Asians are presumed to be destined for success, African-American professionals are thwarted by assumptions that their skills are average at best. Also, African-American women feel that males of their race act more like enemies than peers working toward equality. These women claim that African-American men seem threatened by their accomplishments.

African-American women may be expected to conform to a caretaker stereotype. Nonminorities supposedly feel more comfortable if black women take on roles in which they help employees adjust to stresses of corporate life than if they strive for high performance in formal, top-level positions (Ramos, 1981).

Like Asian women, Native-American women have been stereotyped either as pitiable figures or sexpots. Descriptive phrases include the "poor, overworked squaw" and the "Cherokee princess." Ferguson (1985) says the squaw image is inaccurate because Native-American women had much authority in the tribe and were usually protected and respected by it. Their responsibilities were no more onerous than those of the men.

Women are not the only ones limited by stereotypes. Men have had to contend with the "John Wayne" myth, which requires them to be in control and unemotional. Some men have begun to question this strong, "macho" image. They have decided to become assertive rather than domineering, to show affection more openly, and to seek help from others. Some have begun to reap personal benefits from greater involvement in child rearing.

If women have been viewed as sex objects, men have been considered success objects. Sometimes their worth as individuals has taken a back seat to the value of the income they earn.

As a reaction to the women's movement and because of dissatisfaction with the status quo, men have begun to organize. In the early 1990s, *Iron John* (Bly, 1992) gave further impetus to this movement. In the context of a story, Bly claims that our culture mishandles critical transitions in a boy's life; namely separation from his mother and initiation into the male world. This leads to "father hunger" among men, which causes many social prob-

Men become "soft males" who do not start wars or ravage the earth, but who lack conviction. They are comfortable with decision making by consensus and nonhierarchical organizations but are out of touch with their "deep masculinity." To get in touch, males must do the emotional work needed to connect to the "wildmen" within. The internal "wildmen" are not macho or brutal; rather, they are individuals with deep convictions who also can be spontaneous and are occasionally strong (Bly, 1992).

Men who were deprived of a father's attention try to compensate for that loss through male bonding. To facilitate this, men's centers nationwide sponsor retreats, during which men are encouraged to communicate with other males on a deeper level. Topics like jobs, sports, and cars are banned. Men are urged to get in touch with long-neglected feelings.

Women sometimes wish their bosses would urge them to achieve professionally. Men, on the other hand, get too much pressure to do the same. They are encouraged to be less performance-oriented, but if they follow such advice, peers may question their ambition. Thus, they face a no-win situation.

Since general stereotypes have been discussed, it is appropriate to narrow our focus and examine alleged sex differences between male and female managers. Powell does that in the following article.

"One More Time: Do Female and Male Managers Differ?"
by Gary Powell

EXECUTIVE OVERVIEW

There has been a dramatic change in the "face" of management over the last two decades. That face is now female more than one-third of the time. What are the implications for the practice of management? Most of us are aware of traditional stereotypes about male-female differences, but how well do these stereotypes apply to the managerial ranks? Do male and female managers differ in their basic responses to work situations and their overall effectiveness (and if so, in what ways), or are they really quite similar?

This article reviews the research evidence gathered on these questions since women managers were first noticed by researchers in the mid-1970s. The implications of this review are discussed, and contrasted with recommendations offered in recent articles by Jan Grant in *Organizational Dynamics* and Felice Schwartz in *Harvard Business Review*. The title of the article is styled after the title of Frederick Herzberg's classic 1968 *Harvard Business Review* article, "One More Time: How Do You Motivate Employees?" Herzberg addressed a question that had been addressed many times in the past but had never quite gone away. So does this article.

Do female and male managers differ in the personal qualities they bring to their jobs? Yes, if you believe two recent articles in influential business magazines. Jan Grant, in a 1988 *Organizational Dynamics* article entitled "Women as Managers: What They Can Offer to Organizations"[1] asserted that women have unique qualities that make them particularly well-suited as managers. Instead of forcing women to fit the male model of managerial success, emphasizing such qualities as independence, competitiveness, forcefulness, and analytical thinking, Grant argued that organizations should place greater emphasis on such female qualities as affiliation and attachment, cooperativeness, nurturance, and emotionality.

Felice Schwartz's 1989 *Harvard Business Review* article, "Management Women and the New Facts of Life,"[2] triggered a national debate over the merits of "mommy tracks" (though she did not use this term herself). She proposed that corporations (1) distinguish between "career-primary-women" who put their careers first and "career-and-family" women who seek a balance between career and family, (2) nurture the careers of the former group as potential top executives, and (3) offer flexible work arrangements and family supports to the latter group in exchange for lower opportunities for career advancement. Women were assumed to be more interested in such arrangements, and thereby less likely to be suitable top executives than men; there has been less discussion over the merits of "daddy tracks."

Male and female managers certainly differ in their success within the managerial ranks. Although women have made great strides in entering management since 1970, with the overall proportion of women managers rising from 16% to 40%, the proportion of women who hold top management positions is less than 3%.[3] This could be due simply to the average male manager being older and more experienced than the average female manager. After all, managerial careers invariably start at the bottom. If there were no basic differences between male and female managers, it would be just a matter of time until the proportion of women was about the same at all managerial levels.

But are there basic differences between male and female managers? Traditional sex role stereotypes state that males are more masculine (e.g., self-reliant, aggressive, competitive, decisive) and females more feminine (e.g., sympathetic, gentle, shy, sensitive to the needs of others.)[4] Grant's views of male-female differences mirrored these stereotypes. However, there is disagreement over the applicability of these stereotypes to managers. Three distinct points of view have emerged:

1. No differences. Women who pursue the nontraditional career of manager reject the feminine stereotype and have needs, values, and leadership styles similar to those of men who pursue managerial careers.

2. Stereotypical differences. Female and male managers differ in ways predicted by stereotypes, as a result of early socialization experiences that reinforce masculinity in males and femininity in females.

3. Nonstereotypical differences. Female and male managers differ in ways opposite to stereotypes, because women managers have to be exceptional to compensate for early socialization experiences that are different from those of men.

I recently conducted an extensive review of research on sex differences in management to determine the level of support for each of these viewpoints.[5] I considered four types of possible differences: in behavior, motivation, commitment, and subordinates' responses (see Table 7.1).

THE REVIEW

The two most frequently studied types of managerial behavior are task-oriented and people-oriented behavior.[6] Task-oriented behavior is directed toward subordi-

Table 7.1
Sex Difference in Management: Selected Results

DIMENSION	RESULTS
Behavior	
Task-oriented	No difference.
People-oriented	No difference
Effectiveness ratings	Stereotypical difference in evaluations of managers in laboratory studies: Males favored.
Response to poor performer	Stereotypical difference: Males use normal of equality, whereas females use norm of euality.
Influence strategies	Stereotypical difference: Males use a wider range of strategies, more positive strategies, and less negative strategies. This difference diminishes when women managers have high self-confidence.
Motivation	No difference in some studies. Nonstereotypical difference in other studies: Female motivational profile is closer to that associates with success-ful managers.
Commitment	Inconsistent evidence regarding difference.
Subordinates' Responses	Stereotypical difference in responses to managers in laboratory studies: Managers using style that matches sex role stereotype are favored.

nates' performance and includes initiating work, organizing it, and setting deadlines and standards. People-oriented behavior is directed toward subordinates' welfare and includes seeking to build their self-confidence, making them feel at ease, and soliciting their input about matters that affect them.

There have been numerous studies of whether female and male leaders differ in these two types of behavior, including (1) laboratory studies in which individuals are asked to react to a standardized description of a female or male leader or are led by a female or male leader on a simulated work task, and (2) field studies comparing female and male leaders in actual organizational settings. Laboratory studies control the variable under investigation better, but they provide less information about the manager. Thus, they are more likely to yield results that support stereotypes of managers than field studies.

Sex role stereotypes suggest that men, being masculine, will be higher in task-oriented behavior and women, being feminine, will be higher in people-oriented behavior. However, sex role stereotypes are not supported when the results of different studies are considered as a whole. According to a "meta-analysis" of research studies, male and female leaders exhibit similar amounts of task-oriented behavior regardless of the type of study.

Male leaders have been rated as more effective in laboratory studies, but male and female leaders are seen as similarly effective in "the real world."[7]

There are some possible sex differences in managerial behavior that are under investigation. For example, some evidence supporting the "stereotypical differences" view suggests that female and male managers differ in their responses to poor performers. Males may follow a norm of equity, basing their response on whether they believe the poor performance is caused by lack of ability or lack of effort, and females a norm of equality, treating all poor performers alike regardless of the assumed cause.[8] Other evidence suggests that female and male managers differ in the strategies they use to influence subordinates (see Table 7.1), but that this difference diminishes as women managers gain self-confidence in their jobs.[9] Overall, though, the pattern of research results on sex differences in managerial behavior favors the "no differences" view.

Female managers are at least as motivated as male managers. Some studies have found that female and male managers score essentially the same on psychological tests of motives that predict managerial success, supporting the "no differences" view. When sex differences have been found, they have supported the "nonstereotypical differences" view. For example, in a study of nearly 2,000 managers, women managers reported lower basic needs and higher needs for self-actualization. Compared with males, female managers were more concerned with opportunities for growth, autonomy, and challenge and less concerned with work environment and pay. The women managers were judged to exhibit a "more mature and higher-achieving motivational profile" than their male counterparts.[10]

There is disagreement about whether female and male managers possess different levels of commitment.[11] Some studies have found that women are more committed as a group than males; other studies have found that women are less committed; and still other studies have found no sex difference in commitment. Instead, factors other than sex have been linked more conclusively to commitment. For example, age and education are positively associated with commitment. Greater job satisfaction, more meaningful work, and greater utilization of skills also are associated with stronger commitment.[12]

Even if male and female managers did not differ in any respect, their subordinates still could react to them differently. Subordinates' responses to managers have varied according to the type of study. Some laboratory studies have found that managers are judged more favorably when their behavior fits the appropriate sex role stereotype. Female managers using a people-oriented leadership style have been evaluated more positively than male managers using that style; and male managers using a task-oriented style have been evaluated more positively than female managers using that style. However, subordinates do not respond differently to actual male and female managers, supporting the "no differences" view. Once subordinates have worked for both female and male managers, the effects of stereotypes disappear and managers are treated as individuals rather than representatives of their sex.[13]

In summary, sex differences are absent in task-oriented behavior, people-oriented behavior, effectiveness ratings of actual managers, and subordinates' responses to actual managers. Stereotypical differences in some types of managerial behavior and in some ratings of managers in laboratory studies favor male managers. On the other hand, when differences in motivational profiles appear, they are nonstereotypical and favor female managers. Although results regarding sex differences in commitment are inconclusive, sex differences are not as extensive as other types of differences.

This review supports the "no differences" view of sex differences in management.

There is not much difference between the needs, values, and leadership styles of male and female managers. The sex differences that have been found are few, found in laboratory studies more than field studies, and tend to cancel each other out.

IMPLICATIONS FOR ORGANIZATIONS

The implications of this review are clear: If there are not differences between male and female managers, companies should not act as if there are. Instead, they should follow two principles in their actions:

1. To be gender-blind in their decisions regarding open managerial positions and present or potential managers, except when consciously trying to offset the effects of past discrimination.

2. To try to minimize differences in the job experiences of their male and female managers, so that artificial sex differences in career success do not arise.

Grant based her recommendations on a "stereotypical differences" view. She argued that organizations will benefit from placing greater value on women's special qualities:[14]

These "human resources" skills are critical in helping to stop the tide of alienation, apathy, cynicism, and low morale in organizations. . . . If organizations are to become more humane, less alienating, and more responsive to the individuals who work for them, they will probably need to learn to value process as well as product. Women have an extensive involvement in the processes of our society—an involvement that derives from their greater participation in the reproductive process and their early experience of family life. . . . Thus women may indeed be the most radical force available in bringing about organizational change.

Human resources skills are certainly essential to today's organizations. Corporations that are only concerned with getting a product out and pay little attention to their employees' needs are unlikely to have a committed workforce or to be effective in the long run. However, women are at risk when corporations assume that they have a monopoly on human resource skills. The risk is that they will be placed exclusively in managerial jobs that particularly call for social sensitivity and interpersonal skills in dealing with individuals and special-interest groups, e.g., public relations, human resources management, consumer affairs, corporate social responsibility. These jobs are typically staff functions, peripheral to the more powerful line functions of finance, sales, and production and seldom regarded in exalted terms by line personnel. Women managers are disproportionately found in such jobs, outside the career paths that most frequently lead to top management jobs.[15] Corporations that rely on Grant's assertions about women's special abilities could very well perpetuate this trend.

Thus it is very important that the facts about sex differences in management be disseminated to key decision-makers. When individuals hold on to stereotypical views about sex differences despite the facts, either of two approaches may be tried.

1. Send them to programs such as cultural diversity workshops to make them aware of the ways in which biases related to sex (as well as race, age, etc.) can affect their decisions and to learn how to keep these biases from occurring. For example, Levi Strauss put all of its executives, including the president, through an intense three day program designed to make them examine their attitudes toward women and minorities on the job.[16]

2. Recognize that beliefs and attitudes are difficult to change and focus on changing behavior instead. If people are motivated to be gender-blind in their decision-making by an effective performance appraisal and reward system backed by the CEO, they often come to believe in what they are doing.[17]

Organizations should do whatever they can to equalize the job experiences of equally-qualified female and male managers. This means abandoning the model of a successful career as an uninterrupted sequence of promotions to positions of greater responsibility heading toward the top ranks. All too often, any request to take time out from career for family reasons, either by a woman or a man, is seen as evidence of lack of career commitment.

Schwartz based her recommendations on a real sex difference: More women than men leave work for family reasons due to the demand of maternity and the differing traditions and expectations of the sexes. However, her solution substitutes a different type of sex difference, that such women remain at work with permanently reduced career opportunities. It does not recognize that women's career orientation may change during their careers. Women could temporarily leave the fast track for the mommy track, but then be ready and able to resume the fast track later. Once they were classified as career-and-family, they would find it difficult to be reclassified as career-primary even if their career commitment returned to its original level.

Corporations could offer daddy tracks as well as mommy tracks and accurately believe that they were treating their female and male employees alike. However, if women tended to opt for such programs more than men and anyone who opted for one was held back in pursuing a future managerial career, the programs would contribute to a sex difference in access to top management positions. Automatic restrictions should not be placed on the later career prospects of individuals who choose alternative work arrangements. Those who wish to return to the fast track should be allowed to do so once they demonstrate the necessary skills and commitment.

There are other ways by which organizations can minimize sex differences in managers' job experiences. For example, the majority of both male and female top executives have had one or more mentors, and mentorship has been critical to their advancement and success.[18] However, as Kathy Kram, an expert on the mentoring process, observed, "It's easier for people to mentor people like themselves."[19] Lower-level female managers have greater difficulty in finding mentors than male managers at equivalent levels, due to the smaller number of female top executives. Unless companies do something, this gives lower-level male managers an advantage in getting ahead.

Some companies try to overcome barriers of sex by assigning highly-placed mentors to promising lower-level managers. For example, at the Bank of America, senior executives are asked to serve as mentors for three or four junior managers for a year at a time. Formal mentoring programs also have been implemented at the Jewel Companies, Aetna, Bell Labs, Merrill Lynch, and Federal Express. Such programs do not guarantee career success for the recipients of mentoring, of course. However, they do contribute to making mentors more equally available for male and female managers.[20]

Companies also influence job experiences through the training and development programs that they encourage or require their managers to take. These programs contribute to a sex difference in job experiences if (1) men and women are systematically diagnosed to have different developmental needs and thereby go through different programs, or (2) men and women are deliberately segregated in such programs. Both of these conditions have been advocated and met in the past. For example, in a 1972 article in *Personnel Journal*, Marshall Brenner concluded that[21]

> women will, for the immediate future, generally require different managerial development activities than men. This is based on research showing that, in general, they have different skills and different attitudes toward the managerial role than men do.

This review suggests the opposite, particularly for women and men who are already in management positions. Women managers do not need to be sent off by themselves for "assertiveness training"—they already know how to be assertive.

Instead, they need access to advanced training and development activities, such as executive MBAs or executive leadership workshops, just like male managers do.

Some of the available activities, such as the Executive Women Workshop offered by the Center for Creative Leadership (CCL), are open only to women. In addition, some companies, such as Northwestern Bell, have their own executive leadership programs for women only. Such programs, when attended voluntarily, provide women managers a useful opportunity to "share experiences and ideas with other executive women in a unique environment," as the CCL's catalogue puts it, as well as provide valuable executive training.[22] In general, though, women and men should be recommended for training and development programs according to their individual needs rather than their sex. Almost half of the companies regarded as "the best companies for women" in a recent book rely on training and workshops to develop their high-potential managerial talent. However, many of these companies, including Bidermann Industries, General Mills, Hewitt Associates, Neiman-Marcus, and Pepsi Co., have no special programs for women; they simply assign the best and brightest people regardless of sex.[23]

In conclusion, organizations should not assume that male and female managers differ in personal qualities. They also should make sure that their policies, practices, and programs minimize the creation of sex differences in managers' experiences on the job. There is little reason to believe that either women or men make superior managers, or that women and men are different types of managers. Instead, there are likely to be excellent, average, and poor managerial performers within each sex. Success in today's highly competitive marketplace calls for organizations to make best use of the talent available to them. To do this, they need to identify, develop, encourage, and promote the most effective managers, regardless of sex.

DISCUSSION QUESTIONS

1. Do you think it is just a matter of time until the proportion of women and men at all management levels is the same, or not? Explain.

2. Do you agree or disagree with Powell's view that women are at risk when assumed to have a monopoly on human resource skills? Explain.

3. Should any managers—male or female—have to trade career advancement for greater flexibility to balance personal lives and paid employment? Explain.

4. Do you think organization-sponsored training for managers should be sex-segregated or not? Explain.

VIEWS OF THE "TYPICAL" EXECUTIVE

Although few documented sex-based differences in management style exist, the typical executive is, nonetheless, still described in masculine terms. When most people think of a business executive, despite the fact that 40% of all managers are women, they think of a male. This was true in the 1970s when separate samples of middle managers, supervisors, and business students (Schein, 1973; Powell and Butterfield, 1979) thought successful managers were more like men than women. Males and successful managers, but not females, were considered decisive, firm, unemotional, and logical.

In 1990, Schein repeated the 1973 study, only to discover that male executives' views had changed little in 20 years. As had been the case in the 1970s, subjects thought the average man resembled a successful manager more than the average woman did.

Heilman and colleagues (1989) found that "the correspondence between descriptions of women and successful managers increases dramatically when the women are depicted as managers." Thus, "providing defining information about women diminishes the ascription of traditionally stereotyping attributes." Nevertheless, the same study showed that male managers and successful executives were thought to have more leadership abilities and business skill.

One reason for the latter finding could be that respondents were all male. Results may have changed had more subjects been female, because women, more than men, tend to view females in general as similar to managers (Brenner, Tomkiewicz, and Schein, 1989; Massengill and DiMarco, 1979).

In the reading, Powell said subordinates tend to view supervisors similarly, without considering their gender, after getting to know them as individuals. Heilman et al. (1989) reached opposite conclusions. They argued that employees' perceptions of managerial women do not change as they gain experience working for them.

Kanter (1977) claims employees prefer male bosses because they are perceived to have more power than females. Subordinates dislike working for any powerless manager and may translate such distaste into lowered motivation or active sabotage.

To complicate matters further, Ragins and Sundstrum (1990) contradict the notion that women are viewed as having less power than men. Their research shows that subordinates of both sexes believe male and female bosses with equivalent positions have equal power. The question remains: Do managerial women face special challenges leading subordinates (a) because they are perceived as less powerful than male peers, or (b) due to sexist stereotypes?

Ragins and Sundstrum would answer no to part (a) but Kanter would say yes. Powell (1990), Heilman et al. (1989), and Baron (1984) maintain that sex role stereotypes about female managers vanish after employees work for them. Others disagree. Astrachan (1986) examined working relationships between female bosses and male subordinates, while Henderson and Marples (1986) focused on situations occurring when women reported to younger female supervisors. These studies will be discussed in turn.

REACTIONS OF MALE SUBORDINATES TO FEMALE BOSSES

From the 1960s through the 1980s, male subordinates have been "except"-ers, resisters, or accepters of women bosses. The following passage illustrates the "except"-er view of men who have successfully worked for female executives but still prefer male supervisors. They "esteem their female bosses, but they dismiss their own positive experience as a rare exception, qualifying it with such a phrase as '... but there are few like her' " ("How Men Adjust," 1977).

Men who resist female supervisors may do so for economic, psychological, or sociological reasons, according to Astrachan (1986). Economically, during the massive layoffs of the 1980s, men felt they had enough competition for scarce mid-management jobs from other males without having to vie with women as well. Some viewed the situation as win-lose; if women were promoted, men would not be.

Psychologically, male resisters feared female power. Some men felt uncomfortable dealing with female authority figures. Women's talent, energy, and combination of competence and sexuality was threatening. Even men who supported equality for women were affected. Astrachan (1986) interviewed a successful executive male with a good record for treating women as "true peers" who said:

I have this abiding suspicion that in a lot of areas, women are essentially more capable than men. Maybe part of that is because they're trying harder, because we've had it our way for so long. But in most of the fields I see women in, they really have more on the ball than most of the guys. I'm thinking about real estate, some lawyers, some accountants, some bankers. I only comment on it because I think it's part of what scares men. Whether it's their wife or . . . girlfriend or . . . colleague, they fear "I may find out that she is more capable than I am; perhaps she'll end up earning more than I earn." They don't want this to happen, and as a result, behind the artifice of support, they lay all sorts of traps that keep it from happening.

The sociological reason some men do not want female bosses is that they have been trained to feel superior. Thus, they feel it is their birthright to hold higher positions than women. On Wall Street, for example,

the notion of male superiority is clear in instructions from one firm that a man sign letters to clients that were drafted by a woman trader; in the relegation of women to specialties like retailing and cosmetics, which were deemed "natural" for them, or to public finance, considered "a place for also-rans." (Astrachan, 1986)

Contrary to popular belief, older men seemed to accept female bosses more readily than younger men both in a 1965 *Harvard Business Review* survey and in a 1985 replication (Bowman, Worthy, and Greyser, 1965; Sutton and Moore, 1985). Younger men did not want additional competition. Some older men's impressions of female executives improved partially because their daughters had pursued management careers.

Male respondents to the *Harvard Business Review* survey who were comfortable working for women increased from 27% to 47% from 1965 to 1985. Though positive, this means that more than half of the men still feel awkward with female supervisors. Males who had been supervisors or co-workers of managerial women viewed them more positively than men who had been their subordinates (Powell, 1988).

The following incident shows how executive Jane Evans used a savvy approach to turn initial male resistance into acceptance. After becoming president of Butterick/Vogue Patterns, Evans heard a rumor that seven male vice presidents had threatened to quit because they did not want to work for a woman. She called in the vice presidents, told them they had more to prove to her than she did to them, and then made a bet. If, after one year, they could not say that she was the best boss they had ever had, she would pay them each $10. Otherwise, they would owe her. During the year, one man died, and Jane had to fire another. When she returned to the United States after an overseas trip, Evans was surprised to find a dozen yellow roses and a check for $50 on the seat of her limo at the airport (Blaun, 1988).

Not all men are inflexible about welcoming women as bosses. Accepters generally fall into two categories: those who have changed behavior merely to conform with top management directives, and those who are committed to equal employment opportunity in word and deed. The former group may not have changed their attitudes about women but realize that tapping talent, however packaged, is in their firm's best interest. The latter are true "mensches," Yiddish for "real human beings." Like US West's president, Richard McCormick, they could be expected to make special efforts to include women in such informal networks as golf games, where major business decisions often are made (Konrad, 1990).

REACTIONS OF FEMALE SUBORDINATES TO FEMALE BOSSES

Despite stereotypes that women do not work well together, female executives in the previously mentioned *Harvard Business Review* studies (Bowman, Worthy, and Greyser, 1965; Sutton and Moore, 1985) showed greater approval of women bosses than male counterparts. From 1965 to 1985, the number of female executives who said they would feel at ease working for a woman rose from 75 to 82%. Sixty-one percent of female respondents to a 1993 survey conducted by *Working Woman* said that the boss's gender is not an issue. Overall, of those who think the supervisor's sex matters, 17% want a female boss and 23% favor a male boss (Kruser, 1993). Three-fourths of women earning at least $75,000 believe the supervisor's gender is inconsequential, however.

In response to an earlier survey, 49% of secretaries, most of whom were female, said that the boss's gender was irrelevant. Nearly one-third preferred a male superior, claiming that women bosses "go overboard to exhibit their superiority" (Kagan and Malveaux, 1986). As will be discussed in chapter 11, excessively rigid, domineering behavior could be a reaction by female supervisors to their feelings of powerlessness (Kanter, 1977).

Because many older women took career breaks to raise children and re-entered the workforce years later, it was fairly common in the 1980s for older women to report to younger women. This phenomenon may be short-lived if women's current patterns of taking little or no career break due to childbearing continue (Henderson and Marples, 1986).

When women under age 35 supervise females 10 or more years their senior, generational differences may create added challenges. Older women may resent younger women who are "smart, but not wise." Younger females with more education might act superior, even though their 50-year-old subordinates have a wealth of relevant experience. If tensions develop, they should be dealt with openly and not allowed to fester. Henderson and Marples (1986) suggest that boss and subordinate agree to exchange skills so they can learn from each other in a "spirit of collaboration."

Older women might feel stigmatized by working for a younger female in a society that has, until recently, expected bosses to be older middle-aged males. Nothing has prepared women for this experience. Before the Industrial Revolution, males expected to pass on the family farm to younger men, but women have no similar transition to emulate (Henderson and Marples, 1986).

Though the general public's and subordinates' acceptance of executive women has increased tremendously, small enclaves consider the term "manager" as synonymous with male. Business executives are more likely to be visualized as men, but being male does not make one better qualified for management than does being female. Powell (1988) debunked the myth that males make better managers and then asked "Are better managers masculine?" mainly to be able to answer no. To respond to the question, he traced the origins of various leadership theories, none of which seemed to favor behaviors linked with the stereotypical masculine role over those associated with the so-called feminine role. Readers unfamiliar with the historical development and basic features of leadership theories may wish to consult management principles or organizational behavior texts at this point.

Leadership theories currently in existence have been based on research done primarily on male subjects. A relatively new approach not only is based on studies of both sexes, but also uses stereotypes about women and men, previously described as limiting and potentially harmful, in a positive way. This management style, which combines "masculine" and "feminine" behaviors, is called androgyny.

The word *androgyny* means "man-woman" and is derived from the Greek roots *andr-*, meaning man, and *gynē*, meaning woman. The term describes gender role flexibility. Androgynous individuals have integrated aspects of femininity and masculinity into their self-concept. They are able to enact whatever behavior seems appropriate in a given situation. Their responses need not be consistent with traditional gender roles. For example, androgynous women and men could be both assertive at work and tender or nurturing with loved ones.

Sex researchers have suggested that androgynous individuals approach life with more flexibility than do strongly roled people. They are able to select from a matrix of feminine and masculine behaviors, based not on sex role norms, but rather on what gives them the most comfort and satisfaction in a given situation.

Sargent (1981) believes the most effective management style is androgynous. Leaders must be both competent and caring. Sargent never defines these terms clearly, however. She stops short of advocating high concern for people and production in all situations. Rather, she stresses consistency between androgynous management and the contingency approach, in which the most effective management style depends on the situation. Sargent says managers must be flexible and able to use "traditional" masculine or feminine behaviors when appropriate.

Some believe androgyny encourages sex role stereotyping. Behavior should not be labeled as "masculine" or "feminine" if a sex-role-free society is the goal. Bem (1975) explains the inherent irony:

The concept of androgyny contains an inner contradiction and, hence, the seeds of its own destruction.... Androgyny necessarily presupposes that the concepts of masculinity and femininity themselves have distinct and substantive content. But to the extent that the androgynous message is absorbed by the culture, the concepts of masculinity and femininity will cease to have such content and the distinctions to which they refer will blur into invisibility. Thus, when androgyny becomes a reality, the concept of androgyny will have been transcended.

Recognizing that exceptions exist, Sargent (1981) offers the following suggestions for managers trying to become more androgynous:

Women typically need to work on directing the accomplishment of tasks more forcefully; tempering their expression of feelings with appropriate ... logic and analysis; promoting themselves within an organization by becoming more visible and entrepreneurial; and making their opinions known clearly without backing down in the face of possible disagreement. To develop an androgynous style, most men need to concentrate on ... developing the ability to express ... feelings even when they may expose vulnerability; ... promoting close interpersonal relations through open and honest communication, including listening and feedback; valuing work for its ability to provide ... affiliation with others ... as well as career achievement; and accepting emotion and spontaneity as healthy personal qualities.

SUMMARY

This chapter defined a stereotype as a consistent pattern describing a group's most remembered qualities. Then it explained how stereotypes can harm individuals by forcing them into preset molds. Several sex- and race-based stereotypes were examined.

The reading by Powell concluded that there are no differences in management style or other relevant qualities possessed by male and female executives. In spite of the lack of evidence regarding sex-based distinctions among managers, people still describe executives in "masculine" terms, again due to stereotypes.

Androgyny is an approach to management that blends so-called "feminine" and "masculine" behaviors. By labelling behaviors as "masculine" or "feminine," some say that proponents of androgynous management reinforce stereotypes they are supposedly trying to eliminate.

DISCUSSION QUESTIONS

1. How can stereotypes be harmful? Helpful?

2. Why is the typical executive still described in masculine terms, though few documented sex differences relevant to management exist?

3. Do you think androgyny encourages the sex-role stereotyping it is really trying to eliminate, or not? Explain.

4. If males still hold most top management positions and most positions of power, how could one argue that males have been disadvantaged by stereotypes and the socialization process?

5. Do you think women will attain top level positions in the U.S. military forces or not? Explain.

8 The Socialization Process

OBJECTIVES

After studying this chapter you should be able to:

1. Explain the evidence that indicates that gender roles are not determined innately.
2. List three processes that are a part of gender role learning in early childhood.
3. Explain the circumstances under which gender typing is a nonconscious process.
4. Explain three hypotheses the researchers Maccoby and Jacklin (1974) proposed to analyze parents' influence on the sex role socialization of infants.
5. Explain why one cannot definitely conclude that team sports participation leads to later business success.

In the following article, Riedle counters the belief that gender roles are innate by presenting evidence from Margaret Mead's classic studies of New Guinea societies. Riedle then describes the processes through which young children learn gender roles.

"A Brief Look at Gender Role Socialization"
by Joan E. Riedle

People tend to believe that what is true of their culture is true of every other. Further, when consistency across cultures appears, observed patterns are assumed to be innately determined. For example, people presume that what is true of women's and men's roles in Western culture is true throughout the world and, therefore, that gender roles must be genetically determined. A dramatic example of the fallacy of these beliefs comes from the studies of Margaret Mead (1935; 1963).

Mead studied gender roles evidenced in three northeastern New Guinea societies. She found that each had developed a different conceptualization of the "natural" roles for women and men, none of which matched that of Western culture. In the first two tribes men and women displayed the same temperaments, though different economic and religious roles were allowed. In the mountain-dwelling Arapesh community, both men and women displayed a warm, maternal temperament. Mead described the Arapesh women and men in terms that some Western cultures have considered feminine: nurturant, gentle, unaggressive, and responsive to their community's needs. The river-dwelling Mundugumors were cannibals and headhunters. Both Mundugumor men and women were hostile and competitive, traits some Western cultures have viewed as masculine. In a third tribe, the lake-dwelling Tchambuli, the traditional Western gender roles were reversed. Tchambuli women were hard-working and reliable, running the business of the community, while the men were emotionally and economically dependent and primarily concerned with self-adornment, the arts, and ceremonial life.

The development of such different cultural styles, within a restricted geographic area, defies the idea that gender roles are constant and set by nature. Rather, gender roles may be culturally determined, with Mead's findings vividly illustrating that all cultures do not teach the same behavior patterns. In the following pages I will attempt to explore the processes by which gender-related cultural belief systems are disseminated and address the possibility that such beliefs can be modified.

GENDER ROLE ACQUISITION

Weitzman (1979) divides gender role learning during early childhood into three analytic processes:

1. to *distinguish* between men and women and between boys and girls, and to know what kinds of behavior are characteristic of each;

2. to express appropriate gender role *preferences* for himself or herself; and

3. to *behave* in accordance with gender role standards.

Cognitive social psychology, gender schema theory, and social learning theory may each contribute to an understanding of how these processes are accomplished.

Distinguishing Groups

Cognitive social psychology extends the basic findings about human cognitive processes to social perception. People actively try to find meaning in available information, and a primary method of doing so is by creating categories. It would be extremely difficult to function in a world which contained no categories. How long would a child survive who could not comprehend the category of his or her own "mother"? From each different visual angle she would appear to be a new individual.

People's culture influences the categories they create about people and teaches them to assign more importance to some categorizations than others (Tajfel, 1981). Such importance is conveyed when the culture attaches many associations to the category and assigns to it a functional significance, such as basing roles upon the categorization (Bem, 1983). Through these processes gender categories become "primary," while others, such as eye colors, do not. No other dichotomy in human experience seems to have as many associations as does the distinction between female and male (Bem, 1983). Virtually every culture has perceived differences between men and women and assigned somewhat divergent roles to the sexes. Gender-related associations have been extended to toys, jobs, hobbies, household tasks, inanimate objects (ships are female, the sun is male), and even animal species (dogs are perceived as male; cats as female).

Unfortunately, while categorization enables people to find meaning in stimuli, it also results in perceptual distortions (Tajfel, 1981). Thinking in terms of categories leads people to perceive greater differences between groups than actually exist. Thus, men and women have nothing in common. Thinking in terms of categories also leads people to perceive greater similarity among the members of each category than actually exists. Thus, all men are presumed alike; all women are thought to be the same. In fact, on nearly every characteristic the range of variation within men or within women exceeds the average intersex difference (Hyde, 1985).

The degree of perceptual distortion that results from categorization is somewhat predictable. If the dimension along which the categories are created is one highly valued in the culture, thus personally meaningful to its citizens, distortion is increased. For example, prejudiced subjects tend to exaggerate differences between Blacks and Whites, relative to nonprejudiced respondents (Secord, Bevan, and Katz, 1956). Not every culture places as much importance on the gender dichotomy as Western society does, however. The extent to which cultures exaggerate differences and downplay similarities between women and men may vary, but, generally, men are viewed as somewhat better than women. Though cultures have differed in roles designated as appropriate for women and men, they have consistently assigned the most highly valued roles to men. If women grow potatoes and men grow yams, yams are served at the important ceremonials. Thus, a system of values has been included in cultural belief systems about gender, such that women and their roles are considered inferior to men and men's roles (Tavris and Wade, 1984).

Complete coverage of race and ethnic differences in socialization is beyond the scope of this reading, but must be acknowledged. As one example, the markedly different family structures and role expectations within the Black community (Hyde, 1985) would doubtlessly lead to different patterns of socialization and, consequently, different gender-related associations. Smith and Midlarsky (1985) found Whites to use more stereotypical concepts in their descriptions of women and men than Blacks. Blacks did not characterize women as passive, but many Whites did. Instead of characterizing men as competent and aggressive, Blacks tended to describe men by their roles (e.g., father, truck driver, factory worker). Thus, the teachings of subgroups within a culture also may differ.

Establishing Preference

When discussing categories about groups of people, cognitive psychology replaces the term category with "schema." A schema is a cognitive structure, composed of a network of associations. Schemas organize and guide our perceptions, thus adding efficiency but also distortions.

Bem's gender schema theory (1981; 1983) proposes that, given the importance of gender categories to all known cultures, individuals each have a set of gender-linked associations. The specific content of the schemas, however, is taught and thus can vary across cultures. States Bem (1981), "As children learn the contents of the society's gender schema, they learn which attributes are to be linked with their own sex and, hence, with themselves."

The gender schema becomes a tool for self-evaluation (Bem 1981; 1983). Children's feelings of self-worth are developed through a variety of comparisons, one of which is how well they match the appropriate gender schema. Thus, the male child is motivated to "act like a boy" to compare favorably with his masculine schema and be able to feel good about himself. Out of a desire for high self-esteem, then, comes the preference for gender-typed activities.

Gender-Typed Behavior

While gender schema theory suggests the motivating factor behind gender role acquisition, presumably the specifics of what is acquired will depend on the culture's teachings. Mischel (1966; 1970) addresses the acquisition of sex-typed behaviors through observational learning. He defines sex-typed behaviors empirically as those that elicit different levels of reinforcement for the sexes. Thus, if boys are reinforced more, or punished less, when they shout on the playground, shouting on the playground is defined as a male-typed behavior.

Mischel argues that boys and girls learn the behaviors of both sexes by observing models and then acting in ways for which they anticipate being reinforced. Children are predicted to observe two types of models, those with whom they are in a nurturant relationship and those who are both powerful and willing to provide reinforcement. For girls and boys, the mother has typically met both of these criteria at first. Children quickly learn, however, that males have greater power in Western culture and shift to imitating their fathers. (In single-parent households, the nurturing person serves as the initial nurturant *and* powerful/reinforcing model. As children become aware of cultural differentials in male/female power, they still are expected to gravitate toward masculine-typed behaviors.) Boys should begin to model male-typed behaviors quite readily. Girls are predicted to switch to those patterns as far as reinforcement contingencies permit. Thus, girls will imitate males to the extent that they are allowed while retaining many female-typed behaviors.

GENDER-TYPING: A NONCONSCIOUS PROCESS

Virtually every aspect of our culture contributes to the teaching of gender roles. Parents are not the only models to which children attend. Teachers, neighbors, peers, and media images all contribute. (See Tavris and Wade, 1984; Unger and Crawford, 1992; Weitzman, 1979, for comprehensive reviews of this literature.) For example, studies of books and television programs during the early 1970s show predominantly male characters and females depicted in stereotypical roles. In one survey of 134 grammar-school readers only three working mothers appeared, and the disruptive behavior of one of these mother's sons was attributed to the fact that she was not home during the day to care for him. Currently, preschoolers understand that the categories of boy and girl include personality and behavioral differences (Reis and Wright, 1982). They also are familiar with gender-related occupational stereotypes (Gettys and Cann, 1981). The lessons of our culture have been very consistently and effectively taught, though perhaps not always deliberately.

When all an individual's reference groups agree, persons may develop belief systems of which they are not aware. These implicit belief systems are labelled nonconscious ideologies. Western society's beliefs about women's and men's "natural" roles may be pure examples of such ideologies (Bem and Bem, 1970).

If so, then subtle messages may teach and perpetuate cultural ideologies. Condry and Condry (1976) showed men and women a videotape of a nine-month-old who responded to a jack-in-the-box first by staring and then by becoming agitated and crying. When the child was said to be a girl, adults described her as more fearful and less angry than when the same infant was said to be a boy. Will, Self, and Datan (1976) studied the play behavior of mothers with infants. The women claimed to believe that six-month-old boys and girls were alike and said that they would not treat their own sons and daughters differently. However, mothers who were presented an infant named "Beth" handed her a doll to play with more, and a train to play with less, than did mothers who thought the child was "Adam." Beth and Adam were actually the same child, a boy. Thus, the perceptions and behaviors of parents are biased by the sex of the child, and this may occur at a nonconscious level.

A mechanism for change may exist if our gender schemas become conscious. Bem (1983) suggests that our categories about men and women could be restricted to the areas that truly matter, such as anatomical and reproductive differences. If we did not teach children to extensively differentiate the world in terms of gender (strong boys play football, pretty girls play quietly and win beauty contests), then all other aspects of behavior could remain gender neutral. Perhaps from conscious attempts to restrict the content of gender schemas we can begin to lessen our tendencies to see men and women as different and unequal.

DISCUSSION QUESTIONS

1. Do you agree or disagree with the statement from the article that children's preference for gender-typed activities results from their desire for high self-esteem?

2. If you have siblings of the opposite sex, do you think your parents or caregivers treated you differently while you were growing up? If so, how? Which chores were assigned to you as compared to the duties assigned to the opposite sex siblings? (If you have no siblings of the opposite sex, think of a family you know with children of both sexes. Do the caregivers treat the boys differently than the girls or not? If so, how?)

3. Do you recall anyone suggesting that certain activities or toys would be more appropriate for a child of your sex or not? Explain.

4. Have your ambitions in career choice, job promotion, or everyday matters ever been particularly encouraged or discouraged? If so, to what do you attribute this?

5. Why might stereotypes of "femininity" be inapplicable to minority women?

EARLY PARENT-CHILD INTERACTIONS

In the previous article, Riedle claims that parents vary their treatment of infants by sex. The idea that parents treat boys and girls differently to shape them toward behavior deemed appropriate for their sex was one of three hypotheses Maccoby and Jacklin (1974) proposed when analyzing sex-based socialization.

An alternative hypothesis was that boys and girls stimulate their parents in distinctive ways and elicit different treatment because of inborn variations in traits shown early in life.

These two hypotheses seem contradictory. The first says that parents' behavior is one factor influencing children's socialization. The second suggests that children shape parents. The same parental behavior may evoke varying responses from sons as compared to daughters because of innate, sex-linked differences.

Maccoby and Jacklin's review of 10 socialization studies shows that parents' behavior varies little based on a child's sex. The amount of parent-child interaction and the degree of independence allowed do not depend on the child's sex. Parents do not reward boys more for aggressive or competitive behavior. However, the type of parent-child interaction differs by sex, and differential shaping in dressing the child is evident. Parents encourage sex-typed development of interests by providing sex-typed toys.

Parents do not value domineering behavior in either preschool boys or girls. They try to teach them to satisfy needs without grabbing, hitting, or destroying valuable objects. Parents seem more likely to punish boys for excess aggression, which they regard as a natural tendency that must be controlled.

Maccoby and Jacklin's conclusion regarding the second hypothesis is that there are few biologically based sex differences eliciting different reactions from parents. Preschool boys tend to resist direction and discipline more than girls, however. Boys ages three or four do not respond as readily to mild forms of pressure as girls do. More coercive methods are needed to get them to comply with others' requests.

The third hypothesis Maccoby and Jacklin proposed is that parents base their interactions with a child on their beliefs about what a child of a given sex probably is like. This idea has some support. Parents think boys' typical behavior differs from that of girls but desire similar behaviors from children of both sexes. For example, parents expect boys to be noisy and rough, while girls are assumed to be quiet, neat, and easily upset. Parents want both sexes to be able to care for themselves and to avoid being easily upset. They try to socialize boys and girls in the same direction but believe they are starting at different points.

TEAM SPORTS INVOLVEMENT—EFFECTS ON LATER BUSINESS CAREERS

Before the 1970s, boys had more chances to play team sports than girls. Does participation in such activities help prepare people for business careers?

The public, women's groups, and business executives seem to think so. Hennig and Jardim (1977) claimed that participants in team athletics learn how to work with those they dislike for the good of the team, how to accept criticism, and how to win, lose, and take risks.

Little research supports the link between participation in team sports and later business achievement, however. According to 178 male chief executives in Wisconsin, taking part in student government or forensics predicts success as well as team sports involvement (Karsten and Kleisath, 1986). The three mentioned activities seem to teach cooperation, competition, and communication skills to a greater degree than other extracurricular activities.

Would results obtained from a sample of male managers in one midwestern state generalize to female executives? To find out, a national sample of 170 upper-level executive women in manufacturing firms was surveyed. Most females who responded had had the opportunity to play on unisex sports teams during high school or college. They agreed with male CEOs that forensics, student government, and competitive team sports helped them gain initial positions, but thought that only forensics aided their advancement to executive posts (Karsten and Kleisath, 1987).

One explanation is that the camaraderie one-sex teams created was more advantageous to men than to women. Men developed a group spirit and comfort feelings with other males. Later, in business, they continued to feel comfortable with male colleagues and less at ease with female peers. Because of greater familiarity with and trust of other males, their names were mentioned for promotions.

In the 1970s, participation in all-women sports teams would have had less impact. Even if females experienced camaraderie within the team, there was little carryover into business careers. Until recently, most females did not reach high enough positions to be able to influence promotion of other women.

Female executives saw participation in student government as less important in obtaining current positions than did males. To the women, student government may have been synonymous with politics. Females were more likely to attribute success to hard work than to politics, perhaps as a reaction to previous exclusion from largely male political structures.

It is not surprising that both sexes thought forensics contributed to advancement. Verbal communication skills are considered vital to success in many fields.

Executives of both sexes think involvement in competitive team sports, forensics, and student government is equally beneficial when obtaining initial positions. Men see all three activities as predictors of current success, but women only see a link between forensics and current positions.

If men and women want to cooperate as business colleagues, they must be urged to take part in sex-integrated activities beginning in childhood. More extracurricular activities and college and high school sports teams must actively recruit members of both sexes. Women and men cannot be expected to develop healthy working relationships automatically when they have had little experience interacting to complete tasks during their formative years. Diversity training, discussed in chapter 6, is useful as a remedial measure to facilitate greater comfort among men and women as business peers, but more proactive steps are needed before organizational entry.

Sex-integrated, task-oriented activities earlier in life will lead boys and girls to feel comfortable working together. Later, when they begin business careers, they will view each other as equals and will expect to cooperate to achieve the organization's goals. At that point, diversity training will no longer be necessary.

SUMMARY

Sex role socialization influences human behavior throughout life. As children mature, parents, schools, peers and other influences affect their sex-role development. In the past, girls were steered toward inside, domestic activities, while boys' interests in outdoor, physical play was encouraged. This has changed, but the effects of channeling girls' interests in one direction and boys' in another are still evident in adulthood.

There are few innate differences that elicit varying parental reactions to infant boys and girls. Some studies say parents shape infant behaviors, but others contradict this. Children of both sexes may be socialized to care for themselves, to avoid being easily upset, and to meet their needs without being destructive. Parents may feel they are starting at different points when trying to help a daughter and son achieve these goals.

There is not enough research evidence to support definitively the common belief that participation in team sports leads to future business success. Participation in other extracurricular activities that teach similar lessons may be equally valuable.

DISCUSSION QUESTIONS

1. Are there any other ways women who have not participated in team sports can learn lessons men typically learn from doing so? Explain.
2. If you have ever played on a competitive sports team, explain what you learned from that experience.
3. Describe any sex-integrated, task-oriented activities you took part in during elementary school, high school, or college.
4. Explain how lessons learned through participation in competitive team sports apply in a business setting.
5. What specific actions do you think should be taken to help women and men work together as business colleagues to achieve organizational goals?

9 Career Planning and Mentoring

OBJECTIVES

After studying this chapter you should be able to:

1. Define the terms career and mentoring.
2. Explain the phases of the career planning process.
3. Explain how interest inventories can be used to assist in the self-assessment phase of career development.
4. List five guidelines that should be considered when one is pursuing a chosen career.
5. Explain the importance of transferable skills to those with little recent business experience.
6. Explain advantages and disadvantages of the informal mentoring relationship to both the mentor and protégée.
7. Explain concerns about mentoring that are particularly relevant to women of color.
8. Explain why formal mentoring programs have been criticized.
9. List the stages in the mentoring process.
10. Explain why women have had difficulty obtaining mentors.

Alice: Will you tell me, please, which way I ought to go from here?
Cheshire Cat: That depends a good deal on where you want to get to.
Alice: I don't care.
Cheshire Cat: Then it doesn't matter which way you go.

Lewis Carroll, *Alice in Wonderland*

Unfortunately, this passage may illustrate a typical approach to career planning. In the past, women were less likely than men to plan their careers because they may not have anticipated long periods of employment. Many women in the labor force viewed employment as a job rather than a career until they had worked for 10 years. By then their career plans trailed those of male counterparts.

Employment is no longer optional for many women. They are either heads of households or important contributors to their families' total incomes. Projections show women spending an even greater portion of their lives in paid employment. A married woman with two children can expect to work from 27 to 34 years. Single or divorced women may work even longer. Those working outside the home for so many years should prepare for careers instead of falling into them randomly.

At this point, *career* should be defined. It is a sequence of work-related experiences and activities during a person's lifetime. Choosing a career is no longer a lifetime decision made in one's youth. People evaluate career choices and make changes as necessary. Those entering the workforce in the 1990s may change careers from three to six times. Figure 9.1 depicts the career planning process.

THE CAREER PLANNING PROCESS

The first three steps in this model are similar for most people entering management. Special challenges faced by those changing careers or by women re-entering the labor force will be discussed after these are explained.

Self-Appraisal

Self-appraisal is a crucial step. It is difficult to match oneself appropriately with a career without knowledge of personal interests and abilities. Confronting weaknesses as well as strengths is not easy. Available interest inventories, tests, and techniques can assist in self-appraisal. Well-known devices include the Strong-Campbell Interest Inventory, Holland's Self-Directed Search, and the Myers-Briggs Type Indicator. An inventory developed in the early 1990s is the Kolbe Conative Index, which measures motivation to take a specific action. Most college counseling centers or private career consulting firms administer and interpret these self-appraisal devices.

The Strong-Campbell Interest Inventory compares a person's interests with those of successful people in different fields. People taking the inventory answer questions about occupational interests and receive a profile indicating how similar or dissimilar their responses are to those of experienced professionals in various fields. For example, one person's profile indicated she was very similar to a mathematician or a college professor, moderately similar to a pharmacist, and moderately dissimilar to a physical therapist.

Figure 9.1
Career Planning Process

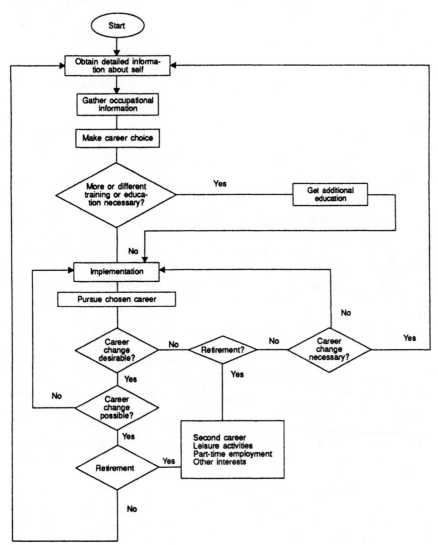

Table 9.1
Occupations Corresponding to Personal Orientations Identified by Holland's Self-Directed Search

Personal Orientation	Corresponding Occupation
Realistic (R)	skilled trades, technical, some service
Investigative (I)	scientific and some technical
Artistic (A)	artistic, musical, literary
Social (S)	educational and social welfare
Conventional (C)	office and clerical
Enterprising (E)	salesperson, business executive

Holland's instrument asks respondents to daydream about occupations that have appealed to them since childhood. They list those occupations and then complete a questionnaire to indicate activities they like or dislike. Activities divide into six major personal orientations: realistic, investigative, artistic, social, enterprising, and conventional. A brief outline of the types of occupations corresponding to each personal orientation appear in Table 9.1.

Respondents score Holland's instrument themselves and determine a three-letter personal orientation code consistent with their occupational preferences. They use *The Occupations Finder* (Holland, 1978) to look for fields associated with their three-letter code. For example, two of the ten occupations corresponding to the code ESA (enterprising, social, artistic) are lawyer and stockbroker.

Holland's Self-Directed Search is not intended to select the one best occupation for each person completing the inventory. Rather, it suggests several occupations consistent with an individual's personal orientation that can be targeted for further investigation.

The Myers-Briggs Type Indicator was developed by a mother and daughter team of psychologists, Katharine C. Briggs and Isabel Briggs Myers. The questionnaire is a forced-choice instrument that asks people how they feel or would act in specific situations. It indicates how people prefer to act along four scales. The first scale shows whether people relate more easily to the inner world of ideas or the outer world of things. The second indicates whether people get information mainly through their senses or through intuition, and the third tells whether respondents make decisions based on fact and logic or based on feelings. The final scale reveals whether people prefer to live in an orderly, systematic way or whether a spontaneous lifestyle is more appealing (Myers, 1987). Scores on the four scales are combined to obtain a four-letter type for each respondent. There are sixteen combinations of dimensions, each with a descriptive profile. Descriptions of preferred management styles are provided for several possible combinations.

There are no correct or incorrect types as determined by the Myers-Briggs questionnaire, though people may have preferred orientations toward either the outer world of things or inner world of ideas. For example, adults are expected to become competent in both spheres. The same is true of preferences measured by the other three scales.

The Myers-Briggs Type Indicator may aid staff development. It can identify individuals with complementary personality types as well as those who will have to work on relationships due to less compatible types. Without blaming anyone, this instrument may point out root causes of ongoing interpersonal conflict. Correctly identifying the problem can start a process aimed at its resolution.

Besides relying on formal methods to gather data about career preferences, people should analyze practical skills and those they enjoy using. Roles students have played in extracurricular activities might indicate skills they possess. Roles in community projects might do the same for others.

People planning careers should focus on skills they enjoy rather than those that are easily marketable. Otherwise, they will find it difficult to compete with those who really enjoy their work.

Occupational Information Gathering

After a thorough self-analysis, one should gather information about various occupations. Researching published sources is one way to do this. General sources include the *Occupational Outlook Handbook* and the *Career Exploration Guide*, both published by the U.S. Department of Labor.

Another way to obtain information about occupations is to conduct an information-gathering interview. Questions to ask and procedures to use while gathering data about occupations during an informational interview include (adapted from Pell and Furbay, 1975):

1. *What is the nature of the work performed?* What would I do on the job? What responsibilities does it entail? Am I qualified for this work? What skills would I use? Does this work interest me? Do I need additional training, or is on-the-job training available?
2. *What are the working conditions?* Will I work with people, data, or things? In an office, outdoors, or on the road? Will I work in a large city or a small town? Do I have a choice? What kind of supervision will I have?
3. *Is this work in harmony with my interests and values?* What are the possibilities for advancement? Can I apply experience gained to other areas with minimal added training?
4. *What kinds of development opportunities would be available in this type of position?*
5. *What is the salary range?*

Interviewing people currently in occupations of interest is another good way to gather data. Suggested steps are to:

1. *Identify People to Interview.* Start with a list of people you already know who might serve as information and/or referral contacts. Consider friends, relatives, co-workers, supervisors, neighbors, and people they know. Also, consider speakers you have heard, people you have read about, and so on. Other resources include professional women's organizations. If you cannot obtain the name of a contact in your field of interest, call an organization and ask who is in charge of a particular department.

2. *Arrange the Interview.* Most people are flattered by requests for information and are usually helpful. You must initiate the contact, however. Screening personnel may try to discourage you by saying that no jobs are available. If this happens, clarify that you are seeking information, not a job.

3. *Prepare for the Interview.* Before the interview, practice stating your interests, values, and skills, so your compatibility with the work environment can be discussed and assessed. Read about the field before conducting informational interviews. Prepare a list of questions for the interview. A few samples follow.

   a. How did you get a job in this field?

   b. What did you do on the job yesterday from morning until evening?

   c. What parts of your job are most interesting?

   d. To which areas may people working in this field be transferred?

   e. What are the basic requirements to get a job in this field?

   f. What suggestions would you give someone entering this field?

   g. How do you think jobs in this occupation will change during the next five years?

   h. What are this company's views about workforce diversity?

4. *Conduct the Interview.* Act professionally and dress appropriately. Try to establish rapport with your contact and indicate an interest in his or her career. Refer to your list of prepared questions, but allow some spontaneity. Before leaving, ask your contact to suggest names of others who might be helpful.

5. *Do Follow-up Work.* Immediately after the interview, record the name, address, and phone number of each contact, the date of the interview, the information gathered, and names of additional referrals. Send a thank-you note to the person you interviewed. Distinguish between how interested you are in the career and how well you liked the interviewee. If, in the future, you decide to pursue a career as a result of an informational interview, send a letter notifying the appropriate individual. You may want to send a cover letter and resume to this person when implementing your job search.

After deciding on an occupation, one should consider the type of organization where one would like to be employed. Some people might prefer to work for a foundation, while others would rather work for a branch of government or a private firm.

A standardized test is required to qualify for most government posts. This ensures at least superficial fairness to women and minorities. Drawbacks to government employment include low prestige and limited advancement possibilities.

If a private sector position is sought, think about preferences regarding type of industry, size of firm, and organizational climate. The challenge of a high-growth industry may be appealing, but an unstable environment may not be desirable. However, in a volatile environment, it is difficult to find a truly stable industry. Flexibility is important. Also, sometimes tradeoffs must be made. Large organizations may have formal selection processes and training programs, but may be impersonal. Small firms may not have established career paths.

Organizational climate refers to management style and culture. Some might be more comfortable in a climate that values workforce diversity, participative decision making, and employee autonomy.

Career Choice

After self-analysis and information gathering, one must choose a career and a specific position. Be focused when seeking a position. Rather than mailing hundreds of resumes, it might be better to target 15 to 20 organizations. Before starting the job search, thoroughly study those firms and their problems. One approach is to conduct an informational interview as previously described.

Pursuit of the Chosen Career

Some guidelines during this phase are to:

1. Gain exposure to different fields through lateral transfer.
2. Develop a skills portfolio and continue to learn but avoid lengthy, low-profile projects.
3. Volunteer for desirable assignments.
4. Keep a variety of options open.
5. Avoid overspecialization so skills do not become obsolete.
6. Network.
7. Know when to leave an organization.

The first three guidelines merit comment; the rest are self-explanatory. The turbulent business environment of the 1990s makes it essential for professionals to develop a variety of skills. The experts do not know which skills will be in most demand in coming years, but they recommend having several that are saleable (Nussbaum, 1991). To cultivate skills, lifelong learning, through formal and informal methods, will be needed.

Careerists of the 1990s should volunteer for assignments inside the organization and in the community. Such experiences represent opportunities to nurture new skills. On the other hand, careerists should avoid long-term projects with little visibility. These may be good for the organization but may sidetrack individuals who need to be concerned about career survival and growth. In managerial careers, lateral moves have become common. Because middle management layers have been cut, few vertical steps remain. Consequently, managers are not promoted upward as often. Responsibilities in current positions change, but the job title stays the same.

SPECIAL CHALLENGES: WOMEN MAKING A CAREER CHANGE, RE-ENTRY WOMEN

Women making a career change into management or re-entering the field may face added challenges. For example, suppose a woman who has been an administrative assistant for 20 years earns a college degree and wants to be a manager. If she is married to someone with dated beliefs about women's workforce roles, it may be difficult to relocate without destroying the relationship. Her opportunities are limited if she is tied to one community. If she finds a management position, others may continue to perceive her as an assistant.

Women re-entering the labor force may lack recent business experience. Though 22-year-old college graduates face similar problems, re-entry women with 15-year-old degrees also may lack confidence in their knowledge of current business practices.

TRANSFERABLE SKILLS

Both re-entry women and 22-year-old college graduates should be aware of their transferable skills. Examples include budgeting, supervising, public speaking, negotiating, and coping with pressure.

Homemakers' and students' experiences translate into management skills. For example, students exercise planning and decision-making functions by choosing a major that will help them achieve career objectives. Similarly, homemakers estimate household income and plan budgets accordingly. After getting a low grade, students may exercise the control function by changing study habits. Homemakers may need to insist that poor quality repair work be corrected (Josefowitz, 1980).   Mentoring and career planning are interrelated. Mentors help advance careers. Supposedly, executives who have mentors are more likely to follow a career plan than those who do not.

MENTORING: DEFINITION AND FEATURES

The term mentor was first used in Greek mythology. Odysseus, who had to leave his son to fight the Trojan War, entrusted him to a wise, caring friend named Mentor. Mentor introduced the king's son to other rulers and taught him how to behave. Thus, mentoring seems to have male origins, but, as Garrison and Comer (1984) point out, "Athena, the Goddess of Love, occasionally would assume Mentor's form, providing the interesting twist of a female in the guise of a male." In the modern business world, a *mentor* is defined as an experienced, productive manager who relates well to a less experienced employee and facilitates his or her personal development.

Others who have studied the process emphasize the emotional bond and personal identification between mentor and protégée (Missirian, 1982). Regarding identification, Thomas (1989) believes mentoring is grounded in it. He says:

The mentor sees part of himself or herself in the subordinate and the subordinate wants to become like the mentor, to take up his or her voice, manner of dress, way of thinking. The two psychologically identify with each other, merging their unconscious fantasies of who they are or might be to the relationship.

This assumes bosses are the mentors and protégées are subordinates, which may not be true. Though immediate supervisors are the most common mentors, division or department heads, the chief executive officer, or peers may assume the role.

Multiple mentors may be desirable. Having many mentors during one's career provides different perspectives and more information. It may be helpful to have supporters in different positions and levels. As Garrison and Comer (1984) point out, "No one can expect that one mentor should or even could, fulfill the multiple developmental career needs that each of us has." Mentors do not have to be in the same geographical location as long as they maintain contact with protégées.

Though most mentors are older than those they are mentoring, age is not a prerequisite either. Large numbers of older women who took a break from careers to raise children have returned to the workforce. Refusing to extend the benefits of mentoring to such women due to their age would be discriminatory.

MENTORING STAGES

Because of personalities, mentoring relationships are unique, but most move through common stages. These are teaching, counseling, organizational intervention, and sponsorship. In the teaching phase, mentors help

Table 9.2
Advantages and Disadvantages of Informal Mentoring Relationships

Advantages	Disadvantages
To Mentor:	

Advantages	Disadvantages
1. Can train successor so mentor is eligible for promotion	1. May be accused of favoritism toward P
2. Satisfies internal need to develop subordinates	2. M's judgment questioned if P doesn't measure up
3. Gains support of P	3. M may feel threatened by P
4. Gains trusted person to whom she or he can delegate work	4. Rumors of or actual sexual involvement

To Protégée:

Advantages	Disadvantages
1. Teaches P about organizational politics and informal aspects of organizational life	1. May be difficult to leave M
	2. Career may stagnate if associated with nonmobile M
2. P has advocate to remove obstacles	3. May experience work overload
3. Boosts P's self-esteem	4. If M fails, P's career may be negatively affected
4. Provides honest criticism	5. Subject to extra scrutiny
5. May aid career advancement	6. Exclusive relationship with one M may cause social isolation
6. M makes sure P gets credit	
7. M ensures P has chance to prove herself or himself	7. Rumors of or actual sexual involvement
	8. Overreliance on M may create dependence

Key: M = mentor, P = protégée

protégées learn the ropes. They explain the organization's culture, politics, and expectations. Mentors invest more of themselves in the counseling stage. They advise on work-related challenges, give pep talks and, to a degree, listen to personal problems. In phase three, organizational intervention, mentors publicly support protégées, recommend them for key assignments, and help them get resources. At this stage, the mentor's reputation suffers if protégées do not fulfill expectations. The last stage, sponsorship, demands even greater personal investment from mentors. They nominate protégées as promotion candidates, and if the protégées fail, consequences to mentors are more severe than during the third phase (Zey, 1985).

ADVANTAGES AND DISADVANTAGES OF MENTORING

Table 9.2 summarizes pros and cons of mentoring relationships to involved parties. Most advantages and disadvantages listed are self-explanatory. Two possible negative aspects of mentoring relationships will be discussed. These are the protégée's difficulty ending the mentoring relationship and office gossip about real or perceived sexual liaisons.

Mentoring relationships will end; they usually last from three to six years. The best way for this to happen is to have the relationship evolve into collegiality. For example, perhaps protégées who previously sent reports to mentors for review now send such documents for information only.

Sometimes former mentors resent protégées whose careers surpass theirs. They may feel angry that mentees no longer need them. They may want to control protégées' careers when this is no longer desirable. When these things happen, trouble results. Resentful former mentors may try to block promotions or refuse to write letters of recommendation for them.

Parties to mentoring relationships that sour might not speak to each other. "Fifty Ways to Leave a Mentor" and "Take My Mentor, Please" are titles of articles that have been written to describe reactions when mentoring relationships end negatively.

Fear of sexual innuendo can prevent the development of productive, nonsexual mentoring relationships. This is unfortunate, because the sexes need to learn to cooperate as colleagues for the organization's good. Mentoring can facilitate this process.

About 20% of mentoring relationships lead to sexual involvement. Most such liaisons are heterosexual, but according to Garrison and Comer (1984),

in a minority of cases, female-female and male-male mentoring relationships also become sexual. Whether male-female, female-female, or male-male, these situations almost always end up in difficulty. However, greater numbers of women experience problems because of innuendos about sexual involvements that do not even occur. In addition, there is the subsequent problem of sexual tension; when two people who might be attracted to each other end up working closely, sexual tension almost inevitably develops.

Garrison and Comer recommend same-sex mentoring relationships to reduce the likelihood of innuendo and sexual liaison. Another advantage of same-sex mentoring is greater psychological identification. People identify with those similar to themselves. Women, in particular, may find that others of their sex have encountered similar challenges. Mentors serve as role models, and those more like the protégée may be more credible.

Historically, men have mentored other males. Females may have been unable to sponsor other women because relatively few have held high-level executive posts. A few women who were management pioneers did not want to extend help downward. Rugged individualism was the motto of these "Queen Bees," whose number is dwindling. Many women have realized the importance of extending help downward to other women struggling to succeed. They consider it a moral obligation. The stereotype that females do not like to help others of their sex is, unfortunately, slow to die.

Men typically have been mentors for women, but the opposite situation is no longer unusual. Women employed in organizations where all top executives are men may prefer male mentors if only to get a better idea of expectations of the top brass. As more women obtain higher positions, it will be interesting to see whether males seek them out as mentors.

GENDER DIFFERENCES IN MENTORING RELATIONSHIPS

Do gender differences exist in mentoring relationships? Burke and McKeen (1990) answer yes. They conclude that women view mentoring as a process involving friendship, while men consider it a task-oriented alliance. In their study, female mentors provided more personal and career counseling than did male counterparts. Female protégées made better use of their mentors' knowledge of the corporate culture.

Do women of color have any special concerns regarding mentoring? Again, the answer is yes. If people are more likely to benefit from a mentoring relationship with someone like themselves, minority women pursuing management careers are at a disadvantage. The shortage of minority executive women has been previously documented elsewhere and will not be repeated here.

Thomas (1989) has described cross-sex, cross-race mentoring relationships involving African-Americans and whites. He contends that racial taboos, reminiscent of the slavery era, still operate subconsciously:

Just as a superior and subordinate can enact the unconsciously experienced dynamics of a parent and child, whites and blacks can enact the history of race relations, with all its difficulty and promise, in their everyday interactions, in the microdynamics of supervision and mentoring, and in career planning.

Some African-American women feel uncomfortable having white male mentors. An African-American managerial woman interviewed in Thomas's study (1989) said she did not like to be seen with white men. To her, it evoked images of being a "white man's slut" and all the connotations that go with it.

Black women with fewer qualms about having white male mentors had to deal with angry, suspicious black men. The men thought their female counterparts were siding with white men against them and accused black females of sleeping with "white dudes" (Thomas, 1989).

It was less objectionable for a white woman to mentor a black man, but the opposite situation was difficult. One black male mentor said his protégée reportedly felt that she would damage her career if she continued to associate with him. Another African-American man was uneasy because of "a lot of history that says black men being somewhat familiar with white women isn't healthy." He continued, "Maybe that is changing, but there is enough history to say that it is something you should have some care around."

White men, in contrast, perceived no problem with cross-race mentoring. "Secure and powerful in ways that women and minorities are not, they [white men] can deny the anxieties created by the relationship between blacks and whites" (Thomas, 1989).

What can be done to deal with history and attitudes that threaten to poison cross-race mentoring? Before they can be left behind, they must be discussed openly. That may be a task for core groups in programs developed to value workforce diversity. Most people would prefer to ignore such issues, but they must be confronted if people of various races are to work together effectively.

OBTAINING MENTORS

What should people do if they decide it is worthwhile to have mentors? They need to publicize their career goals. This is especially important for women, because not everyone will assume they want to get ahead. They should volunteer for projects that will provide visibility throughout the organization. Dunbar (1990) tells those seeking mentors to set up an appointment with the chosen executive and try to build a relationship by volunteering to work on the executive's pet projects. The direct question, "Will you be my mentor?" may not be appropriate. A statement such as, "I'd like to stop in for a few minutes occasionally to get your feedback," is preferable. Prospective protégées should not be offended personally if potential mentors nix the relationship because they lack time.

Due to the socialization process, stereotyping, and tokenism, it is sometimes more difficult for women than men to obtain mentors. An Oregon chapter of the American Leadership Forum has tried to remedy that situation by launching a pilot project to pair 50 women seeking career advancement with more experienced businesswomen.

The U.S. Small Business Administration has set up another mentoring program specifically geared to needs of potential entrepreneurial women. The Small Business Administration's program is open to all women, and formalized minority mentorship programs are popping up nationwide. College students, entry-level professionals, and entrepreneurs now have access to a host of programs. However, the problem Nkomo (1988) describes in an appropriately titled article, "Race and Sex: The Forgotten Case of the Black Female Manager," may be happening with respect to mentoring. Programs for women exist, as do programs for minorities, but few are available to deal with unique issues that women of color face.

FORMAL MENTORING PROGRAMS

Formal mentoring programs were first mentioned in the previous paragraph. Until that point, the focus was on informal arrangements. Kizelos (1990) castigates formal mentoring programs. He says forced coupling can fuel discontent, anger, resentment, and suspicion, and claims that good relationships must develop naturally, not at gunpoint.

Furthermore, assuming that any experienced employee would like to be a mentor is a mistake. People in a career stage characterized by "generativity" might welcome a chance to assist others, but that stage no longer can be predicted by age or length of service.

Hennefrund (1986) criticizes formal mentoring programs as Band-Aid solutions within organizational cultures that need overhauling. If the culture does not support development, mentoring programs will have little effect. Their popularity stems from the fact that they are easier to evaluate, at least on paper, than more far-reaching changes in an organization's culture.

On the positive side, formal mentoring programs ensure the inclusion of women and minorities. Another advantage is that they assist recruitment by making applicants feel that the company cares about employees' development needs. Mentoring programs can be invaluable in firms combining cultures, such as a company with Japanese management and American workers, and in merged firms. In the latter case, pairing employees in acquired and acquiring firms may be desirable. That way those whose firm was bought can learn about the acquiring company's culture.

Some formal mentoring programs seem narrow. For example, the steps Lawrie (1987) recommends to set up a program reduce mentoring to a form of training. He suggests developing a mentor-protégée match for jobs in which the incumbent is ready to retire or expects to be reassigned. Also, the human resource department, which probably would coordinate a formal program, should assess protégées' job and organizational knowledge. Finally, only those who enjoy teaching, are good at their jobs, are respected throughout the organization, and want to be mentors should assume that role.

SUMMARY

Career planning and mentoring are intertwined. Developing a career plan and talking to others about it may attract the attention of a mentor. That individual's assistance may facilitate career advancement.

In the volatile business environment of the 1990s, career planning is a challenge. Flexibility has become crucial. People must plan careers, but also must have contingency plans. They must update their skills.

Steps in career planning are self-assessment, occupational information gathering, the initial career choice, and pursuit of the chosen career. Several inventories, including the Strong-Campbell Interest Inventory, Holland's Self-Directed Search, and the Myers-Briggs Type Indicator, are available to aid individuals in the self-assessment stage. The informational interview is a helpful tool in the occupational information-gathering stage.

Those who re-enter organizations after career breaks face added challenges. They need to emphasize transferable skills they have learned through life experiences.

An initial career choice must be evaluated periodically. Sometimes a career change is not desired but becomes necessary. In other circumstances a prior career choice may no longer be consistent with one's values and goals. In such a situation, is a career change possible? Because of financial risks involved, it may not be. On the other hand, if a career change is necessary or desired and seems feasible, an individual must appraise his or her strengths, weaknesses, and interests and search for occupational information.

Retirement does not signal the end of life. Retirees regularly pursue second careers, accept part-time employment, travel, or develop interests in a wide range of leisure activities.

A mentor is a more experienced employee who helps a less experienced employee learn about informal organizational processes. Mentors are trusted advisors who provide constructive criticisms to protégées and may eventually recommend them for desirable assignments or promotion.

Informal mentoring relationships have several advantages and disadvantages. Protégées benefit by having a chance to prove themselves and having an advocate to remove career obstacles. Mentors gain protégées to whom they can delegate work. The mentoring arrangement satisfies the mentor's developmental needs.

On the other hand, a protégée's careers may be harmed by a mentor who fails or stagnates. Protégées may be overloaded with work, or their work may be subjected to extreme scrutiny. They may become socially isolated or too dependent on mentors. Mentors may feel threatened by successful protégées or may have their judgment questioned if the protégée fails.

DISCUSSION QUESTIONS

1. How do you think career planning for women and men is similar? Different?

2. What could you do (what have you done) to plan your career more effectively?

3. Since unforeseen circumstances may arise in your life to upset career plans, of what value are these plans?

4. What additional career planning challenges do you think Hispanic women might face? African-American women? Native-American women?

5. As a protégée, would you prefer a same-sex mentor or not? Does the mentor's sex matter? Explain.

6. Overall, do you feel informal mentoring programs are beneficial or harmful to people interested in career advancement? Formal programs? Explain.

10 Networking

OBJECTIVES

After studying this chapter you should be able to:

1. Define the term networking.
2. Explain why women's networks developed.
3. Explain five advantages of networking.
4. Explain why informal networking seems less advantageous to women than to men.
5. Give an example of an intraorganizational and an interorganizational network.
6. Explain issues related to membership requirements of networks.

Networking is a process of developing and nurturing contacts with others who provide social support, career advice, and feedback. According to Mueller (1987), networks are "seedbeds in which individuals can risk stretching their creativity." They are nonhierarchical and usually do not have formal rules. Communication links within networks resemble spider's webs.

HISTORY OF NETWORKING

Networking exists in various cultures. For example, when aborigines in Australia meet on a trail, it is customary for them to stop and talk. During their conversation, they try to identify a relative in common. If they succeed, it means they are friends. If they fail, they are expected to fight. Reportedly, the verbal search for a mutual ancestor sometimes continues for days (Michaelson, 1988).

Women's clubs have been around since the 1830s (Editors of *Working Woman*, 1984). Unlike those organizations, which met social needs of upper-class women, current women's networks formed to serve females in business and the professions.

Women's networks began in earnest in the 1970s. In retrospect, some contend the networks of 20 years ago were characterized by a "hard-sell" approach, which is no longer effective. Crossen (1990) says, "The self-conscious glad-handing style of formal networks, so popular in the late '70s and '80s, now seems contrived." In the 1970s, women were eager to obtain and use any "intelligence" they believed would aid career advancement. Twenty years later, some have adopted a more subtle approach to networking. Women still use contacts to get ahead, but they may not obviously promote themselves immediately. Rather, they may wait for an opportune moment to make requests or mention accomplishments (Crossen, 1990).

Both the women's movement and the "good old boys' network," present in business, spurred the growth of women's networks. In the 1970s, females began to reap benefits from the push for women's rights in the previous decade. They started to gain momentum in nontraditional careers, including management. Many felt excluded from male groups that met on golf courses, at clubs, or in bars to exchange career-related information informally.

GOOD OLD BOYS' NETWORK

The old boys' network is "not simply a clique, not quite an elite, not exactly a trade union but with some of the qualities of all these alliances" (Mueller, 1987). Beginning in youth, males seem to get exposure to a wider range of networks than females (Feiring and Coates, 1987). Until the current generation, males were more likely than female counterparts to play on school sports teams or to graduate from prestigious colleges.

Both sports and school connections seem to have created a bond for men. Team sports participation is not the only way students develop camaraderie and learn lessons applicable to business, but it is an important means through which they learn to cooperate to achieve a common goal. The experience of lacrosse players, who are mainly sons of wealthy, East Coast families in the United States, illustrates this point. An international arbitrage executive at Morgan Stanley and former captain of the lacrosse team at Wharton, Don MacLeod, explains the importance of the lacrosse connection. He says it provides entree to the business world. Former lacrosse players gravitate to large cities and use the sport to establish rapport with prospective employers (Salzman, 1986).

Similarly, Harvard graduates, most of whom have been males until recently, help other alums obtain jobs or secure financing for business ventures. The president of the Harvard Club even used influence of lawyers on the club's board to have shoplifting charges against a Taiwanese graduate student at Harvard dropped ("The Old School," 1986).

Other examples of old boys' networks that have recently been sex-integrated include community service groups like Rotary, private clubs, and some fraternities. Before 1987, when women became eligible for membership in Rotary, a woman could be a speaker at a Rotary meeting but was not allowed to join. That has since changed, but one professional woman's husband was invited to join Rotary as a result of a speech *she* had given at a meeting.

By the early 1990s, large private clubs had to be integrated and many fraternities at Ivy League schools had agreed to admit women. In the late 1980s, courts ruled that private clubs that serve meals and have 400 or more members must allow women to join. In 1991, Yale's Skull and Bones secret society voted to admit women.

ATTITUDINAL BARRIERS TO NETWORKING

The old boys' network has been second nature to men for years. Many women have become comfortable with informal networking relatively recently. To do this, some had to overcome attitudinal barriers. Such obstacles included a belief that getting a job or promotion because of *who* you know is less desirable than obtaining it due to *what* you know. Another barrier that had to be surmounted was the idea that using others for career advice or social support is manipulative, if not unethical. Potential networkers had to be convinced that an exchange of information or skills is mutual. They would not be using other people in a negative sense; they would give as well as receive.

BENEFITS OF NETWORKING

When they are convinced that networking is not only respectable but also valuable, both sexes gain from the process. Potential benefits include enhanced managerial performance, feedback, social support, career change assistance, empowerment, and a chance to acquire influence.

People become better managers by nurturing peer linkages. By communicating with peers in other departments, managers find out what is happening in other organizational areas. Because they interact with people in other units, they are more likely to view the organization as a system and focus on its overall objectives. Maintaining contacts with colleagues also allows executives to learn from others' experiences and resolve conflicts at early stages.

Networkers can learn from the feedback they receive from others. This information might pertain more to an executive's image, interpersonal skills, or political savvy than to task performance. Such knowledge might be particularly valuable to women, who tend to get less feedback from male bosses than male counterparts.

The importance of social support, defined as an exchange of emotional or material nurturing or caretaking (Feiring and Coates, 1987), should not be underrated. Olson and Lippitt (1985) contend that "our professional growth and mental health depend on finding close colleagues."

A major advantage of networks is that they provide social support. They help new employees assimilate more quickly, not only by familiarizing them with technical and social aspects of the job but also by providing a sense of belonging to the group. In addition, co-workers transmit the organization's behavioral norms and expectations (Bhatnagar, 1988).

The support that informal connections provide serves as a buffer against excess stress. This buffer effect, in turn, enhances wellness. Some have argued that traditional socialization patterns for women, which emphasize social support and intensive contacts, may actually give females a health advantage as compared to males (Feiring and Coates, 1987).

Social support is more difficult to obtain, but perhaps even more essential, for women entering work groups in which they are outnumbered by men. Social support is more difficult to obtain because, as Brass (1985) points out, co-workers prefer to interact with others of the same sex. Many feel uncomfortable interacting with opposite sex peers in an informal, yet work-related, setting. Thus, women employed in departments where most peers are male may be excluded from informal gatherings, not because of malicious intent, but because people prefer to interact with those similar to themselves. Such exclusion is nonetheless harmful to women. It leads to social isolation and may contribute to turnover.

One woman who helped plan a conference hosted by her department was excluded from a party to celebrate the event's success. She was the only woman involved in planning the conference and was employed in a department comprised of 20% women and 80% men. Her male colleagues simply forgot to include her or did not think she would be interested in their gathering. She had reasonably good rapport with the men in her department and later told them, assertively but good-naturedly, that she had not appreciated being excluded. They assured her that it would not happen again.

Just as it is important for women to be part of men's groups, they also must have groups of their own. Dr. Pauline Bart, a sociologist quoted in *Women's Networks* (Kleiman, 1980), claims it is vital for women to have a circle of female friends. She says, "Without networks women don't know there are other women around. You think you are the only one. It's very important to know that you are not unique, that more than just one woman at a time can rise to the top" (Kleiman, 1980).

Supportive relationships, such as those cultivated through networking, are especially vital to women of color. Denton (1990) says that African-

American women in the professions are at particular risk of stress due to paradoxes created by having to function in a white male culture. Organizational bonding requires participation in socioeconomic rituals both during and outside working hours. Because of race and sex, "black women have less opportunity for participation in these rituals and subsequently are excluded from organizational exchanges and alliances which such participation brings" (Denton, 1990).

Networking helps those who want—or are forced—to change careers. Dunbar (1991) urges people in such situations to consider cross-conference mingling. This involves attending conferences and meeting others in a person's area of expertise but in a different industry or sector. For example, a university professor of engineering might attend a conference geared to engineers in the private sector.

Employee empowerment has been cited as an advantage of networking. The process encourages people to take control of their professional development and to share with others hints that enhanced their careers (Solomon, 1991).

A final advantage of networks is that they help people acquire influence within organizations. It is essential for those pursuing upward mobility to gain influence, and active networking allows them to do this in at least three ways. It enhances visibility, speeds up the process of finding a mentor, and yields valuable information. The links among networking, visibility, and mentorship require no further explanation. Information gleaned from a network may give people ideas for new products or better service, provide an understanding of organizational politics, or knowledge of potential new hires, promotions, or job openings. Information about job openings is crucial, since 75% of all jobs are obtained through personal contacts (Bhatnagar, 1988).

POSSIBLE REASONS INFORMAL NETWORKING IS LESS ADVANTAGEOUS TO WOMEN THAN TO MEN

Though advantages of networking accrue to anyone who uses the technique, women tend not to benefit from informal relationships as much as men do. Brass (1985) suggests three reasons for this. First, as mentioned earlier, people prefer to interact with those similar to themselves. Gender is not the only relevant characteristic, however. Some men and women in the same occupation may be more like each other in values and economic class than two women or two men who do different types of work.

Proximity might moderate the tendency for people to interact with those who are similar to themselves. Other things being equal, those in adjacent offices are more likely to associate informally than those occupying offices in the top and bottom floors of a skyscraper.

A second reason women gain less than men from networks is because they have difficulty gaining acceptance in men's networks, particularly those of the "dominant coalition." As compared to that powerful group, women are still perceived to lack influence, and are therefore excluded (Brass, 1985). Men have not been integrated into females' networks very well either, but that has not seemed to cause a problem regarding males' power and influence.

The lack of mingling cannot be attributed to inter-sex behavioral differences. Brass (1985) hypothesized that as relative newcomers to organizations, women might be less aware of informal networks or less skillful at building them than are men. In a study of nonsupervisory employees in the newspaper industry, however, he found that women and men developed networks limited to members of their own sex equally well.

Though others have since criticized the notion that balanced sex ratios within occupations would automatically shatter the glass ceiling for executive women, Brass (1985) believes such a balance within work groups might facilitate more interaction between men and women. He urges women who want to increase their workplace clout to join mixed-sex work groups. His recommendation assumes that men are still more powerful than women in organizations, which, if less than ideal, may reflect reality.

In terms of acquiring influence, Brass (1985) believes it is a mistake to urge women to form networks with other females in an organization. He denounces unisex networks as unnecessary.

Besides being unnecessary, an extreme view is that exclusively female networks harm women's careers. According to a study reported in the *Wall Street Journal*, "the 'Old Girl network,' though valuable for helping women share business contacts, may hurt their careers by keeping them in lower-paid, female-dominated professions" ("Women's Job Contacts," 1991). When women network primarily with others of their sex, they tend to find out about jobs in occupations where women predominate. They do not get as much information about jobs in areas that have been considered non-traditional for females. Thus, networking only with other women may perpetuate occupational segregation.

The third reason women derive fewer benefits from informal relationships is because they purposely have been excluded from networks of powerful men. Remnants of such exclusion remain, as evidenced by the fact that 27% of respondents to a 1991 survey of members of the National Association of Female Executives (NAFE) felt left out of business and civic groups. Over 40% of the primarily female subjects said women felt uncomfortable in those organizations, and nearly 80% admitted that the old boys' network thrived in their industry (Smith, 1991).

PREREQUISITES TO EFFECTIVE NETWORKING

Some qualities and skills that are necessary for effective networking include self-esteem, the ability to introduce oneself to others and to motivate them, and a willingness to exchange favors. The first two prerequisites are related. Before introducing themselves to others, people need to think they have something valuable to offer. To believe they have worthwhile skills and talents to share, people need to have a positive self-concept.

When introducing themselves to others, successful networkers must be able to explain their current position concisely. They also must be able to state career goals succinctly and discuss their interests.

Networkers must be willing to do favors, but they also must know when to ask for specific help. They must realize that successful networking involves both giving and receiving. Networkers who have "markers" to call should not be reluctant to do so (George, 1988).

Besides being able to speak positively about themselves, networkers must be able to motivate others. Listening to peers, discovering their talents, and showing sincere interest in them can facilitate this process.

TIPS FOR SUCCESSFUL NETWORKING

Before listing some dos and don'ts for effective networking, a few caveats are in order. First, networking is not a cure-all. The process should not be expected to substitute for excellent performance. People should not expect a network to become their personal placement office. Though peer linkages are irreplaceable in generating job leads, people should not presume contacts automatically will result in challenging careers. Having stated those cautions, the following are practical suggestions to help those who wish to begin or expand their networks.

Be Polite and Use Others' Time Wisely

Sometimes, rude networkers irritate high-level executives. They dislike networkers who demand lengthy interviews based on a "vague, tenuous connection" (Sonnenberg, 1990). To avoid being seen as brash, networkers must be considerate of others' time. When telephoning a contact, they should ask whether or not it is a good time to talk. They should prepare specific questions ahead of time and should limit telephone calls to half an hour. Networkers should not make requests of others that they would not have time to fulfill. When providing a name of a contact to others, networkers should inform the contact so she or he will not be surprised. Finally, a thank-you note for a favor done always is a good idea. Besides being courteous, it gives people another chance to bring their name to the contact's attention.

Take the Initiative and Avoid Discouragement

Successful networkers must learn to introduce themselves to strangers. This may seem uncomfortable, but it should get easier with practice. Also, networkers should remember that most experiences leading to growth require discomfort. Those who wish to develop peer connections must overcome fear of rejection and learn not to take a "brush-off" personally.

Make the Most of All Networking Opportunities

Some forget that volunteer activities and even parties may facilitate networking. They may believe it is inappropriate to cultivate contacts at such events. Making new acquaintances or renewing friendships that may evolve into part of a business network is perfectly acceptable. In fact, fostering potential contacts, whether developed at social or business functions, represents judicious use of time.

Some refrain from networking because it takes too much time. People with families may prefer to interact with them at the end of a day rather than with professional peers. However, the beauty of networking is that it can be done anywhere with any group.

Many people belong to groups unrelated to the firm that employs them. For example, business executives may serve on hospital or library boards of directors because of a personal interest in those organizations. Parents may assume leadership roles in Girl Scouts, Boy Scouts, or similar groups due to their children's affiliation. All such organizations represent untapped networking potential. By developing contacts made through groups that they would join anyway, people are able to expand their networks with no additional time commitment.

Avoid Playing "Business Bumper Cars"

Some approach networking as a game of "business bumper cars" (Sonnenberg, 1990). Their goal is to join many organizations and to meet lots of people superficially. Sonnenberg suggests a more selective approach. He believes it is better to become actively involved in a few organizations than to be an in-name-only member of dozens.

Use Business Cards Effectively

When business cards are exchanged, too often they are either lost or stuffed in a drawer to be forgotten. To make them more useful, Pearson (1989) recommends that the recipient of a card write something about the giver's interests on the back of the card to jog the receiver's memory. Then the receiver should organize business cards for easy access later.

Network before Contacts Are Needed

Though networking is almost always helpful during a job search, people should not wait until they are unemployed to make contacts. Like most friendships, networking relationships develop gradually. They require mutual respect, trust, and the right interpersonal chemistry (Pearson, 1989).

Call to Stay in Touch

If a person has not heard from a contact for a few months, a brief telephone call is appropriate. A lunch invitation might facilitate a more in-depth conversation.

TYPES OF NETWORKS

There are several types of networks for people who are currently working and for those not presently employed due to either personal choice or layoffs. These include *intraorganizational* and *interorganizational* networks. Those limited to one company are intraorganizational. They may be vertical, including all women in the company, regardless of occupation, or horizontal, including only those in related fields. Even networks confined to one organization vary in focus. For example, 3M's Women's Advisory Committee emphasizes policies that affect women (Farish, 1987). HISPA, a 2,000-member association of Hispanic employees at AT&T, also stresses policy change and has held a meeting with the chief executive officer of the firm to state its views. HISPA goes beyond policy recommendations, however. It also promotes harmony among cultures, interacts with the community to raise scholarship funds, and works with AT&T recruiters to attract more Hispanic college students to the firm (Solomon, 1991).

The Black Professional Association, one of three networks within Avon Products, Inc., takes a somewhat different approach. That group emphasizes career education and has its own academy that presents workshops on topics selected by members, such as personal growth and career development (Solomon, 1991).

Honeywell's Women's Council also promotes education as a means to achieve career mobility. The council has conducted workshops on topics ranging from leadership to child care (Farish, 1987).

Interorganizational networks have members employed by different organizations, and, again, may be horizontal or vertical. Two examples of horizontal, interorganizational networks are the National Association of Female Executives and the International Alliance, an association of professional and executive women. NAFE members who wish to become contacts provide their names, title, telephone numbers, and mailing addresses, which are published in *The Executive Female*. They also receive a packet of networking suggestions. Among other things, the International Alliance advocates women's promotion into top executive positions and promotes greater acknowledgment of women's business achievements.

Vertical interorganizational networks may be open to interested women in a certain geographical area. An example of a vertical interorganizational network is the Professional Women's Network, headquartered in a northeastern Iowa community. It is geographically based and accepts members from the tristate area, which also includes southwest Wisconsin and northwest Illinois.

THE MECHANICS OF NETWORKING

Specific issues networks must resolve are membership requirements, recruitment procedures, and meeting format. Regarding membership, should any working woman be allowed to join or only those above a certain level? Some dislike an elitist group. Unless there are some restrictions, however, networks might not help potential executives. They need to be able to meet others facing similar challenges. TEMPO, in Milwaukee, Wisconsin, is an example of an elitist network. Membership is by invitation only, and prospective members must be women who hold full-time paid positions.

Should male executives be asked to join women's networks? A decade ago, some answered no in the short run but yes in the long run. People were aware that the proper long-term response to women's exclusion from the old boy network was not to banish men. Some believed that in the short run women would feel more comfortable initially developing skills and exchanging information in an all-female group.

For many, this thinking has changed. Since men still have more power in organizations, networking with them may be very valuable. If the sexes do not begin to make connections at a professional level, they will never achieve true collegiality.

Current popular advice is that any professional—male or female—should belong to a national, professional association that holds conferences and disseminates state-of-the-art occupational information. Women may want to join a local network that exists to provide support to its members.

Networks differ in degree of structure of their meetings. Some groups meet over lunch or dinner. Members analyze career-related problems and issues in a relaxed setting. Such discussions are confidential, and members must refrain from put-downs or destructive criticism.

Some groups begin meetings by asking members to state accomplishments since the last session. Others feature a program or speaker. The specific format depends on the group's composition.

One network, comprised of training and development professionals of both sexes, structures its meetings as follows. When members enter the room, they may write any "brainstorming requests" on an easel placed near the door. Brainstorming requests are simply problems a person would like the whole group to address. Examples include "how to cope with an authoritarian boss" or "how to run conflict resolution workshops." Four to six requests are picked, arbitrarily, to be discussed at each meeting.

During the first part of the meeting, newcomers are introduced and members take turns sharing a fact about themselves or professional lives that has changed since the last meeting. Then members have an informal dinner. Trays are provided, and small groups continue their conversations. After dinner, chosen brainstorming requests are discussed. The last part of the meeting features a speaker, case discussion, or book review (Olson and Lippitt, 1985).

SUMMARY

Networks are groups of people who rely on each other for career advice and support. Historically, the "good old boys' " network has helped men find jobs initially and make career progress. Women decided that it would be advantageous to form networks to advance their careers too.

Attitudinal barriers to the networking process include beliefs that using people for career advice is manipulative and that getting a job based on personal connections is undesirable. If they can overcome attitudinal obstacles, people can reap the benefits of networking. These include enhanced performance, feedback, social support, career change assistance, empowerment, and a chance to acquire influence.

Various types of networks exist. They can be horizontal or vertical, intraorganizational or interorganizational.

Network membership policies may be restrictive or open. Some limit membership to executive women employed full-time and earning more than a specified figure. Others are open to any working women or men.

Meeting formats vary in the degree of structure. Some meetings feature a shared meal and informal conversation, while others include a formal presentation by a guest speaker.

DISCUSSION QUESTIONS

1. Talk to someone who is a member of a network. Ask that person why she or he joined and what she or he has learned from membership.
2. Are networks solely for women still necessary? Desirable? Explain your answer.

11 Power and Assertiveness

OBJECTIVES

After studying this chapter you should be able to:

1. Define power, influence, tokenism, reward, coercive, referent, expert, and legitimate power.
2. Explain which power sources would be appropriate in an organization designed to be consistent with feminist principles.
3. Distinguish among passive, assertive, and aggressive behavior.
4. Apply scripting, a technique designed to increase assertiveness, to a situation in your life.
5. Explain the types of words or phrases those who wish to be powerful communicators should avoid.
6. Explain two offensive and two defensive strategies used in organizational politics.
7. Explain the process through which a "double deviant" becomes a token.
8. Explain two sources of and two effects of powerlessness.
9. Compare the effects of tokenism on women and men.
10. Explain structural changes that can empower managers.

DEFINITIONS AND CHARACTERISTICS

Power is the potential ability to get people to change attitudes or behavior; *influence* is the actual ability to do so. The distinction between these terms is like the difference between potential and kinetic energy; the former is dormant capacity, while the latter is energy in motion.

To some, power has negative connotations evoking Machiavellian images. It is seen as vulgar and distasteful. Though power can be abused, the term should not be equated with offensive practices. As will be seen later, extending power downward can benefit individuals and the organization. To be effective, managers need power.

Organizational power and political tactics are not necessarily foundations of modern business school programs, but at least one former vice president of a major firm believes they should be. According to Mary Cunningham Agee (1984), "In business school they taught us about cash flow, not about corporate politics; about return on equity, not about egos and pride. My experience taught me that [courses on power] should have been every bit as much a part of the core curriculum as Production, Marketing, and Finance."

Detractors accused Cunningham, who in 1980 was the highest ranking vice president of Bendix, of an inappropriate relationship with her boss, William Agee. Due to rumors, Cunningham left Bendix for a position as vice president for strategic planning at Seagrams. She described the allegations as resulting from "blatant sexism." Perhaps they were the outcome of behind-the-scenes political maneuvers as well.

Just as no set of traits predicts which individuals will become leaders, no characteristics definitively identify powerful people. However, they are commonly described as visible, credible, professional, and enthusiastic individuals who can maintain the proper perspective. Powerful people make themselves and their competence known. They develop networks inside and outside the organization and use internal and external media to publicize accomplishments. The powerful are likely to be true to their word; when they commit themselves to a project, it gets done. They are believable.

Powerful people conduct themselves professionally using appropriate etiquette. They have fun but are aware that company parties are extensions of work. They avoid drinking excessively or telling demeaning stories at such functions.

Rules of organizational etiquette have changed, and leaders who wish to be powerful may have to learn new behaviors. The following guidelines, adapted from *Effective Human Relations in Organizations* (Reece and Brandt, 1990), may be helpful:

1. When a male manager visits a female executive, she should rise from her desk to greet him, and vice versa.

2. Those conducting meetings should not assume women will take minutes or answer the telephone; neither should it be assumed that men enjoy repairing office equipment.

3. In a business setting, women should open their own car doors.

4. The person who invites another to a restaurant for a meal should pay the bill.

5. The person who reaches a door first should open it, and the person standing toward the front of an elevator should get off first.

6. Men should not assume women dislike discussing topics like sports or cars.

7. Anyone with a free hand should help a person with a load that is too heavy.

Most of the preceding suggestions are common sense, but people who were raised in an environment featuring rigid sex roles may have to adjust to them. Adopting these guidelines alone does not ensure power, but boorishness or inappropriate sexist behaviors may detract from it.

Powerful individuals are motivated; they maintain high energy levels. They refuse to become mired in details but, instead, see the overall picture.

The amount of power available can be viewed as fixed or infinite. If the quantity of power is assumed to be unchanging, then giving it away reduces one's own supply. On the other hand, if power is unlimited, sharing it causes it to multiply. Empowering others increases the total amount available and has a positive impact on the organization.

If effective leaders need power, how do they acquire it? French and Raven (1959) identified six power bases that managers can develop, namely legitimate, reward, coercive, referent, expert, and information power. *Legitimate power* is vested in one's position. In a manufacturing firm, for example, a vice president has more legitimate power than a first line supervisor. In a university, an academic dean has more clout than a faculty member.

Along with formal authority based on job title, managers have the ability to punish employees for failing to meet requirements and to provide desirable outcomes to those performing satisfactorily. The former capacity is called *coercive power*, and should be used cautiously, as a last resort. Overreliance on coercive methods is not recommended, because it may backfire. Punishing employees may extinguish one undesirable behavior, but another equally harmful behavior may replace it.

When using *reward power*, leaders must make sure their perceptions of what constitutes a reward agrees with that of subordinates. Otherwise, this too may have undesirable effects. For example, a professor in an organizational behavior course with an enrollment of 500 tried to apply principles taught in class by publicly commending a student for an outstanding test score. To give the student attention, which the professor considered a reward, she invited him to the front of the lecture hall to participate in a class demonstration. Rather than being motivated by the added attention, this student felt embarrassed. To make matters worse, while he was in the front of the classroom, a jealous peer stole his notebook.

Expert and *referent power* transcend the hierarchy. Regardless of their position, people seek out "experts" because of their knowledge and technical competence. The following example shows how expert power helped a woman employed as a draftsperson find her niche in a firm.

One day the CEO walked through the drafting department in a panic; the company needed someone to take a photograph on short notice and no local photographers were available. Jan volunteered that she had amateur camera equipment at home and would be glad to attempt the shot. As the firm grew to national importance, the company began to rely on Jan's photographic expertise. Ultimately, she became [its] full-time photographer, shooting oil wells in the North Sea and other exotic locations. (Duke and Sitterly, 1988)

People are attracted to those with *referent power*. Such individuals have charisma. People enjoy being around them and may look up to them. Women as different as Oprah Winfrey, former British prime minister Margaret Thatcher, and Mother Teresa of Calcutta all have referent power.

Information power is based on general knowledge and facts about the organization, its constituencies, and its products and services. Information power does not depend on holding a particular hierarchical position but on familiarity with facts that may either be withheld or shared.

An organization structured to be consistent with feminist principles, described in chapter 1, would not rely mainly on coercive or legitimate power. Most feminists would abhor the strategy of dominance and subjugation that coercive power implies. They would not be impressed by power based solely on one's hierarchical position. They would prefer that power be based on information and expertise, at whatever level they would be found in organizations.

Both structural and behavioral power sources exist. Decentralization of authority and few hierarchical levels are structural power sources. Both are features of organic systems, explained in chapter 1, and are not found in mechanistic organizations.

Behavioral power sources focus on steps individuals can take to increase their clout. Some tactics, discussed more thoroughly in previous chapters, include networking and obtaining a mentor. Others, to be described in the following paragraphs, involve becoming more assertive, modifying communications, and playing politics effectively.

BECOMING ASSERTIVE

Before explaining techniques to increase assertiveness, it is useful to distinguish among assertive, passive, and aggressive behavior. *Assertiveness* means communicating one's needs and wants clearly while respecting others' needs. *Aggressiveness* means stating one's needs and wants without regard for others' rights. Aggressive individuals insist on their position or way of doing things even if they must trample on the rights of others. Those with *passive behavior* fail to mention their needs or do so in such a self-deprecating way that no one pays attention to them.

Some men have been socialized toward aggressive behavior, and some women have been raised to be passive. In business, assertiveness is more appropriate than either of the other two behaviors. Using assertive communication can make it easier to gain resources for one's department or for volunteer projects. It also is beneficial when asking for a pay raise or protesting unjust criticism.

Assertiveness training can help those who experience difficulty in self-initiation, limit setting, or in the expression of feelings. Self-initiation is the ability to introduce oneself to a stranger, start a conversation, or let others know what one wants to do. Limit setting means telling others what one is unwilling to do. Saying no to an unreasonable request is an example of limit setting.

Until recently, many men were socialized in ways that discouraged them from expressing positive feelings, and women were not encouraged to vent negative emotions. Some men were uncomfortable voicing appreciation or expressing their love for family members. Women, on the other hand, may have felt guilty for becoming angry. In reality, it is healthy for both sexes to learn to verbalize a wide range of feelings appropriately.

The following dialogue between co-workers illustrates passive, aggressive, and assertive responses to a request for help. Carol lacks time to assist her colleagues because of her own work demands. How might she respond to a co-worker's request for help?

Carol's co-worker: Just the person I wanted to see! Will you help out with this market research project? Your statistical expertise is sorely needed. We want to finish the project next week.

Carol's passive response: Well (hesitating), I've been a little busy... but I suppose I could handle it.

Carol's aggressive response: Why do you have to ask me to do your dirty work? I'm snowed under as it is. It would help if the ignoramuses in your department would take a statistics course themselves. Why did you hire them if they can't do the job? I'm sick of being your patsy.

Carol's assertive response: I just won't be able to fit it into my schedule. I am currently working on three other projects that must be completed by next week too.

Certain nonverbal cues are associated with passive, assertive, and aggressive behavior. When a statement is made passively, eye contact quality is poor. There may be little contact, or the person may look downward, or glance away. A slumped posture and whining voice characterize passive communication. Assertive communicators maintain direct eye contact, stand up straight, and speak in firm, moderate tones. Aggressive individuals may have sharp, raspy voices and may place their hands on their hips and glare at the person to whom they are speaking.

Increasing one's assertiveness involves behavior change. Before modifying behavior, people must be aware of their current patterns. Just as weight loss program participants sometimes monitor food intake for a specified time, those trying to assert themselves should log situations in which they acted passively, aggressively, and assertively. This should be done for about two weeks.

Exercises or tests can be used to assess assertiveness. One such device is the Assertiveness Quotient Test, reproduced here from Baron (1979). Take the test and score it according to the directions following the test.

Assertiveness Quotient Test

Write the number 10 before the statement if the characteristic or situation is very important to you and you experience the feeling or need quite intensely and perhaps quite often.

Write the number 5 before the statement or situation if you experience the characteristic, feeling, or need occasionally and if it is of average concern to you.

Write a zero (0) before the statement if you experience the situation or characteristic seldom or never and if it is of almost no consequence to you as a feeling or need.

1. Do not try to get ahead of others in a line.
2. Getting the job done is more important than the feelings of others.
3. Give encouragement and praise willingly.
4. Easy going.
5. Make fun of others.
6. Show affection easily.
7. Don't want to get involved.
8. Get revenge for injuries or insults.
9. Compliment others on taste, accomplishments, etc.
10. Reluctant to voice opinions.
11. Interested in violence or tragedy.
12. Want to influence or persuade others to your way of thinking without dismissing others' ideas.
13. Willing to help others before considering personal priorities.
14. Critical of others.
15. Don't mind dressing differently from others.
16. Readily do favors for other people when asked.
17. Blame others when things go wrong.
18. Seek suggestions and help from others when you honestly feel those suggestions will be helpful.

19. Have few opinions on topics of discussion.

20. Prefer to do things your own way.

21. Express opinions and viewpoints easily.

22. Prefer to wait until styles are well established before trying them.

23. Jealous or envious of others.

24. Easy to meet new people in new situations.

25. Fearful of authority.

26. Choose to do things for self rather than for others.

27. Consider many viewpoints before making up your mind.

28. Prefer to take directions from someone.

29. More interested in things than people.

30. Willing to settle arguments.

31. Let others get credit for doing things.

32. Be the center of attention.

33. Make positive statements about your own accomplishments or achievements when appropriate.

34. Opinions easily swayed by others.

35. Don't like people to get too close to you.

36. Accept criticism from others.

37. Follow the suggestions of others.

38. When given poor service, complain loudly to person who serviced you.

39. Be able to admit mistakes.

40. Uncomfortable around wealthy, educated, or prestigious people.

41. When dissatisfied with someone, verbally or physically attack them.

42. Without embarrassment, ask a physician all questions for which you want answers.

43. Difficulty maintaining eye contact.

44. Frequently show anger toward others with little provocation.

45. Speak up readily in groups.

SCORING THE ASSERTIVENESS QUOTIENT TEST (BARON, 1979)

The assertiveness quotient is not a psychological test. There are no standards by which to measure your results. However, the results may give you some guidelines about which type of behavior is more prevalent in your life and give you an incentive to become more assertive and less passive and aggressive. Statement 1 on the assertiveness quotient test and every third statement thereafter are "passive." Similarly, item 2 on the test and every third statement thereafter are aggressive; statement 3 and every third thereafter are assertive. Sum your scores on items 1, 4, 7 . . . 43.

The total is your score on the passive scale. The sum of items 2, 5, 8 ... 44 is your score on the aggressive scale, and the sum of items 3, 6, 9 ... 45 represents your score on the assertive scale. If you have many "10" answers (between eight and ten) under the passive statements, this indicates that you need some assertive behavior in these areas; you are reacting more passively than assertive behavior indicates. A score of 80 to 120 on any scale indicates that you are somewhat locked into that type of communication. Above 110 indicates that you are highly passive, aggressive, or assertive.

Besides taking tests and keeping logs to assess initial assertiveness levels, people should think about how they typically handle employees with problematic behavior. They should write down their response and analyze it for signs of aggression or passivity. Then they should consider other possible ways to respond (Morgan and Baker, 1985).

THE SCRIPTING TECHNIQUE

A scripting technique, attributed to James Waters, formalizes the analysis of behavior for signs of assertive, passive, or aggressive communication (Morgan and Baker, 1985). Variations of scripting have either four or six phases. The four basic stages include a description of the situation, expression of feelings, a request for behavior change, and a statement of positive consequences to the party who changes behavior. In the expanded version, an expression of empathy with the other person follows the expression of feelings, and negotiation of the change precedes the statement of positive consequences.

In the first stage of the basic scripting process, people prepare a written description of a situation in which they acted either passively or aggressively and later realized assertive behavior would have been preferable. The description should be as objective as possible.

In the next step, people communicate feelings being careful to avoid accusatory statements or generalizations beginning with "You always..." or "You never...." Those phrases should be avoided because they trigger receiver defensiveness. A statement of feelings usually does not provoke such hostility.

In the third step, people state a behavior change they would like from the other person. The desired change must be specific. It should be something the other person is able to do. The other party should not be asked to modify behavior drastically overnight.

Finally, those trying to become more assertive should state positive consequences that will occur if the other person modifies his or her behavior. These must be realistic, and the assertive people must deliver them. Otherwise, they will lose credibility.

An example of the scripting technique, adapted from *Asserting Yourself: A Practical Guide for Positive Change* (Bower and Bower, 1976), follows.

Joyce was a new supervisor replacing George Jones, who had retired. She inherited George's administrative assistant, Ann, who had never worked for a woman before. For the first three weeks, Ann made comments like, "That's not the way Mr. Jones would have done this," or "Mr. Jones was a better planner." Joyce accurately interpreted these comments as criticisms that were interfering with her performance.

Joyce: I find it annoying to be reminded constantly that George Jones did things differently. I know he had his way of doing things, but I would like to try some of my ideas. Please stop telling me how George Jones did things. If you would stop mentioning George, I could implement some new plans more quickly. To do that, I'd welcome your ideas.

CONSEQUENCES OF ASSERTIVE BEHAVIOR

Becoming assertive has positive and negative consequences. It gives people another behavioral option and provides a greater sense of control. On the other hand, adopting this new behavior may strain relationships. Family or "significant others" may not understand the change or may dislike it, especially if they have benefitted from previous passivity. They may purposely mislabel the new behavior as aggression to pressure people to revert to nonassertive ways (Cammaert and Larsen, 1979). They do this out of fear of loss and change. Family and friends may have been content with the old relationship, in which they could dump extra work and emotional "garbage" on passive individuals. Those learning assertiveness should examine their behavior if accused of being aggressive. Sometimes previously suppressed anger and frustration surfaces, causing them to overshoot the mark.

SITUATIONS IN WHICH ASSERTIVE BEHAVIOR SHOULD BE USED

People working on assertiveness skills should not feel compelled to use them in all situations. They can ask four questions to determine whether it is worthwhile. These are:

1. How important is it to be assertive in this instance?
2. How will I feel later if I am nonassertive?
3. What are the costs of assertiveness?
4. Is it appropriate to be assertive now?

POWER AND COMMUNICATION

Increasing assertiveness is one way people can become more powerful verbal communicators. Before listing recommendations to improve oral communications, essentials of the communication process will be reviewed. *Communication* is the transmittal of understanding (Ivancevich, Szilagyi, and Wallace, 1977). A sender encodes a message and transmits it, through a channel, to a receiver, who then decodes it. Feedback from receiver to sender completes the loop and creates two-way communication. Without feedback, one-way communication exists.

Communication can be verbal, nonverbal, or written. Verbal, or oral, communication is spoken; nonverbal includes body posture and gestures and facial expressions. Memos, letters, and reports are examples of written business communication.

Potential master communicators should avoid fillers, diminutives, flowery adjectives, or disclaimers. Fillers are speech segments like "uh" or "um." They are distracting to listeners. If fillers are overused, listeners pay more attention to them than to the content of the message. According to Hunsaker and Hunsaker (1990), fillers "signal uncertainty and lack of preparation. [They] also open the door for interruption and allow others to take away the speaker's right to speak."

Diminutives are words like "little," "tiny," "only," or "just." Overuse of such words may indicate weakness or a low self-concept. When accompanied by nonverbal signals such a hesitating manner and slumped posture, those who approach the boss with, "I know you're busy, but this will *only* take a *little* time" will not be considered forceful leaders. Besides diminutives, this example also contains a disclaimer, namely the phrase, "I know you're busy, but. . . . " Other examples of disclaimers are "You'll probably think this is a crazy idea, but . . . " or "It's not my place to say this, but. . . . " Those who make such statements habitually seem defensive (Rogers, 1989).

"Fantastic," "magnificent," "dreadful," "gorgeous," and "awful" are too subjective for routine business communication. Specific, meaningful adjectives are preferable.

Sometimes apologies are necessary, but they should not be overdone. Rogers (1989) says that for some, "I'm sorry" becomes a mantra. Instead of overapologizing, she recommends focusing on problem solving.

Supervisors prefer employees who get the job done to those who say they will try. While exerting one's best efforts even if falling short of the mark is admirable, employees interested in power enhancement should not speak tentatively. Think of the difference in tone between "Well, I'll try . . . " and "Consider it done!" The second statement packs more punch.

Tag questions transform statements into queries. They connote hesitancy and dependence. Instead of saying, "This project needs to be done by October 1," a questioning intonation is used at the end of the sentence. This makes the speaker seem unsure and detracts from her or his power.

Suggestions about voice, pitch, and volume seem culturally dependent. Bias against high-pitched voices can harm careers based on an uncontrollable factor that is not job-related. Some women have been socialized to speak quietly, but in business, speaking softly indicates a person's message is unimportant or that the individual has low self-esteem. Talking too loudly also is unacceptable. Beverly Edgehill, an African-American executive, is accustomed to turning up the volume off the job. She claims a friend can tell when she is going to attend a board of directors meeting where all the members are white women because Beverly "turns down the volume and starts talking all proper" (Ray, 1988).

Though speech patterns can be altered, should women and minorities have to do so to fit in and advance in the current business culture? By the year 2000, the answer ought to be no. With the predicted influx of women and minorities, corporate America must learn to accept cultural variations in style of speech. Programs to manage diversity should help people become more comfortable with differences in volume, pitch, and manner of speaking, at least within a range.

Whether or not people allow others to invade their personal space, how often and in which circumstances they smile, and the type of gestures they use affect others' perceptions of their power. Supervisors should not allow subordinates to move so close, physically, that they invade the former's personal space. Females permit others to reduce their personal space more than males do, but managerial women should be wary of this. Allowing subordinates to invade one's personal space signifies low power.

For women, to smile or not presents a dilemma. If they smile too much, their seriousness is questioned. If they rarely smile, women may seem cold or worse. Men are not expected to smile as much as women; if they do, it makes them seem more approachable.

Small, close-to-the-body gestures connote weakness; large, expansive gestures indicate power. Allowing personal belongings to take up more, rather than less space, and being physically large makes people seem forceful. The latter finding is a disadvantage for women, most of whom are physically smaller than most men.

To make written communication more potent, it should be concise and specific. Memos should get to the point. Simple words should replace multisyllabic ones, and writers should use the active voice more often than the passive.

In written and spoken communications, companies that want to empower all employees should use nonsexist, inclusive terms. Masculine pronouns are no longer universally accepted as generic terms designed to include both sexes. Alternatives are available. Sentences containing "he," "his," or "him" may be rewritten using plurals "they," "their," and "them." Another option would be to use "s/he," meaning "she or he."

Gender-neutral equivalents to words like "manpower" and "workmen's compensation" exist. The U.S. government has replaced "manpower" with "staffing." More than ten years ago, workmen's compensation became workers' compensation. Major publishers have developed manuals intended to promote nonsexist communications. One of the first was McGraw-Hill's *Guidelines for Equal Treatment of the Sexes* (1974).

In spoken conversation, business executives must be aware that the term "girl" may be considered demeaning when used to describe adult females. In an era when women make up almost half the labor force and 80% of new entrants to the workforce in the next 18 years are projected to be women or minorities, organizations can ill afford to alienate even a segment of the female workforce by condoning disparaging speech.

To some, the controversy over nonsexist language is much ado over nothing. To others, it is important because language reflects inner beliefs. Describing executives and other leaders in exclusively masculine terms reinforces the idea that it is appropriate for men, but not women, to have power. When occupational titles are masculine, children visualize a male jobholder. For example, to a child, the word "policeman" evokes a male image. It may be more difficult for children who grow up hearing male-oriented job titles to accept women as firefighters, letter carriers, and police officers. By extension, their gut reaction may be to balk at female incumbents in occupations previously viewed as male bastions, such as management.

Paradoxically, powerful communicators also are sensitive. They respect others' feelings and would not purposely use exclusionary oral or written language.

POWER AND ORGANIZATIONAL POLITICS

Besides learning to be forceful and empathetic communicators, powerful managers should adopt behaviors used by savvy politicians. Organizational politics are here to stay, and executives will not change that fact by disdaining them, wishing them away, or refusing to play the game. Their best bet is to learn the rules because, as Kennedy (1989) says, "Thinking that hard work alone brings success brands you a political neophyte."

If hard work is insufficient, what else is needed? Astute political players will adopt at least three offensive and three defensive strategies. Offensively, they should remain visible, build alliances, and stand up for their beliefs. Publicizing accomplishments and participating in informal and formal company functions are vital for managers seeking power through politics. Getting to know co-workers is important because "in organizational life, familiarity breeds acceptance and interest, not contempt" (Kennedy, 1989).

Alliance building also is crucial. Isolates may lack support for sound proposals. Managers must cultivate allies not only from among their peers but also at different levels. When making connections, secretarial and maintenance staff should not be overlooked. Their support is valuable, and it would be foolish to alienate them.

Powerful managers do not play dead when encountering opposition. They do not fight every battle—only the important ones. Executives who are perceived as constantly giving in to avoid conflict may not be promoted.

Defensive political strategies include safeguarding one's turf, considering hidden agendas, and recognizing signs of sabotage. The first strategy means noticing when parts of one's job responsibilities are being reassigned, and taking corrective action. During the downsizing decade of the 1980s, this was especially important. Managers who appeared indifferent about real-location of their duties soon could have been without a job.

Executives must recognize signs of sabotage without becoming paranoid. Three signals that something is wrong are reductions in the amount of network-supplied information, unusual questions from the boss about future educational plans, and conversations that end abruptly when one joins the group (Kennedy, 1989). When "intelligence" dries up, offer to trade a piece of information with a network member to find out the reason. If supervisors ask about developmental plans, tactfully inquire why they want to know. If a group repeatedly clams up when a manager appears, she or he should ask one member for an explanation. The more vehement the denial, the more the manager should suspect that something is amiss. The executive should then identify and confront the culprit, leaving the impression that the sole motive is to clarify the record (Kennedy, 1989).

TOKENISM

Besides avoiding political minefields and practicing power-enhancing be-haviors, executives must realize that factors beyond their control may create "bureaucratic powerlessness" (Kanter, 1977). Tokenism is one such factor, which occurs when the sex ratio within an occupation is skewed. This means that 85% or more are of one sex, and 15% or less are of the other. Because at least 95% of CEOs of major U.S. firms are men, at the highest corporate levels, tokenism could still be a problem. Laws (1975) has defined tokenism as a promise of career mobility that the predominant group makes to the underrepresented group. The quality and amount of mobility are both lim-ited, however.

Much literature on tokenism depicts men as the dominant group and women as tokens. According to A Tale of O, a film produced by a consulting firm owned by Kanter, an authority on tokenism, the idea of dominant and excluded classes can be extended to other groups. The film suggests that any class that differs from the majority and makes up 15% or less of the studied population could be considered a token group. Thus, a person with disabilities in the midst of able-bodied individuals, a person over age 65 surrounded by 30-year-olds, or one Hispanic in an otherwise Caucasian work group would be tokens.

Yoder (1991) disputes the generalizability of Kanter's theory of dominants and tokens. She claims it only applies to women in occupations stereotypically considered appropriate for males. Kanter and other later researchers only studied females in occupations statistically dominated by men. Furthermore, they examined situations in which "workers studied represented either the first group of women ever admitted to the institution or a first-time, significant numeric surge, both of which could be regarded as intrusive by the higher status dominant group of male workers" (Yoder, 1991).

New studies are needed to extend Kanter's work by isolating effects of numerical imbalance in an occupation from other factors. Specific variables of concern are the gender mix of jobholders, an occupation's perceived gender inappropriateness, and "intrusiveness." Intrusiveness is an influx of minorities into a majority-dominated occupation. This surge threatens the dominant group, which reacts with increased discrimination against minorities to "limit their power gains" (Yoder, 1991).

Regarding gender mix, evidence (Fairhurst and Snavely, 1983; Ott, 1989) shows that women, but not men, experience negative effects of tokenism, namely social isolation, visibility, and encapsulation into stereotypical gender roles. Yoder (1991) reports that "the visibility afforded token men may work to their advantage, enhancing their opportunities for promotion." She concludes that "the negative consequences of tokenism seem only to occur for members of social categories that are of lower status relative to the majority."

Male tokens seem immune to negative effects of working in a field considered appropriate for females. Women in male-dominated occupations feel performance pressures, and are stereotyped and isolated, but male nurses report no such experiences (Ott, 1989).

While studying the first group of female West Point graduates, researchers found that they experienced harmful effects of tokenism regardless of whether or not their presence was thought intrusive (Yoder, Adams, and Prince, 1983). Negative treatment of female West Point graduates was attributed to gender and perceived occupational inappropriateness.

Yoder's constructive criticism should not obscure the impact of Kanter's work on the study of gender in organizations. By focusing on numerical imbalance, Kanter shifted attention from the misguided idea that managerial success eluded women because of their inherent deficiencies. With hindsight, it is easier to see that numeric imbalance may be one of several factors that thwart women's progress.

Keeping criticisms of Kanter's ideas in mind, it is worthwhile to recount her concept of the process by which individuals become tokens. To understand that process, the terms primary and double deviant must be explained. *Primary deviants* are those who are not members of the dominant class. *Double deviants* are "uppity" primary deviants. They are not content with second-rate status; they want the same opportunities as the dominant group. In her analysis of academia, which has implications for business, Laws (1975) views men as the predominant class, primary deviants as those "born female," and double deviants as women who aspire to equality with men. Yoder (1991) defines primary deviants as women whose strong career commitment differs from gender norms and double deviants as those "who deviate a second time by aspiring to succeed in a domain defined as appropriate for men."

Double deviants turn into tokens by being sponsored by dominant group members and striking a role bargain with them. Three elements of the role bargain are exceptionalism, individualism, and merit (Kanter, 1977). First, sponsors convince double deviants that they are exceptions. Making them believe they are better than, and therefore unlike, most other primary deviants reinforces the idea that the primary deviants are less valuable.

Sponsors also assure deviants that individualism and merit count. In the United States, stories of rugged individualism are appealing. People like to hear about those who have "pulled themselves up by the bootstraps." Sponsors urge deviants to accept the outdated notion that hard work alone leads to success. If they believe that myth, they also must conclude that failure is caused by lack of hard work. Using such logic, the dominant group would hold deviants responsible for their own failure.

Sponsors may brainwash deviants to think that the dominant class has achieved its status. If deviants accept this merit principle, they buy into two ideas. The first is that the dominant group must remain exclusive because of its high standards, and the second is that excellence will be rewarded. Deviants who have outstanding performance but who are not rewarded may blame themselves. This is unfortunate, since the real reason why their efforts were not recognized has nothing to do with them. Rather it is the fault of a system that seeks excuses to relegate some to second-class status.

The transformation of deviants to tokens is not complete until they and their sponsors agree on roles and attitudes. They concur that sponsors are not prejudiced and decide that tokens will defend sponsors.

The final task is to integrate tokens into the dominant class in a way that does not threaten the latter. When this is accomplished, the sponsor and token will "know that the token cannot completely escape ... deviant origins, and cannot participate completely in the dominant group" (Laws, 1975). Thus the dominant group retains control.

After deviants have become tokens, sponsors marginalize them. Tokens are simultaneously isolated socially and overloaded with assignments as a result of visibility. They are stereotyped as helpers, sex objects, mascots, or militants. When tokens are female, "helper" may be synonymous with mother. Kanter (1977) identifies three dangers to women who assume the "mother" role. They may be stereotyped as emotional specialists or rewarded mainly for service. Finally, if these women are critical, others may fear them. If female tokens stray from the "good, nonjudgmental" mother image, they will lose rewards.

If viewing female tokens as mothers puts women into a familiar context for men, so does thinking of them as sex objects. Male sponsors tend to overprotect tokens they see as mothers or sex objects, which damages their careers.

The mascot, or pet, also may be overprotected. This person has a great sense of humor. According to Kanter (1977), "she has to admire male displays but not enter into them. Shows of competence on her part are treated as special and complimented just because they are unexpected, a kind of look-what-she-does-and-she's-only-a-woman attitude."

Because militants do not fit into familiar categories, sponsors distrust them. In the male-female scheme, militants are strong-willed women. Their work and opinions may be scrutinized carefully in attempts to cause them to fail. This overexposure to which militants are subjected may affect other tokens as well. As individuals who differ from the norm, they gain attention, not because of competence, but because they stand out. Ever-present visibility, though advantageous initially, may cause long-term stress. It is more difficult for those who are visible to hide mistakes.

Tokens also may be asked to serve on committees as spokespersons for their groups. Since there are relatively few of them, this can lead to overload. It perpetuates the myth that tokens all have the same opinion on various issues.

OTHER FACTORS CONTRIBUTING TO POWERLESSNESS

As stated earlier, other factors besides tokenism may contribute to bu-reaucratic powerlessness. One such factor is sole reliance on position power.

Often, first line supervisors have position power but nothing else. Their performance reviews depend on how well subordinates do their jobs. For that reason, supervisors feel they have limited ability to confront employees. If employees resent confrontation, and therefore reduce quantity and quality of services or products, supervisors get blamed. Though dependent on sub-ordinates, supervisors may not be able to discipline them for ineffectiveness. Middle managers may retain that authority. If they refuse to delegate power to first line supervisors, the supervisors may feel like puppets (Kanter, 1977).

Employees lose respect for bosses who must check with higher authorities before making decisions. If employees jump the chain of command, more trouble will follow. As Kanter states (1977), "Nothing diminishes leaders' power more than subordinates' knowledge that they can always go over their heads, or that what they promise has no real clout."

Like first line supervisors, managers of advisory or staff departments, which contribute indirectly to production of goods or services, also are dependent. They cannot force other department heads to heed their advice but must rely on persuasion. A dwindling number of supervisors regard staff departments' advice as an infringement. For example, in the early 1970s, when human resource managers first counseled line managers to consider equal employment opportunity when hiring, some resented the intrusion.

EFFECTS OF POWERLESSNESS

Powerless managers respond predictably. They act domineering to cover up anxiety and feelings of inferiority. To prove they still have clout, powerless managers dominate subordinates. According to a study of Air Force officers (Hetzler, 1955), those

of lower status and advancement potential favored more directive, rigid, and authoritarian techniques of leadership, seeking control over subordinates. Subordinates were their primary frame of reference for their own status assessment and enhancement and so they found it important to "lord it over" group members.

Powerless supervisors overemphasize rules. They enforce the letter of the law at first so they can reward friends by easing up later.

Managers without power are overcontrolling and territorial. If they have just been promoted from technical areas, they may supervise employees too closely, correcting the smallest mistakes. Supervisors without clout are more likely to use coercion to control subordinates. In circular fashion, when subordinates resist, such managers become even more forceful.

Because they have little power, such managers place a high priority on defending the territory they do have. If executives get too concerned about protecting their own domains, however, the organization suffers. This is because it is impossible, in those circumstances, to acknowledge the interrelatedness of all units and their impact on the whole organization. According to Kanter (1977):

As each manager protects his or her own domain, the sense of helplessness and powerlessness of other administrators in intersecting units increases. They ... respond by redoubling their domination over their territory and ... workers. The result can be "suboptimization": each subgroup optimizing only its own goals and forgetting about wider system interests.

As mentioned previously, people sometimes stereotype managerial women as overcontrolling, territorial, and bossy. Kanter suggests that any manager—male or female—could be expected to exhibit such behaviors when faced with bureaucratic powerlessness. She concludes that powerlessness, not gender, produces domineering actions that subordinates dislike.

Now that possible causes of some undesirable supervisory behaviors have been identified, what can be done to change them? Kanter proposes unconventional approaches. She suggests empowering those lacking clout. Superficially, this may seem unwise. Why reward managers who dominate others? If given more power, wouldn't they abuse it? The opposite is true.

Empowerment breaks the powerlessness cycle. It involves flattening the hierarchy, decentralizing authority, facilitating decision making at lower levels, and assigning activities that increase power. Kanter (1977) also proposes a number balancing strategy, which Yoder claims is ineffective.

Flattening the hierarchy by removing excess levels leads to more accurate and speedy communication. It should be easier for employees to get answers from a manager two levels above them than from an executive five steps higher. Also, there is an inverse relationship between job satisfaction and the number of hierarchical levels. Increased satisfaction is associated with flatter companies (Crozier, 1964).

A decentralization strategy pushes formal authority downward. Work groups become more independent and may therefore feel more responsible for completing a whole piece of work.

Facilitating decision making at the bottom requires managers to take additional steps. All parties must commit themselves to open communication. Managers must make information more widely available. Kanter (1977) suggests formalizing sponsor-protégée relationships, which are similar to mentor-mentee relationships discussed in chapter 10. Pitfalls of such "arranged marriages" also were summarized in that chapter.

Activities that are extraordinary, relevant, or straddle departments are power-enhancers. Extraordinary activities involve crisis or uncertainty. Kanter (1977) stops short of saying that some organizations create crises to allow managers to demonstrate their ability, but contends that satisfactory performance of routine activities is not enough to generate power. Liaison positions are examples of those that straddle departments. These jobs require incumbents to network with different units regularly, thereby helping them to develop alliances with others. Relevant activities deal with pressing organizational problems.

The numbers-balancing route to empowerment should be viewed with skepticism. According to this idea, as the ratio between token and dominant groups approaches equality, former tokens will no longer be treated badly. Unfortunately, this scenario may be too simple and too optimistic. Yoder (1991) believes that "when numbers of a low-status group increase substantially across the occupation, the reaction is stepped up harassment, blocked mobility, and lower wages."

SUMMARY

Power is the potential ability to change behavior or attitudes. Some believe the amount of power is fixed, but others consider it unlimited.

Increasing assertiveness, modifying communication patterns, and playing politics can increase one's power. Managers who learn power-enhancing behaviors may be thwarted by barriers inherent in an organization's structure. These obstacles, which include token status and employment in certain staff positions, result in bureaucratic powerlessness. Territoriality and over-controlling behavior are two negative consequences of such powerlessness.

Members of a group that is not numerically dominant become tokens through a role bargain with the dominant group. That class limits the extent of the token's participation in its activities; the token remains an outsider.

Structural changes can empower the powerless. Some power-enhancing actions are to flatten the hierarchy, decentralize decision making, and place people in liaison positions or positions involved with extraordinary or relevant activities.

DISCUSSION QUESTIONS

1. Do you believe the amount of power is fixed or infinite? Explain.

2. Does assertiveness training have real merit or is it a passing fad? Explain.

3. Pick one situation or incident in which you wished you had been more assertive. Write a replay of that situation using the scripting technique described in this chapter. (The steps in this technique are to describe the situation objectively, use "I" statements to explain your feelings about it, state the desired behavior change, and explain positive consequences of this change.)

4. Do you use any nonverbal communication methods that either enhance or detract from the message you are trying to convey? Explain.

5. Do you think women and minorities should have to adjust speech patterns to advance and be accepted in business, or not? Explain.

12   Balancing Career and Family/Personal Life

OBJECTIVES

After studying this chapter you should be able to:

1. Distinguish between a dual-career and dual-earner couple.
2. Explain three advantages and three potential problems associated with a dual-career lifestyle.
3. Explain positive strategies dual-career couples can use to cope with challenges inherent in their lifestyle.
4. Explain why companies may have to change their cultures to be more hospitable to workers' family needs.
5. Explain common management beliefs that may create obstacles to family-supportive programs.
6. Explain advantages and disadvantages to employers and employees of an on-site child care center.

Just as the nature of a career has changed dramatically, so has family life. The meaning of the term "family" also has become ambiguous. The 1950s "Ozzie and Harriet" model of employed father, stay-at-home mother, and a few children has not been the norm for years. During the 1980s, it was partially replaced by the dual-career couple with children, as exemplified by the Claire and Cliff Huxtable family on "The Cosby Show." Many family constellations coexist in the contemporary scene. These include single parents, "blended" families, and former empty-nesters whose grown children have returned home. Some unmarried couples have registered as "domestic partners" so they can be considered family for purposes of coverage under each other's employee benefits plans.

In a discussion of career/family issues, singles may feel excluded. Their need to have a personal life away from work should not be overlooked. Also, those who have living parents or other older relatives may need to make decisions regarding elder care.

DUAL-CAREER COUPLES

The focus in this chapter will be to explore issues unique to dual-career couples. First, the distinction between a dual-career and dual-earner couple will be explained. In a *dual-career* arrangement, both partners are deeply committed to their work and to a love relationship. They have an advanced education and expect opportunities for development, promotion, and greater responsibilities. These individuals are ego-involved in their work. They may value the paycheck to an extent, but are more interested in self-fulfillment. Their positions are professional, technical, or managerial. *Dual-earner* couples, on the other hand, are both employed mainly because they need the income. They do not seek fulfillment from their jobs and have not taken advanced training to obtain current positions.

In 1990, 65% of all marriages had two incomes (Connelly, 1990), and that figure is projected to grow to 81% by 1995 (Reynolds and Bennett, 1991). Data on the number of dual-career couples, as defined in the previous paragraph, are not as readily available. In 1982, they made up 10% of all married couples (Newgren, Kellogg, and Gardner, 1987). The fact that the number of dual-career couples has increased is obvious. A burgeoning percentage of highly educated women in the workforce has contributed to this trend. Forty-five percent of those in the labor force are women, and they earned half the master's degrees and one-third of all doctoral and professional degrees in 1989 (Collie, 1989).

Though it may have been novel, in the recent past, for both spouses to pursue a career, having two wage earners in a family was fairly common. For people of color, it was often an economic necessity. This was particularly true for African-American women: "The prohibition against the employment of women never extended to them. . . . African-Americans have never had access to a family wage, and both men and women have had to work throughout their life cycle" (Mullings, 1986).

African-American women have toiled alongside men of their race since slavery. When they tried to withdraw from the labor force after emancipation and demanded that a wage to support the entire family be paid to their husbands, African-American women were accused of being lazy. An official of the Freedmen's Bureau attributed financial problems black families had in that era to the "evils of female loaferism" (Gutman, cited in Mullings, 1986).

Society expected African-American women to be employed and raise a family simultaneously. The way they balanced these roles during the era when the norm for married white women was to stay home was not a topic deemed worthy of serious research.

Ironically, the slavery legacy created greater equality between the sexes among African-Americans. As Mullings (1986) states, "disenfranchisement of both men and women meant that the enslaved family possessed no means by which one gender could control the other." Apparently, there is still some carryover. Wilson and her colleagues (1990) report that "both black men and women are socialized to expect mothers to share in providing financial support and making family decisions. Black men are generally supportive of this egalitarian relationship and expect a marriage in which husbands assist in household tasks and child care duties."

There was little interest in the dual-career phenomenon until it affected middle- to upper-class white women. That began to happen after Title VII of the Civil Rights Act was passed.

Dual-career couples can be classified according to whose career takes precedence, or according to the way spouses' career paths are related. Using the former scheme, relationships can be dubbed *unequal, pre-egalitarian*, or *fully egalitarian*.

The unequal relationship can take on two forms. In the first, the facetious suggestion is that the woman has two jobs—one at work and one at home (Bem, 1987). She is expected to be successful in her career and to care for the home as well. Without any role modifications, this sets her up to be a discouraged perfectionist, a superwoman, or to go insane. In this version of the unequal situation, the male partner may talk about equality, but that is as far as it goes. The second form of the unequal arrangement is matriarchy. In this situation, the woman's career is most important, and her spouse knows it.

Unequal relationships simplify marital decision making, because both partners know, for example, who will relocate to accept a promotion and who will follow. The problem is that someday the self-sacrificing spouse may tire of being the follower. If neither spouse has anticipated this, both will need to spend much time communicating with each other and re-evaluating roles for the relationship to survive.

In the pre-egalitarian couple, the husband "helps" with household tasks, but the wife is the administrator. She determines what needs to be done, by whom, and when. Bem (1987) argues that planning and organizing take more mental energy than physically performing tasks. This explains why a woman who assumes the household manager role seems more harried than her husband. He may shop for groceries, but she probably made the list. He may pick up their son Chris from Scouts and take Chris to the after-school sitter's, but she probably registered Chris for Scouts and arranged for after-school child care. In a fully egalitarian marriage, either spouse would do these things. In the pre-egalitarian set-up, usually the woman does them, which explains why she seems so hassled. "And when the woman's sympathetic but puzzled husband tries to alleviate her distress [he doesn't] even notice the giveaway line: 'I'll be happy to take on more of the work, honey. Just tell me what you want me to do' " (Bem, 1987).

In egalitarian partnerships, the goal is to minimize gender-related division of labor. One dual-career couple developed the following way to do this:

First, they discussed all the chores and crossed off tasks that neither of them cared about. Next, they delegated everything to someone else where they would be able to find and pay an outsider to do the work. Then, they bargained with each other to take the tasks that they personally abhorred. Once the emotionally charged duties were disposed of, they equitably divided the remaining work. (Lee, 1981)

Spouses' career paths may be parallel, competitive, disparate, or joint. In parallel careers both spouses are on different tracks in the same field. For example, a couple might be interested in management. The husband is a human resource manager, and the wife is a production manager. If both spouses attend medical school together, their careers could be competitive. Careers are called disparate if they have nothing in common. If spouses are co-owners of a firm or co-authors, they have joint careers.

Whether committed to a relationship or not, all career-oriented individuals must make decisions about further job advancement and personal goals. Such decisions become more complex when one is part of a two-career couple. If only adults' needs must be considered, the net impact of two positions is positive (Stoner and Hartmann, 1990). Paid employment at managerial or professional levels can be combined successfully with parenthood, however. In a survey sent to 1,500 executive women, 30% said having children enhanced their careers, the same percentage said their children's presence detracted from job advancement, and 40% thought kids had no effect. Respondents who believed becoming parents aided career progress attributed their ability to combine multiple roles to shared home responsibilities, availability of adequate and convenient child care, and family-provided emotional support (Stoner and Hartman, 1990).

No one has suggested that fatherhood and employment in a professional or administrative capacity are incompatible. In fact, the opposite is true. Not long ago, men were socialized to believe that by providing for their families economically, they were, by definition, "good fathers."

Until recently, however, career and motherhood were perceived as incompatible. Women could choose one or the other, but trying to do both supposedly would produce chaos. This view has changed. Seventy-one percent of managerial women responding to a 1983 survey agreed that it is possible to combine a demanding career with successful family life including husband and children (Baron, 1984). In a later study of career-committed women and their husbands, 87% were optimistic about blending careers and family life, though they admitted it was difficult (Baron, 1987).

Those concerned with balancing career and family are usually referring to the situation faced by a dual-career couple with children. Her career, his career, nurturant child care, and high-quality family life all are important.

ADVANTAGES OF A TWO-CAREER LIFESTYLE

What are the advantages associated with a two-career lifestyle? The following rewarding features will be discussed in turn.

1. Both parties can satisfy affiliation and achievement needs and experience greater self-fulfillment.
2. Greater financial resources.
3. Mutual empathy.
4. More equal power and influence within the relationship.
5. Multiple roles provide a buffer.
6. Neither partner is the sole breadwinner.

In the past, Western society generally permitted women to satisfy love and belongingness needs to a greater degree than men. Females met these needs by caring for their families. Unless they remained single or chose to flout societal norms, they had little outlet for achievement, except in domestic tasks. Males, on the other hand, were pushed to move to the highest possible position, regardless of their true wishes. Except with their wives or "significant others," they did not feel free to express emotions or show vulnerability.

If a dual-career lifestyle allows both sexes to meet achievement and affiliation needs, the partners will be more fulfilled. They will move toward self-actualization. As this occurs, couples may adopt a holistic approach to human existence. This approach respects the fundamental unity and wholeness of persons. It recognizes that each person has unique needs. Individuals cannot be fragmented and only permitted to be half of themselves. The either/or dichotomy that says good mothers cannot be good managers or that subtly suggests that involved fathers are not executive material must be rejected. In an ideal setting, this would be replaced by a systems view, which would recognize that each role a person assumes has an impact on every other role and on the individual's overall functioning. Thus, to maximize employee and manager well-being, work would not be all-encompassing. Time at work would be intense, and productivity would have to be maintained, but at all life stages, balance would be the goal. Interspersed with work would be time for leisure activities, dialogue with friends and family, and personal reflection.

Though dual-career couples are not motivated mainly by financial incentives, added income will provide for luxuries as well as enable them to buy services required to maintain their lifestyle. Financial independence for each party ensures that a loveless relationship will not continue solely because one partner is economically dependent.

Because both know what it is like to be employed at a professional level, they should be able to understand each other's work-related frustrations and triumphs better. Perhaps one partner is embroiled in a politicized situation, or maybe his or her firm is being restructured. A spouse who has encountered similar situations previously is likely to be more empathetic because he or she has "been there."

Though Hochschild and Machung (1989) contend that most employed women do a "second shift" of housework and child care, and that their husbands do substantially less than half of such work, change is occurring. Of necessity, some fathers are getting more involved in their children's daily lives. This could have a positive effect on the family. If Dad finds out what it's like to care for little Janie or Joey for more than a few hours, he may have more respect for the service mothers typically provided in past generations. In addition, he and his wife will be able to share the tribulations and joys of child rearing more fully.

Too often, the value of work done by full-time homemakers has been devalued. Despite significant contributions, the fact that their spouses (usually male) brought home the paycheck may have given the wage-earning partner more power in the relationship. Like it or not, a common parody of the Golden Rule, namely, "she or he who has the gold rules," might apply here. When women regularly contribute their earnings to replenish the "gold," spouses tend to give their opinions more weight.

Multiple roles can have a buffer effect. If things are not going well at work, dual careerists can take refuge in family roles. The converse is true to an extent, but workaholism is not recommended as an antidote to personal problems. It is better to confront difficulties than to escape from them through compulsive behavior.

Instead of sapping energy, Baruch and Barnett (1986) argue, multiple roles can energize. Their ideas may be consistent with social identity theory, which provides a basis for work and family life compatibility. According to social identity theory, people have many different roles. Once committed, they continue to invest in a role, even if net costs exceed net rewards. Role conflict occurs when values associated with identities are so different that they "can be enacted only in situations that are sharply separated by time and place" (Allen, Wilder, and Atkinson, 1983). For example, if "values, such as ambition and mastery, expressed in the manager role, differ from values, such as interdependence and nurturance, expressed in the parent role, then a person will need to relinquish the manager identity . . . to be a mother or father" (Lobel, 1991).

There are two ways to reconcile work and family roles without conflict. Either they must be separated, which is not always possible, or "consistent personal values" must be applied to both the parent and employee/manager role. The following example illustrates what this means, assuming work and family roles are equally important to the decision maker.

A person may be trying to meet an important work deadline when his or her child becomes sick. If in both domains helping others when necessary is given priority over enforcement of rules...then the individual will be able to attend to the sick child and expect that the work deadline could be changed. (Lobel, 1991)

Even if missing a deadline would lead to negative consequences, having consistent values would reduce stress associated with making such a decision. Thus, a person can "achieve balance without interrole conflict" by "expressing a consistent philosophy of life in the enactment of two different roles...not by a clear overinvestment in one role at the expense of the other...but by self-consistency" (Lobel, 1991).

Finally, in times of downsizing, it may be wise to have two employed professionals in a household. If one spouse is laid off, circumstances will not be as dire if the other still has a job that pays well. When the breadwinner responsibility is shared, it is less stressful than when one spouse must bear it alone.

POTENTIAL PROBLEMS ASSOCIATED WITH A TWO-CAREER LIFESTYLE

Having discussed advantages of a two-career lifestyle, it is appropriate to consider potential problems. These include:

1. Overload.
2. Identity dilemmas.
3. Potential for role conflict.
4. Daily transition problems.
5. Special situations.

Overload occurs when spouses have too much to do. Women in two-career marriages supposedly experience overload more often than men. Extreme time pressure characterizes this situation, as do physical and mental exhaustion. If warning signs are not heeded, spouses may develop negative feelings toward each other. A spouse who feels he or she is doing more than a fair share of "home work" and child care may grow resentful. Spouses may crave emotional support at the end of the day, but both are too tired to provide it. Sometimes dysfunctional competition can arise between spouses.

Partners in a dual-career relationship hardly have enough time for each other and children, if any. They need social support from friends and extended family, yet rarely are able to nurture such relationships. The difficulties couples have maintaining contacts outside the nuclear family are "social network dilemmas" (Rapoport and Rapoport, 1976).

Identity dilemmas occur when disparities exist between internalized, early socialization experiences and one's current desires. For example, women who internalized the idea that "good" mothers had to be physically present with preschool children most of the time would experience an identity dilemma if they decided to return to work six weeks after childbirth. Males who had internalized the idea that they must be breadwinners would encounter an identity dilemma if they wished to take a six-month parental leave after the birth or adoption of their child.

Though *role conflict* does not have to be part of the dual-career experience, it can be, particularly under a utilitarian approach to role investment. A win-lose mentality underlies that approach. Greater investment in one's work role is thought to necessitate less commitment to the family role, and vice versa. Utilitarianism reduces the decision to become more involved in work or family to a system of rewards and costs. This theory states:

When net family rewards (rewards minus costs) are lower in value than net career rewards, the individual will invest more heavily in career than family. When net family rewards are equal to net career rewards, the value of career rewards minus career costs (foregoing family rewards) approaches zero. (Lobel, 1991)

The latter situation provokes the most stress and role conflict.

Daily transitions occur when one leaves the family/personal domain and begins work, and when one ends work and re-enters the personal/family realm. Transitions can be anticipatory, discrete, or lagged, and gender differences in transition styles exist (Hall and Richter, 1988). Those with *anticipatory transition styles* are already thinking of work before they start it. They may physically be present with their spouse or family, but their minds are on the job. Those with *discrete styles* arrive physically and mentally at the same time. They do not start thinking about work until they begin it. At the end of the day, they do not think about family roles ahead of time, but when with family or friends, neither do they have a need to mull over the work day. Finally, it takes a while for the minds of those with *lagged styles* to catch up with their bodies. When they begin work, their thoughts may be on unresolved personal or family issues. After work, it may take time before they are ready to focus on relationship concerns again.

If spouses in a two-career marriage have different transition styles, it is easy to understand how conflicts arise. Gender distinctions in transition styles further complicate the issue (Hall and Richter, 1988). Though exceptions exist, men tend to delay the shift between work and home orientation. They take time to "unwind" by reading the newspaper, for example. Many women make a discrete transition between work and family roles. When putting on their "home selves" they immediately launch into family-related tasks. They become impatient with spouses who are still in transition.

The time during which women cross the work-to-home boundary is the most hectic part of the day. Some have referred to it as "arsenic hour." If there are children, they demand attention. Because of prior socialization, women may feel self-induced pressure to attend to household tasks.

In this situation, it might be preferable for women consciously to adopt a lagged transition style. A former student, now a colleague, described how she handled the transition between work and home 20 years ago when she was employed full-time, married, and assumed more than half the responsibility for the couple's four children. After picking up the children at the babysitter's, she asked them to play in the downstairs recreation room for a few minutes while she had a cup of coffee and collected her thoughts.

Another female partner in a two-career relationship would, after picking up her two preschoolers at the child care provider's, sit down, relax, and take the time to be physically and emotionally present with them before beginning household chores. This example illustrates a discrete transition style with respect to children and lagged only regarding housework. Nevertheless, for the woman in question, it reduced stress, allowed her to satisfy her children's needs, and eased the psychological move from work to home.

In both these examples, the reader might wonder why mom, not dad, picked up the kids at the end of the day. Perhaps that was most suitable for those particular couples. On the other hand, maybe these examples reflect reality in that most couples do not function within fully equalitarian relationships. Many are moving in that direction, however. For instance, Baron (1987) noted that 59% of the husbands of career-minded women surveyed said they took their children to appointments and child care providers.

Usually the end of the day transition is more problematic for couples than the morning move from home to work. Hall and Richter (1988) studied dual-career couples in which both spouses worked during daytime hours and were employed at workplaces away from home. If telecommuting is widely adopted, people may move, psychologically, from home to work domains, but they may stay in the same place.

In the morning, the main task is getting out the door. Many people perceive more options regarding activities they pursue after returning home. As one man whom Hall and Richter (1988) interviewed commented:

Morning is always so rushed. You have to get up and get to work...you don't have free time in the morning. When I come (home), I have much more choice of what to do. Whenever there is a choice there is always a conflict as to what choice should be made (children, wife, personal time). So I'd say the evenings are more difficult than the mornings. The mornings take care of themselves.

Special situations for two-career couples include relocation, birth or adoption of a child, ill children, extra work demands, "special needs" children, and blended families. All except the last two will be discussed in turn. Issues confronted by blended families or by those who have children with special needs are beyond the scope of this book. Managers should be sensitive to such families' concerns and should provide confidential referrals to professional counselors if necessary.

Futurist Marvin Cetron, as quoted in *Personnel Administrator* (Collie, 1989), said: "Perhaps the greatest disruption to a family's routine is transfer. All the family's support systems must be re-established at a new location and if a traveling spouse has difficulty finding a job, the transfer must be accomplished with less income." Besides monetary cost, dual-career couples must answer questions such as: Whose career will take precedence when? Will the partners take turns accepting moves requiring relocation? Will such decisions be made solely on economic grounds? If so, will the spouse with lower income grow resentful? How will this affect family life?

Because it is difficult to answer questions like these, professional and managerial partners in two-career relationships have become reluctant to accept transfers. Though individuals who turn down opportunities demanding relocation may not wish to discuss their reasons, 31% of companies surveyed thought a spouse's reluctance to leave a job was a prime factor (Collie, 1989).

In 1989, 75% of American firms provided some relocation assistance to spouses or partners of transferred employees. Usually this was done informally through referral. Some companies relaxed anti-nepotism rules so they could employ mates of transferees.

Within the United States, transferring a professional employee whose spouse wants to remain employed is challenging enough. It can become a headache when a partner in a dual-career relationship accepts an overseas assignment.

Sometimes it is impossible to find suitable employment for a spouse, in which case a few major multinational employers provide payments to partially offset lost income. If both partners are employed by multinationals, the firms might coordinate benefits or cooperate to find the trailing spouse a job. Another option, as in the case of domestic transfer, is to drop anti-nepotism rules and find work for the spouse in the same firm.

In 1986, multinational firms identified the management of dual-career couples on international assignments as one of the five most important international human resource challenges for the decade ahead. At the time, however, none of the companies had a well-organized program for dealing with dual-career couples sent abroad (Reynolds and Bennett, 1991).

Some companies provide counseling for two-career families in which the spouse of an employee transferred abroad has not found suitable employment. This is necessary because the divorce rate, even among American couples in a one-career family, is higher than average when the breadwinner accepts an overseas assignment. When both parties previously had high-powered careers, "the negative impact on the accompanying spouse's career continuity, self-esteem, and identity can be personally and professionally devastating" (Reynolds and Bennett, 1991).

One solution some two-career couples have adopted to deal with foreign or domestic transfers is a commuter marriage. For some, this means a weekly flight from the Midwest to one of the coasts, or from Moscow to London. For others, it may involve a few hours by car to meet a spouse on the weekends and for vacations. Long-term effects of commuter marriages on the individuals and the couple have yet to be assessed. The success of such relationships depends on the partners' personalities and commitment. Some believe commuter marriages keep romance alive and prevent spouses from taking each other for granted. Also they avoid situations where one partner always must make career sacrifices for the other.

On the negative side, commuter relationships are stressful, expensive, and carry a social stigma. Besides the hassle, long-distance telephone bills and the price of airline tickets can mount rapidly. In addition, there are two residences to maintain.

Commuter marriages may not be socially acceptable. Ms. Steen, a developer of historic sites in St. Paul, Minnesota, married to Mr. Ebel, a congressional aide in Washington, D.C., said friends avoided asking her to go out because they didn't know what to make of her. Was she married or single? During the commuter phase of the relationship, she claimed she felt like a widow (Dahl, 1985). Her husband eventually decided to find a job in St. Paul.

Commuter marriages seem to work best when only the lives of two adults must be meshed. Children make the situation even more complex.

The birth of a child is a special situation in the lives of a dual-career couple that warrants extra attention. Because of physical changes that occur in the woman's body (unless new "reproductive technologies" like surrogate motherhood are used) and the fact that she will be unable to work temporarily due to childbirth, she is affected more directly.

As recently as the early 1980s, pregnant executives reported chauvinistic attitudes among some colleagues who did not consider it appropriate for them to continue working in the third trimester. One pregnant manager, Amanda Brown-Olmstead, felt she lost ground professionally and described client's reactions as "Aha, I knew she was a woman" ("When the Mother-to-Be Is an Executive," 1983).

Finding appropriate business clothing during pregnancy was a problem women mentioned during the 1980s. Until mid-decade, it was difficult for those outside major metropolitan areas to find suits designed for expectant women.

Despite chauvinistic attitudes and other minor difficulties, executive women said pregnancy was among the least of their worries. Balancing career and parenthood after the child's birth was an issue of greater concern.

Taking a leave of absence creates some difficulties. Women feel a break in organizational attachment and are outside the corporate mainstream. When they return to the office, others assume new mothers will not be able to work as long as they did before parenthood. Highly successful executive females feel as if they again must prove themselves after a parental leave. Some resent this, feeling that they "paid their dues" earlier.

Career-oriented women develop elaborate procedures to prevent family life from intruding unduly into the workplace. Despite these steps, companies assume new mothers are unable to participate in meetings after hours and in extra work functions and therefore exclude them (Stoner and Hartman, 1990). As Hall (1990) pointed out, "Even when a woman makes all of the personal accommodations needed to continue to work at the same pace she did before she became a parent, she is often perceived and treated as a 'mommy tracker.' " The following remarks of a computer account executive are typical:

Once you have that baby, you're seen differently. I had everything set up to support high-powered work, a live-in sitter, a husband who saw my career as the primary one, a job I absolutely loved. Yet I noticed I wasn't being sent to training seminars anymore. I wasn't being given the "plum" assignments anymore. I wasn't put on projects that involved travel. After a while, I realized that I was on an involuntary mommy track! (Hall, 1990)

The problems new mothers experience relate to stereotypes supervisors and peers hold about the career commitment of women with children. The blank stares such supervisors probably would give if asked if they make similar assumptions about the work commitment of new fathers illustrates the depth of the problem. Gender stereotypes involving this issue are still pervasive, but are beginning to change as employers, out of necessity, seek ways to become more family-friendly.

When children are sick, a parent may have to miss work. Determining who will stay home can create controversy. As Friedman mentions in the reading for this chapter, some firms now allow employees to use sick leave when caring for ill children. Others have set up care centers for mildly ill children.

Sometimes spouses in two-career couples both get hit by extra work demands at the same time. Because a dual-career lifestyle contains enough stressors under the best circumstances, the wise couple should negotiate with employers to avoid this situation. If that fails, they need to maintain a long-term view and a sense of humor. Otherwise family life will suffer. For example, an untenured professor felt pressure to publish articles at the same time as her spouse, a medical technologist, was asked to work extra shifts at a hospital because of understaffing due to downsizing. The couple had a two-year-old child at the time. They pulled through the three-month stint of being overworked by setting priorities and by realizing that the situation was temporary.

Career and family issues are best discussed before individuals become committed to a relationship. Even that, however, is no guarantee that relationship/career dynamics will evolve as anticipated since people change. Flexibility is especially important for those planning to become part of dual-career marriages, with or without children.

Coping mechanisms for special situations two-career partners might face already have been discussed. Negative measures, such as blaming, scapegoating, emotionally withdrawing from a spouse, and relying too heavily on alcohol or drugs, have been detailed elsewhere and will only be mentioned in passing.

Two other less desirable options are to try to "do it all" by becoming "superman" or "superwoman," or to compartmentalize work and family roles. The first option should be rejected as a stop-gap measure that leads to burnout. Lobel (1991) would agree that separating work and family roles may reduce interrole conflict, but also would say that this is not always possible.

Hall and Richter (1988) think most people would prefer work and home life to be separate. In their words, "Work is literally moving into the home. Unless the employee can set clear boundaries, both physical and psychological, such arrangements can increase rather than decrease work and family stress."

To illustrate their point, think of a parent's predicament when trying to respond to an important work-related phone call in the evening. Noting that mom (or dad) is preoccupied with the telephone, preschoolers Janie and Joey take the opportunity to climb up on the cupboard (which mom or dad otherwise would not allow) to find a hidden treat. They argue about who gets two crackers and who gets three. One pushes the other, who falls off the cupboard and starts screaming. Meanwhile mom (or dad) is trying to have an intelligent telephone conversation with a client. Granted, the parent could go soothe the children and return the call later. If the client has children too, she or he might understand, but the situation has compromised the parent's professionalism. The permeable boundaries between home and work in this example "epitomize *role conflict*, as a person engaged in a specific role is called upon to operate in another role simultaneously" (Hall and Richter, 1988).

POSITIVE COPING STRATEGIES FOR TWO-CAREER COUPLES

Despite arguments of advocates, compartmentalization of work and home roles remains unpopular. Few try to separate the two, and attempts to do so relate negatively to job satisfaction (Gray, 1983). Positive general coping strategies for dual-career couples include setting priorities, reducing standards of perfectionism, delegating, planning leisure, joining or forming a support group, and enlisting the employer's support.

Prioritization involves determining that one role is more important than the other and making decisions affecting that basic choice. Since two-career partners are sometimes overachievers, they may need to be reminded that the world will not end if they miss one meeting or if all the beds in the house are unmade at 7:00 A.M.

Though perfectionism is not necessary, some chores must get done, and a certain level of cleanliness must be maintained. Recognizing this, two-career couples should delegate chores to family members or hire others to do them. If they dislike yard work or housecleaning, they should pay someone to do those tasks. With two professional level incomes, this should not overburden the family budget.

It is important to be able to look forward to relaxation times. Because of their greater financial resources, two-career couples may be able to afford vacations more often. Coordinating schedules so all family members can relax together may be difficult, however. More frequent extended weekends may be easier to schedule than one two-week vacation. Dual-career families who want to stay close should schedule family time regularly. If they mark family events on a calendar, they are less likely to be overlooked.

Support groups are very important for dual-career couples. Spouses need people who will listen to their joys and difficulties empathetically and nonjudgmentally. Ideally, extended families might serve this purpose. Otherwise, similarly situated couples or formal support groups might be helpful.

Finally, two-career couples should try to get employer support in scheduling accommodations and services to facilitate the career/parenthood combination. Human resource managers have called the 1990s the decade of family-related benefits, and many employers are receptive to parents' needs. Some researchers have called for more than receptivity; they demand a basic change in the "work-family prioritization paradigm."

According to Stoner and Hartman (1990),

We must accept the legitimacy of work-family coexistence and attempt to build a managerial paradigm that upholds and uplifts the value of family rather than relegating it to a second class status. It is ironic that corporations that work so hard to build an internal "family" culture will accept and actively utilize a managerial system that obscures the significance of their managers' biological families.

Equal valuation of work and family is a goal worth pursuing. Employers who accommodate workers' family needs by implementing policies such as parental leave, and by starting child care and elder care programs, are moving in that direction. In the following article, Friedman reviews programs companies have adopted to become more family-friendly.

"Work and Family: The New Strategic Plan"
by Dana E. Friedman

EXECUTIVE SUMMARY

A growing number of employers have begun responding to the family needs of their workers. Concerns about labor shortages, productivity and global competitiveness create the bottom-line reasons for a business response to families. About 5,400 employers have addressed employees' child care needs with on-site centers, referral programs and financial assistance. Several hundred employers provide elder care support, usually through counselling and referral services, and long term care insurance. Flexibility, through flextime, job sharing and work-at-home is also important to employees with family needs. These programs eventually led companies to create a "family friendly" culture through corporate communications, management training programs, designation of a "manager of work-family programs," and incorporation of family concerns into the strategic plan of organization.

The future is not what it was, a business executive recently declared. A shrinking labor pool, global competitiveness, and a new set of social concerns have caused many companies to reconsider and restructure the status quo. One of the most dramatic changes involves the new interface between the worlds of work and family life. Today's worker is faced with a constant struggle to remain productive at work while tending to hearth and home. Corporations have begun to realize that their ability to recruit and retain a productive workforce depends, in large part, on their attention to employees' family needs.

Serious corporate interest in work and family concerns began with a handful of companies sponsoring on-site child care centers in the late 1970's. Throughout the 1980's interest mushroomed into numerous kinds of child care support—referral, financial assistance, and sick child care, to the point where there are today over 5,000 employers providing some form of child care support. Towards the latter part of the decade, elder care emerged and several hundred corporations are today experimenting with various kinds of counselling programs and long-term care insurance.

As we head into the 1990's, companies have begun to accept the real challenge posed by the work-family nexus which is to respond to employees' needs for greater flexibility. This has led to a resurgence of alternative work schedules, from flextime to job sharing, work-at-home options, and parental leave. It has also created a move from management by objectives to management by subjectives as supervisors assume more discretion while implementing flexible work policies. The work-family innovations of the 1990's will be in the areas of management training and strategic planning that incorporate sensitivity to employee's work and family conflicts and avoid career penalties for those taking advantage of family-friendly policies.

This article will review the basic dimensions of the corporate response to the family needs of workers, including child care, elder care and alternative work schedules. It will conclude with the facets of the corporate culture that inhibit or foster a more flexible and family-friendly workplace.

THE CORPORATE RESPONSE TO CHILD CARE

The first on-site child care center was developed by a manufacturer of soldiers' clothing during the Civil War. Women were needed in the war effort and someone

Table 12.1
Growth of Employer Supported Child Care

Year	Number of Companies
1982	600
1984	1,500
1986	2,500
1988	3,300
1990	5,400

had to provide for their children while they worked. This obvious need during national emergencies presented itself to employers again during World War I and with government assistance, during World War II. Nearly 3,000 child care centers were established at or near war plants during World War II under the Lanham Act. Some of the child care innovations begun in the war are the cornerstones of child care programs today. Unfortunately, the clean laundry and hot meals that the centers used to send home with the children have been forgotten (Krug, Palmour and Ballassai, 1972).

Industry's interest in child care remained dormant during the Ozzie and Harriet days of the 1950's, despite the fact that many women remained in the labor force. During the 1960's corporate interest reappeared, but under the guise of corporate social responsibility. Stride Rite Corporation in Roxbury, Massachusetts opened a center to ease some of the racial tensions in the community. Others found the child care center an ideal way to improve community relations and distribute foundation funds (Friedman, 1983).

During the 1970's there was scattered corporate experimentation with child care, but serious activity did not occur until the 1980's. Much of the growth in employer-supported child care during the early 1980's can be attributed to the Reagan administration. The former President made it both necessary and fashionable for the business community to play a larger role in the child care delivery system. By cutting back on social services, the nonprofit community was forced to look to other funding sources. At the same time, public-private partnerships encouraged by a Republican White House sanctioned business investments in social programs. Between 1983 and 1985, the White House sponsored 33 breakfasts for corporate CEO's to educate them about child care. During that period, the number of employers providing child care support tripled (Friedman, 1986).

These and other education efforts, as well as an improvement in the economy led to significant growth in employer-supported child care during the 1980's as Table 12.1 indicates. The rise from 600 employers in 1982 to an estimated 5,400 today is dramatic in absolute terms, but it represents only 12% of the 44,000 employers with more than 100 employees.

In addition to an increase in the number of employers supporting child care, there was also an increase in the variety of their responses. While the on-site child care center worked for some, it was found inappropriate for many and other options were explored.

Individual company responses often reflect the inadequacies of the child care market. Some employers find it necessary to help increase the supply of care with the creation of new services; others provide greater access to existing programs

Table 12.2
Estimated Prevalence of Various Child Care Options Provided by Employers

Option	Estimated Number
On- or near-site centers	1,200
by Hospitals	800
by Corporations	200
by Government	200
Family day care, school-age care and sick child care	100
Resource and referral services	1,500
Discounts, vouchers	100
Dependent care assistance plans in flexible benefits	2,500
	5,400

Source: Friedman, 1990b

through resource and referral services; and many choose to address the affordability of care by providing various types of financial assistance. Through all of these strategies, companies try to improve the quality of services.

CREATING NEW SERVICES

Provision of on- or near-site child care continues to grow. As seen in Table 12.2, of the 5,400 employers providing some form of child care support, 1,200 do so by sponsoring a child care center. Most of these (800) are sponsored by hospitals, and only 200 are sponsored by corporations and another 200 are sponsored by government agencies. The growth in the provision of the on-site center is due largely to developers who create child care centers in office parks as an amenity to attract companies, and to government agencies that often create multiple centers. For instance, the State of New York has 36 centers for state employees. Others are working together in a consortium arrangement, sharing the costs, risks and benefits of having a quality center conveniently located to employees.

The on-site center is not feasible for the majority of employers. Many firms are too small and don't have the resources or the labor pool to fill it (Berkeley Planning Associates, 1988).

The commuting patterns of employees and the costs of downtown space make it difficult for companies in large urban areas to create centers that employees want to use or can afford. Other worksites, such as chemical plants, may be inappropriate for children.

Some firms have tried to increase the supply of care by focusing on family day care, a neighborhood arrangement in the private home of the provider. Younger children (under age 3) are most often cared for in family day care homes (Hofferth, 1989). American Express, for instance, provides funds to family day care associations and to resource and referral agencies to recruit, train and help get licensed new family day care homes. Mervyns and Target Stores, subsidiaries of Dayton Hudson, have embarked on a three-year effort to increase the supply and quality of family day care in 30 communities where they have stores.

School-age care is another concern of parents and therefore of growing concern to companies. Millions of children return to empty homes at the end of the day and many parents do not have access to telephones to make sure they are home safely (Coolsen, Seligson, and Garbarino, 1986). Some companies have helped create a phone-in service that children can call when they arrive home or when they need assistance or someone to talk to. Other companies offer after-school services as part of their on-site child care centers or help create such services in schools, YWCA's and other community agencies.

Recently, companies have become concerned with the absences created by parents staying home with sick children. Some firms have created sick child care centers or emergency family day care homes that care for mildly ill or recuperating children. Others, such as a consortium of seven companies in New York City, have developed an in-home service that sends trained providers into the child's home in an emergency. Still new, the success of these initiatives has been varied. Parents may be unwilling to bring their children to a strange location when they are sick.

Others may be reluctant to have a stranger come into the home. Realizing that some parents want to and should be with their sick children, companies are revising their sick leave policies to permit employees to stay home with them. One advantage of this policy is that workers stop lying about the reasons for their absence, admitting that it is their children and not they who are ill (Friedman, 1990a). A recent Conference Board survey of 521 large companies found that two-thirds of large companies offered sick leave for family members, although 59% of the sick leave was unpaid (Christensen, 1989).

PROVIDING INFORMATION

About 300 resource and referral agencies around the country help parents shorten their search time and make them wiser consumers of the care they purchase. About 1,500 companies contract with these agencies to provide counselling and referrals to the employees (Friedman and Kolben, 1990).

IBM created the first nationwide network of referral services which at least 35 other national corporations now use. Most employers who provide such services also contribute funds to the resource and referral agencies for the development of new services. Within five years of the efforts of IBM and the other companies contributing to a nationwide referral service, over 50,000 new child care programs were created, most of which are family day care homes (Friedman and Kolben, 1990).

Companies also provide information to employees through parenting seminars, caregiver fairs, employee support groups, handbooks, videos, parent resource libraries and company newsletters. Some firms have expanded their employee assistance programs to include a wide range of family issues.

HELPING PARENTS PAY

The real cost of providing quality child care in the U.S. is between $6,000 and $8,000. Parents pay somewhere between $2,000 and $3,000 of these costs per year with low staff wages accounting for the difference (Child Care Employee Project, 1989). The cost depends on the form of care used, the age of the child and the location of the program. In the Northeast, it is not uncommon to find centers where the parent fees are $6,000 per year, and infant care as high as $10,000.

To help employees absorb this cost, some employers contract with individual providers for an employee discount. Other companies subsidize child care costs as a program of the employee's choosing. Retail chains and firms in other service industries have begun to revive interest in the direct subsidy because of their difficulty in recruiting female labor. At lower ends of the pay scale, these women are less likely to benefit from a flexible benefits plan (Friedman, 1985).

The most popular child care option for companies is the Dependent Care Assistance Plan (DCAP) that is authorized under Section 129 of the Internal Revenue Code. This provision enables employees to use before-tax dollars to purchase dependent care services.

DCAPs are the most popular form of child care support from the business community because the company only assumes administrative costs (Friedman, 1985).

In the beginning stage of employer-supported child care, companies offered one option. Then they began to realize that employees had a diversity of child care needs and that one program would not satisfy many needs. Further, the shortcomings in the child care market made some options less useful without additional support. For instance, referral programs are less effective when there is a shortage of child care programs in the community. Today, most employers package a set of child care responses to meet a variety of needs among their employees.

CORPORATE RESPONSES TO ELDER CARE

Several hundred employers have begun to respond to employees who provide care to an aging relative. Elder care support is likely to flourish in the coming years as all sectors of society grapple with a rapidly aging society. In 1986, 30 million Americans were over age 65, accounting for 12% of the population. By the year 2030, the number will double and senior citizens will comprise 20% of the population (Stone, Cafferata and Sangl, 1986). The baby boomers will become responsible for their aging parents just as they are ready to assume leadership positions in business and government. The need for attention to this problem will be pushed by the people in power—a new dimension to advocacy that child care has not experienced.

Contrary to popular belief, most elderly people do not live in institutions. About 75% of the aged live with their children or nearby (Administration on Aging, 1987). Caring for elderly parents is not new; combining it with a career is. Roughly 20% of any workforce might have some caregiving responsibilities for an aging relative (Friedman, 1990a). A survey at The Travelers Companies found caregivers providing roughly 10 hours of care per week. About 10% provided 35 hours of care each week. A substantial portion—between one-third and one-half of caregivers—are responsible for an elderly relative living more than 50 miles away (The Travelers Companies, 1985).

Elder care needs may be more complex than child care. Caregivers may need to provide transportation, housekeeping services, bathing, personal services, shopping, cooking, and paperwork. They are forced to use company time for researching and conferring with doctors, finding home health care, visiting nursing homes, and applying for Medicare. In a survey conducted by the New York Business Group on Health, two-thirds of companies reported excessive telephone use by caregivers and half felt that these employees were less productive (Warshaw, 1986).

After 20 years since the passage of the Older Americans Act, there is a network of services upon which companies can build, unlike the child care system. Most of the companies responding to elder care provide information to their employees about available services, the aging process or company policy. Some information efforts are intended to reduce stress by making employees more knowledgeable about the services they might purchase. Some companies, such as Hallmark and Marriott Corporation, contract with a community-based organization or geriatric care manager to counsel employees about the helpful services. Several agencies now offer referral services to multi-site companies by contracting with referral specialists across the country. IBM, Arthur Andersen, American Express and Johnson & Johnson have this type of nationwide service. Cross-country referrals can also be helpful to single-site firms whose employees provide elder care support to relatives in other cities.

Other informational aids are provided by companies in an effort to help their employees with their caregiving needs. An expanded employee assistance program can help, as can seminars, support groups and caregiver fairs.

Although companies are concerned about increasing benefit costs, several employers have tried to help employees offset the costs of elder care. Dependent care accounts can be used for elderly relatives as well as children, although the regulations require that the aging relative live in the employee's home and that the employee provide more than 50% of the elder's financial support. These stipulations significantly limit the use of this pre-tax savings program for elder care (Friedman, 1986).

A company can subsidize directly a portion of the elder care costs. Vouchers can be applied to adult day care centers or in-home health services. The costs of long-term care may be exorbitant and a growing number of companies such as John Hancock, Procter and Gamble, and American Express offer long-term care insurance that covers the employee and their parents in time of need. Employees are usually expected to pay the full premium for these policies, but they are less expensive than what employees could purchase on their own in the market (Levin, 1988).

One of the most innovative responses to elder care was introduced by the Stride Rite Corporation which opened an on-site intergenerational day care center for the children and parents of employees. Due to the demographic realities of caregiving, replication of this initiative will be limited, although greater contributions to the community to create intergenerational services are likely.

CORPORATE RESPONSES TO FLEXIBILITY

Of all the benefit options or policy changes a company might contemplate, employees seem overwhelmingly to prefer ways to make their work schedules more flexible. They desire genuinely flexible flextime, that is, a program that allows large windows of start and stop times. They also want sick leave for family members, half-day vacations, work at home, part-time work with pro-rated benefits, and job sharing. While the child care and elder care programs can reduce much of the worry about dependents while people work, the greatest stress may be caused by the rigidity of the work day and one's inability to handle emergencies or to schedule needed appointments.

FLEXTIME

In 1985, 12.3% of the workforce, or 9.1 million full-time wage and salary workers, were on flextime. Based on a 1988 Conference Board survey, 50% of the 521 large companies responding offered flextime. About half plan to increase flextime availability in the near future (Christensen, 1989). In earlier years, flextime was not implemented to accommodate family needs. It was more likely to be a response to concerns about tardiness, commuting problems or morale. A growing body of literature suggests that flextime also can address employees' family needs (Pierce, Newstrom and Dunham, 1989).

While flextime will not reduce the total number of hours worked, it makes possible more conveniently arranged hours that may permit more time spent on activities outside work (Winnett, 1985). In a 1981 study by the Office of Personnel Management where 325,000 employees were studied, flextime users spent more time with their families, more time on household chores, and more time in children's school activities. The freedom to set their own work schedules enabled employees to spend less money for babysitting services. In a study at two federal agencies where flextime users were compared to a control group, it was found that flextime users generally came to work earlier and gained increased family time in the evening. The data strongly suggest that alternative work schedules may enhance the quality of family relationships (Bohen and Viveros-Long, 1981).

The ability for flextime to reduce work-family conflicts also leads to fewer negative work behaviors. One study, however, found that this may be less true for mothers. The authors conclude that, "The magnitude of the logistical energy and time demands on families with two employed parents or a single parent, cannot be dramatically altered by minor changes in daily work schedules" (Bohen et al., 1981). The flextime schedule under evaluation at this federal agency allowed variations of only one-half hour at either end of the day. A restricted program of fixed flextime would have little effect on work-family stress. Research has also shown that the effects of flextime may not be seen for several years (Pierce et al., 1989).

PART-TIME WORK

Employers might offer part-time work as a way to keep valued employees who prefer a reduced work schedule. They might also develop a part-time workforce in order to reduce labor costs. Part-time workers rarely receive company benefits, such as health insurance, maternity leave or pension coverage (Christensen, 1989). Some companies that rely on part-time workers are having difficulty recruiting them and are beginning to pro-rate benefits.

For instance, Shawmut Bank in Boston developed "mothers' hours" that enabled tellers to work from 9:00 A.M. to 3:00 P.M. with summer months off (Bureau of National Affairs, 1986). A survey by Catalyst (1983) indicated that women prefer part-time work as a transition following maternity leave and a growing number of companies now permit reduced hours for a period of time after leave.

New Ways to Work, a national organization advocating alternative work schedules, has found job sharing to be a viable option for people with family needs. While many companies have one or two job sharing teams, very few encourage employees to pursue this option. It has been found to be enormously beneficial to employees whose work styles are compatible. Companies also report that they get far more than one full-time job accomplished with this arrangement (Olmsted and Smith, 1983).

WORK AT HOME

Although frequently called telecommuting, the option of working at home need not involve a computer. A growing number of jobs can be accomplished outside

the office, but they require management that does not equate presence with performance. There must be trust between the employee and the supervisor that the
work can get done without supervision. According to telecommuting specialist Gil
Gordon, between 200 and 300 companies have eight to ten workers on some type
of home-based work arrangement (Christensen, 1985).

Parents who work at home admit that this option does not preclude the need for
child care assistance. It is difficult to be productive with a two-year-old tugging at
one's sleeve. This arrangement, however, does provide employees with the most
flexibility in the design of the work day. Work can go on in the evenings after the
children are in bed.

THE NEED TO CHANGE THE CULTURE

Companies are beginning to recognize that several child care or elder care programs are not going to have their desired effects if they are implemented in a culture
hostile to families. Utilization will be low if employees believe that their careers
will be negatively affected if they take advantage of available programs. Flexibility
is, therefore, impossible to implement if managers do not understand why and how
they can be supportive of families and still meet production quotas. The most progressive firms in the country have recognized this problem and are beginning to
make conscious efforts to change the culture and create a more family-friendly
environment.

Companies may do this with symbolic changes such as altering the company
credo as Johnson & Johnson did. Their new language says, "We must be mindful
of ways to help employees with their family responsibilities." Others have made
sure that everyone knows that there is commitment from the top. The CEO might
issue a letter or create a videotape made to express reasons for wanting a more
family-supportive work environment. The seriousness of the work-family commitment might be embodied in a handbook that lists all of the ways that a company
recognizes and supports the family needs of employees. The handbook might include
things that have been around for a long time, such as the company picnic or benefits
for dependents.

Another way to express company commitment is to have a visible individual
responsible for the range of work-family initiatives. The newest title in human resources is "manager of dependent care" or "manager of work-family programs." At
Herman Miller, there is a Vice President for People. At the DuPont Companies there
is a Director of Workforce Partnering. In addition to coordinating the work-family
initiatives, this person assures that all programs will be coordinated, communicated,
and adequately funded.

The greatest change in the culture might be achieved through management training. If flexibility is the goal, the natural by-product of that pursuit is discretion.
Managers are no longer given one set policy to be applied evenly to all employees.
Now there are choices depending on the work and family circumstances of the
employee. If managers are unclear about how to implement flexibility, they will
not, and the efforts of management to create a more family-supportive workplace
will not occur.

Some of the management beliefs that must be dealt with in management training
and that may create the greatest obstacles to becoming more family supportive are
listed below.

- Keep your personal problems at home. Obviously, when there is no one at home, it becomes increasingly difficult and unrealistic to adhere to this concept.

- Given them an inch and they will take a mile. This is based on the assumption that employees will abuse whatever privileges they are given. The idea that by giving them more time off they can be even more productive is counterintuitive to most managers.

- Equity means the same. Many managers believe that what you do for one you must do for everyone. They are not used to dealing with the kind of diversity that currently exists. They may also be afraid that if they do not provide exactly the same response to all employees, they will invite a law suit.

- Benefit programs are provided for long-term income security and protection. Companies are used to responding to catastrophes. Yet, work-family problems call upon programs to respond not to the tragedies of life, but rather, to the drudgeries of life. It's the day-to-day hassles that must be addressed and this is new to managers.

- Benefit programs can only satisfy workers and make them happy; they cannot make people more productive. According to Frederick Herzberg's (1966) theories of motivation, benefits are extrinsic to work and cannot motivate people to perform better. However, his research was conducted on male workers in the 1950's. It is likely that different things motivate the workers of today.

- Presence equals performance. The only way a manager can feel comfortable knowing that workers are doing their job is if they are sitting at their desks. This strongly held conviction is what prevents managers from granting time off or work-at-home options. Again, it seems counterintuitive that employees could actually produce more if given more time away from the office.

- Hours equal output. Many managers measure, through time sheets and other quantifiable indicators, the number of hours that an employee works. The employee's performance rating is based on the number of hours of worked. Product quality, efficiency, and level of effort are omitted from the equation.

As companies struggle to understand the new values of today's workers, they will eventually come to terms with the need to treat people differently than they have in the past. Some of this will be forced by the "sellers' market" created by the labor shortage. Employees will be able to request and receive some of the accommodations they desire (Freedman, 1989).

What began as a move to create a little child care center has burgeoned into a major overhaul of the work environment, a redefinition of work and a new partnership between employees and managers. Work and family issues are not some passing fad. They are a symbol of the more significant way in which the business objectives of organizations must be redefined to include non-work factors. As a result they provide strong evidence of the need for a company's strategic plan to embrace not just employees, but their family members as well.

DISCUSSION QUESTIONS

1. What does Friedman mean by the phrase "management by subjectives"?
2. If you would like to have children (or already have them), what child care arrangements do you think you would prefer? Why?
3. What are the pros and cons of an intergenerational day care center for children and parents of employees?
4. Comment on the phrase "mothers' hours" that Shawmut Bank in Boston used to describe hours from 9:00 A.M. to 3:00 P.M. during the school year with summers off. What does the phrase tell you about societal beliefs?
5. Does equity mean treating all employees exactly the same? Explain.

Friedman describes many corporate initiatives designed to facilitate work-family balance. She does not mention family leaves, however. In 1993, President Clinton signed the Family and Medical Leave Act. This law allows employees to be absent from work without pay for up to 12 weeks following the birth or adoption of a child. Leave also may be taken to cope with employees' own serious illness or that of a parent, spouse, or child. Employees are entitled to either their old positions or comparable posts when they return to work. Their health insurance must be continued for the duration of the leave.

The Family and Medical Leave Act covers firms with 50 or more employees, which means that 95% of all U.S. companies, or 25 million employees, are not protected (O'Brien, Gupta, and Marsh, 1993). Even among businesses employing 50 or more people, other exemptions apply. For example, employers are not required to grant leave to those who have been employed less than one year or to those who have worked less than 25 hours per week during the previous 12 months. The highest paid 10% of a firm's labor force, called "key" employees, also are exempt.

Employees who wish to exercise their rights under the Family and Medical Leave Act have some responsibilities. They must give their employees 30 days notice of absences that can be anticipated. They also must furnish a physician's statement to verify their own or a family member's serious illness.

The 1993 family leave law does not supersede similar legislation previously passed in 32 states (O'Brien, Gupta, and Marsh, 1993). Firms must comply with the statute that offers greater protection to employees.

MYTHS RELATED TO CHILD CARE

Besides discussing measures to make companies sensitive to family concerns, Friedman lists management beliefs that are obstacles to such heightened awareness. In addition to these general attitudes, myths specifically related to child care exist. Two are that relatives and friends can provide child care, and that daycare is a women's issue. First, many families with young children live great distances from relatives. Living closer, besides being impractical, would not solve the problem because grandparents, aunts, and uncles may be in the labor force too. The same is true of friends and neighbors.

Second, child care is an employee concern, not a women's issue. Hall (1990) cites several studies to show that, though women spend more time caring for children than men, fathers are becoming more involved. For example, 37% of mothers and 36% of fathers surveyed reported "a lot of stress" trying to mesh work and family roles. Eleven percent of the women and none of the men encountered "extreme stress," however. A 1988 DuPont study showed similar numbers of men and women concerned about work/family balance. Seventy percent of fathers under age 35 employed by a large Minneapolis firm said they experienced severe work/family conflicts. Sixty percent said such issues affected their career goals, causing them to turn down promotions to be able to spend more time with their families.

In the reading, Friedman (1990) claimed that an on-site child care center was not feasible for many employers. However, the advantages to the firm of having such a center should not be underestimated. On-site child care centers help companies recruit and retain workers and generate positive publicity. They could be expected to improve morale and reduce turnover and absenteeism. Direct, positive effects on productivity are more difficult to document, but some have argued that such gains might occur too.

On-site centers benefit employees who need child care in several ways. They give workers peace of mind, reduce stress related to juggling work and family roles, and can cut commuting time.

Hall and Richter (1988) identified the only drawback to on-site care from the employee's viewpoint. Though they supported other child care arrangements, Hall and Richter warned employers that

too permeable a boundary between work setting and a child care facility leads employees to feel guilty if they are not there at lunch time and to feel not totally separate from their children during work hours. They could possibly feel too accessible, which could interfere with work concentration.

Potential drawbacks of corporate-sponsored on-site child care centers to employer and employees also must be considered. Initial costs of establishing and staffing centers, and licensing and liability issues, are disadvantages employers frequently mention. Employers can get liability insurance, which is an added, but necessary, cost. Certain staff-to-child ratios, equipment adequacy, and facility safety standards must be met for licensing purposes. Though employers might dispute the need for some regulations, they would want to maintain safe facilities with reputations as wholesome, stimulating places for children. They would do this for ethical reasons as well as to reap previously mentioned benefits like positive public relations and a recruiting edge.

Costs of child care centers do not have to be overwhelming, particularly if existing space can be used and if the center is designed to be self-supporting eventually. A California bank was able to recoup its initial investment in a child care center in five years (Ritter, 1990), and other firms should be able to do likewise.

SUMMARY

To retain a qualified workforce in the 1990s, businesses must become sensitive to employees' needs to balance work and their family or personal lives. Balance is important to all workers, but particularly so to the growing number of two-career couples. Both partners in such couples are strongly committed to each other and to a profession.

Advantages of a dual-career lifestyle include a holistic approach in which both partners achieve affiliation and achievement needs, mutual empathy, and financial independence. Overload, stress, lack of time, identity dilemmas, role conflict, and daily transition problems are some challenges. To cope with these, couples can prioritize tasks, delegate less desirable duties, reduce perfectionist standards, interact with a support group, and set aside relaxation time.

Employers have begun to make organizations more family-friendly. They should ensure that the corporate culture supports families so specific programs do not operate within a hostile climate. Specific family-friendly programs include resource and referral systems for child and elder care, on-site dependent care, after-school programs, and care for sick children. Flexible work arrangements also help employees manage family responsibilities.

DISCUSSION QUESTIONS

1. Do you think work life and family/personal life should be integrated or separated? Explain.
2. Would you ever want to be part of (or if you already have been, would you want to again be part of) a dual-career relationship? Explain, citing advantages and disadvantages of that lifestyle.
3. Interview a dual-career couple. Ask them to explain three ways they cope with challenges inherent in their lifestyle. Report findings in class.

13   Stress Management

OBJECTIVES

After studying this chapter you should be able to:

1. Define stress in two different ways.
2. List three categories of stressors.
3. Explain what is meant by a "Type A" personality.
4. Explain tactics to develop resilience.
5. Explain the circumstances in which the paid employee role can yield health benefits for women.

STRESS: DEFINITIONS, SYMPTOMS, AND EFFECTS

Stress is a physiological state of the individual that, in itself, is neither good nor bad. Barnett and Baruch (1986) define it as a lack of fit between resources, meaning personal coping mechanisms, and expectations of self and others.

Distress refers to the negative effects of stress, which include everything from headaches, insomnia, and irritability to high blood pressure and increased heart attack risk. Other physical stress symptoms are shortness of breath, ulcers, colitis, skin conditions like hives, and backaches.

A short attention span, overconcern about money, increasing negativism, an inability to cope with routine problems, and loss of a sense of humor are mental stress indicators (Duke and Sitterly, 1988). Concentration may be impossible for those with shortened attention spans. Formerly interesting tasks are considered boring.

Unless one is independently wealthy, some money concerns are inevitable. Extreme worry may either signal underlying problems or reflect concerns over job security or financial obligations.

Cynicism and negativism may be signs of stress. When previously confident people doubt themselves or begin to view change as a threat instead of a challenge, it should cause concern.

For individuals under stress, routine tasks seem overwhelming. People may request help on activities they used to do alone.

Loss of a sense of humor can be devastating. It indicates stress exists and reduces one's ability to cope. Peers' comments that would have been dismissed with laughter under normal circumstances may be taken too seriously.

Women and men seem to exhibit different stress symptoms. Women show signs of low emotional well-being and are treated for mental illness more often than men. They have higher reported depression rates than male counterparts and are more likely to have headaches and upset stomachs. Men, on the other hand, have higher rates of heart disease and cirrhosis of the liver. They are more likely than women to commit suicide (Jick and Mitz, 1985).

Some worry that as more women reach top executive positions formerly held by men, they will suffer from stress-related symptoms to the same degree. For example, by the early 1990s, lung cancer, formerly afflicting more men than women, became more prevalent among females than breast cancer. A National Heart, Lung, and Blood Institute study showed a rising coronary disease rate among married working women. Among employed women, the incidence of heart ailments rose with the number of children they had. Mental health does not seem affected by women's employment, however. Professional women seem to have higher self-esteem and better mental health than homemakers.

Contrary to popular belief, stress is not always bad. Its positive effects are called *eustress*. Sometimes stress can stimulate better performance, as depicted in Figure 13.1. Performance is low at both extremely low and at very high stress levels. Performance peaks with a moderate amount of stress. This general model does not consider individual differences in stress tolerance, however, which may limit its value.

The graph on the left in Figure 13.1 shows how stress levels and task complexity are related. For most people, stress is lowest when tasks are moderately complex. If they are too easy, most people experience boredom, which produces stress. On the other hand, extremely complicated tasks may cause frustration.

Events creating stress are called *stressors*. People differ in perceptions of whether or not events are stressors and in their tolerance to them. Even one person's tolerance varies over time.

Stressors can be categorized as organizational and extraorganizational

Figure 13.1
Stress, Performance, and Task Complexity

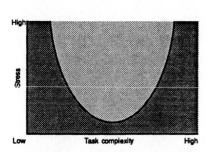
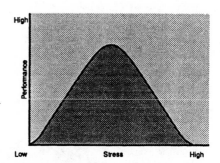

Source: Figures 7 and 8 in R. Dunham, Stress. In L.. Cummings, and R. Dunham, (eds.), Introduction to organizational behavior: Text and readings (pp. 593-594) Homewood, IL: Richard D. Irwin, 1980.

(Nelson and Quick, 1985). A third category, gender-based stressors, will be introduced here. Gender-based stressors can be either internal or external to the organization. Those that are internal (organizational) include discrimination, stereotyping, and possibly tokenism. These were discussed earlier. To the extent that women and men have different occupations, they are subject to varying stressors. Women are overrepresented in jobs characterized by high demands and low control (Jick and Mitz, 1985). Such features create built-in strain.

Outside the organization, Nelson and Quick (1985) contend that career/ family conflicts can be stressors. Those responsible for both children and a career can experience biculturalism similar to that which people of color encounter in white society. Single parents or dual-career couples with children may feel a part of both home and work worlds. Functioning in both realms may add strain.

However, Braicker (1988), reporting on results of a national survey of employed women ages 18 to 54, says that "an involving and satisfying career actually may contribute to a woman's appreciation and enjoyment of her family." Barnett and Baruch (1987) expand on this theme. They claim that human energy is unlimited and that, rather than causing distress, multiple roles energize people. For women, the wife and mother role has been assumed primary, and the employee role has been considered secondary. The employee role was blamed for women's distress. In reality, the mother/ wife role, with its high demands and low control, can cause strain. If the employee role includes stimulating work on a variety of tasks, a chance to learn, a sense of accomplishment, and a good fit between the employee's interests and skills and job requirements, it yields health benefits for women (Barnett, 1987).

For men, the employee role has been presumed primary, and the husband/

father role was either ignored or assumed secondary. Until recently, men regarded paid employment as the means through which they fulfilled their family role as breadwinner. Thus, they experienced no conflict between primary and secondary roles.

In fact, family roles are important to men's well-being. The husband role has been linked with longevity in males, and marriage seems to have more health benefits for men than for women (Barnett and Baruch, 1987).

For both sexes, multiple roles seem to have a buffer effect. People can emphasize family roles when work roles become difficult, and vice versa, at least to an extent.

Organizational stressors are job, role, interpersonal, and environmental. Job stressors include work overload or work that is either too challenging or not demanding enough. Managerial work is stressful because of overload and too much challenge (Colligan, Smith, and Hurrell, 1977). Particularly stressful features of executive jobs include low decision-making latitude and having to appraise employees' performance.

Role demands include role conflict, which has been discussed earlier, and *ambiguity*, which means uncertainty about tasks to be done or the best methods to accomplish them. New managers experience much ambiguity.

Interpersonal stressors are challenges related to getting along with supervisors, peers, and subordinates. Subordinates who distrust supervisors' motives may become dissatisfied with their jobs and may experience role ambiguity (French and Caplan, 1970). In addition, the following supervisory behaviors, which McGuigan (1986) identifies, can induce tension among subordinates and should be avoided.

1. Calling frequent, lengthy meetings and then criticizing employees for not spending enough time getting work out.
2. Setting unachievable goals in the mistaken belief that it will make employees try harder.
3. Putting employees on the spot, especially in front of others, rather than giving them time to research answers to questions.
4. Repeatedly taking employees off one project to work on others, requiring them to juggle many projects at the same time.
5. Reminding employees of past mistakes when correcting them for current errors.

Drawing on French and Caplan's (1972) work, Whetton and Cameron (1991) report that "the highest levels of encounter stress exist among managers who interact frequently with other people and who have responsibility for individuals in the workplace." Other researchers have associated heart disease with responsibility for subordinates at work (Wardwell, Hyman, and Bahusen, 1964).

Peer relationships are not stress-free for managers. Colleagues may exert group pressure. They may punish a nonconforming individual, thereby creating tension in that person (Nelson and Quick, 1985).

In all relationships, the possibility of conflict exists. Functional conflict, in which people work through differences, ultimately is productive. There are many causes of dysfunctional conflict, which produces stress and is, by definition, counterproductive.

Environmental stressors refer to things like noise, poor ventilation, and uncomfortable temperatures at the workplace. Other stressors in this category are long working hours, office politics, and a poor organizational climate (Kornhauser, 1965; Cooper and Marshall, 1978).

Stressors thus far described relate to an organization. Events in one's personal life also can create stress. Holmes and Rahe (1967) developed the Social Readjustment Rating Scale (SRRS) to help people evaluate the amount of stress in their lives in a given year. The SRRS includes a few organizational stressors, but most are personal. Examples of scale items are death of spouse, the addition of a new family member, and an outstanding personal achievement. Each event is weighted. For instance, a spouse's death counts 100, and a minor violation of the law, such as getting a speeding ticket, counts 11.

As reported by Craeger (1991), a researcher named Witkin revised the social readjustment rating, taking into account stressors that supposedly affect women differently than men, and adding items not found in the original scale. Major holidays seem more stressful for women who assume responsibility for entertaining, meal preparation, and the purchase of gifts in addition to their jobs in the workforce. If these duties were shared with spouses or significant others, presumably they would be less burdensome. New sources of stress that were not listed in the 1967 scale include being a single parent, raising teens, becoming a crime victim, and developing a chemical dependency.

The total SRRS score is linked with the probability of becoming seriously ill or being injured in the next two years, assuming people do not change their response to stress. The higher the score, the greater the chance. For example, those scoring 300 or above have an 80% chance of getting ill in the near future.

High SRRS scores do not always lead to injury or illness. Effective techniques to cope with, if not eliminate, stress can moderate general tendencies. Some object to the notion that major life events are the most important stressors. They argue that minor annoyances like traffic jams or constant disagreements with peers or relatives can be more taxing over time. They contend, further, that some people cope well with life's major problems and are more vexed by less weighty but more frequent irritants (Schaefer, Coyne, and Lazarus, 1981).

How does the body react to stress initially? It releases hormones, including adrenaline, that cause the heart and respiration rate and blood pressure to rise. The body prepares either to confront the situation or withdraw from it, which is called the "fight or flight" response. Regardless of whether the stressor is a traffic jam or a disagreement with a boss, the body's reaction is the same.

THE TYPE A PERSONALITY AND STRESS

Many personality types exist, but one associated with dysfunctional stress is Type A. Time-conscious and competitive, Type A individuals are impatient, achievement-oriented worriers. They interrupt others and finish their sentences. Their speech is explosive, and they sometimes experience free-floating hostility. Men with a Type A personality are more likely to develop heart disease. Their chance of recovering from heart attacks is high, however, because once put on a health regimen, they follow it with the same zeal with which they previously pursued other activities.

Nelson and Quick (1985) showed that "executive women reported no higher incidence of coronary heart disease than housewives, even though they reported more stress." The same researchers, however, "found that their sample of women managers were predominantly Type A individuals, with the more extreme Type A's in the higher managerial positions."

There is a debate over which features of Type A personalities are most harmful. Some claim impatience, competitiveness, and anger are most detrimental, while others say hostility is most problematic (Greenberg, 1987).

Regardless of which aspects are most harmful, Type A behavior is counterproductive. It works against the development of resilience in the following way:

When stressors are encountered, arousal levels increase, and the tendency is to combat them by increasing arousal levels (effort) even further.... The trouble is, at high arousal levels, coping patterns become more primitive. Patterns of response... learned most recently are the first to disappear. The ability to distinguish among fine ... stimuli actually deteriorates, so the coping strategies of individuals ... become less and less effective. (Whetton and Cameron, 1991)

EFFECTIVE WAYS TO DEAL WITH STRESS

If Type A behaviors are ineffective in dealing with stress, what measures work? Eliminating stressors is most constructive; if this is impossible, people should become more resilient. Short-term coping techniques provide immediate help for those under stress.

Even if it is possible to eradicate stressors, the process may take a long time and is not easy. Time management and delegation are methods to get rid of stressors that occur because managers have too much to do (Whetton and Cameron, 1991).

Developing resilience helps individuals withstand stress and is fairly effective. This requires a moderate amount of time. Two types of resilience are physical and psychosocial/emotional. A proper diet, an adequate amount of sleep, and regular exercise are necessary to maintain physical well-being. To summarize, dietary recommendations are to eat many whole grains, fresh fruits and vegetables, and other high-fiber foods. Those striving to have a healthy diet should avoid overindulging in processed foods made with sugar and white flour, caffeine, alcohol, salt, and fat.

Aerobic exercise can improve cardiovascular fitness under two conditions. It must be done for 20-30 minutes 3 or 4 times a week, and a person's heart rate must increase to 60-80% of capacity and stay at that level during the exercise session. Bicycling, jogging, and brisk walking are examples of aerobic exercise. Besides being good for the heart, regular exercise improves mental wellness. This occurs because the brain produces endorphins during vigorous exercise, which relax the body (Whetton and Cameron, 1991).

There are many ways to cultivate psychosocial/emotional resilience. Relaxing, adopting a "small wins" strategy, depersonalizing criticism, learning to "let go," and joining or starting support groups enhance well-being (Whetton and Cameron, 1991). In addition, to remain emotionally fit, people must be able to release emotions and to remain tranquil despite life's adversities (Cranwell-Ward, 1990).

To relax fully, people need to get into a comfortable position in a quiet place and concentrate on a certain word or phrase to prevent their minds from wandering. Deep relaxation takes practice, but reduces Type A behavior over time. "Using the automotive analogy, individuals who use deep relaxation exercises find that when stress occurs, their engines don't rev up as high and they return to idle faster" (Whetton and Cameron, 1991). Prerequisites for deep relaxation are a quiet place, comfortable body position, mental focus, and a passive attitude.

Relaxation also may include biofeedback and positive self-talk. Sitterly and Duke (1988) guide people through the biofeedback process by giving the following directions:

Close your eyes and . . . block . . . sounds or distractions that keep you from concentrating on your body. . . . Clench your fists and release the muscles as slowly as you can. Repeat each step twice for about 5 seconds. Bend your elbows and tense your upper arm muscles. Release slowly as before. . . . Follow the same exercise for other parts of your body.

Sitterly and Duke (1988) conclude that "after doing every step twice, you should feel less tension . . . and a general feeling of relaxation."

Positive self-talk includes encouraging phrases such as "You can do it." Also called autogenic messages, positive self-talk can be used to "reprogram" thoughts when in a stressful situation (Sitterly and Duke, 1988).

A small wins strategy contributes to psychosocial/emotional resilience. This strategy, which boosts confidence and generates optimism, involves experiencing a minor triumph while coping with a major stressor. For example, a child unable to walk on land due to a physical disability celebrated the fact that he could walk unassisted when neck deep in water in a swimming pool. Though a small triumph, this enhanced the child's self-esteem.

People personalize criticism because of fear of failure. To minimize this fear, they should focus on the goal and view mistakes as inevitabilities from which they can learn rather than as results of personal shortcomings (Carr-Ruffino, 1985). People should think of business as a game, abandon a tense need to achieve a goal, and concentrate on the process. Such an approach emphasizes solving the problem rather than dwelling on its possible causes.

"Letting go" is accepting the possibility that a problem's outcome may not be one's preferred solution. This strategy is important for those who have a tension-producing need for a specific outcome. The overriding need and accompanying fear of failure can sabotage their best efforts to achieve a coveted goal. They still may desire a particular result, but when they abandon the need to have it, they are more likely to have the relaxed concentration necessary to obtain it (Carr-Ruffino, 1985).

Support groups help to build psychosocial/emotional resilience. Support systems are important to dual-career couples, as mentioned in chapter 12, but they are not the only ones who can benefit from support systems. Everyone needs people with whom they feel comfortable venting frustrations and sharing half-formed ideas.

Being able to do this is vital professionally and personally. At work, employees and managers cultivate social support through networking, mentoring, and task team involvement. Networking and mentoring were discussed previously. Reporting on Shaw's 1976 work, Whetton and Cameron (1991) point out advantages of task teams. In their words, "Members of highly cohesive teams communicate with one another more frequently and more positively and report higher satisfaction, lower stress, and higher performance levels than do individuals who do not feel as though they are part of a work team."

Personally, burying feelings instead of discussing them has a corrosive effect. It can create anxiety and undermine self-esteem. To maintain emotional health, it is important to be able to vent feelings to either a trained counselor or a nonjudgmental friend (Cranwell-Ward, 1990).

To remain tranquil, sometimes stoicism is necessary. People must realize and accept the fact that they are not immune from adversity. Some unpleasantness in life is inevitable and beyond anyone's control. When faced with a loved one's sudden injury or illness, for example, it might be more helpful in the long run to maintain some emotional distance and inner peace than to become consumed by others' emotional turmoil (Cranwell-Ward, 1990).

So far, two methods to deal with stressors have been proposed. The first is to eradicate them; the second is to develop resilience to withstand their effects. The final approach is to cope with remaining stressors. Coping mechanisms have been described as "quick fixes" that do not adequately address underlying issues. Nevertheless, people resort to coping methods first, probably because they require the least effort. Unfortunately, short-term coping tactics are relatively ineffective ways to deal with stress.

Short-run techniques include visualization, rehearsal, and breathing exercises. Visualization ranges from focusing on something pleasant to seeing oneself achieving long-run goals. However, one must guard against developing an overriding need to meet such objectives. Rehearsal means reviewing how one intends to conduct a conversation. This can be done mentally or shared with a trusted friend. Inhaling and then exhaling for ten seconds is a simple breathing exercise to supply more oxygen to the brain. Consciously attending to the breathing process allows a person to regain control (Duke and Sitterly, 1988).

To this point, coping mechanisms have been discussed in general without mentioning gender differences in their use. There is conflicting evidence on the issue of whether women and men appraise and cope with stress differently. One idea is that women are socialized to evaluate stressful events less confidently than men. This could explain their higher incidence of stress symptoms. Another notion is that men often do not interpret stress symptoms as signs of underlying problems. For example, they are not as likely as women to believe that depression symptoms signal emotional difficulties. Perhaps the sexes have similar stress symptoms, but only women construe them as signs of strain (Jick and Mitz, 1985).

SUMMARY

Stress, in itself, is neither good nor bad. It has been defined as a gap between one's coping mechanisms and the expectations of self and others, and as a physiological state. Distress refers to negative effects of stress and eustress to its positive impact.

Stress is low when tasks are moderately complex; at either extreme of complexity, stress is higher. Performance is high when there is a moderate amount of stress as opposed to too little or too much. Stressors can stem from factors outside or inside the organization. Some feel that the biculturalism experienced by those involved in both work and family spheres is an external stressor. Others say that multiple roles energize and that family roles serve as buffers when work roles become difficult, and vice versa.

Major events and minor hassles in one's personal life also are external stressors. Inside an organization, employees may deal with job, role, interpersonal, and environmental stressors.

Most regard Type A behavior as a counterproductive way to deal with stress. Other approaches are to eliminate stressors, develop resilience, and use short-run tactics such as visualization, rehearsal, and breathing techniques.

DISCUSSION QUESTIONS

1. Identify one stressor you have experienced in the past or are experiencing now. Explain the methods you could use to deal with that stressor effectively.

2. What methods would you recommend Type A individuals use to deal with stress more effectively? Why?

3. Give an example of the use of a "small wins" strategy in your life or in the life of someone you know.

4. Do you agree or disagree with the idea that multiple roles can energize people? Explain.

14 Time Management

OBJECTIVES

After studying this chapter you should be able to:

1. Define "tyranny of the urgent," activity trap, expert system, delegation, reverse delegation, polychronic and monochronic activity levels.
2. Explain two advantages of time management.
3. Explain how goal setting is related to time management.
4. List tactics designed to minimize interruptions.
5. Explain how to avoid procrastination when tackling major projects.
6. Explain the circumstances in which technology can save time for managers.
7. Explain tactics for becoming better organized at home and at work.
8. Explain guidelines for conducting efficient and effective meetings.
9. Explain the importance of an appropriate match between personal and organizational time styles.

Time is a valuable resource. No one seems to have enough of it, but everyone has all there is (Schwartz and Mackenzie, 1977). Unlike other resources, time is unrenewable. It cannot be saved; after a moment passes, it cannot be reclaimed. If time is used to contribute to personal and organizational goals, however, it has been spent effectively.

Guidelines for effective time use apply to both sexes. The only difference is that some women have had to juggle more roles than their male counterparts due to socialization. Regardless of employment status, white, middle-class women have been assumed to be responsible for maintaining a household and nurturing ties with extended family. This is beginning to change, but until necessary duties unrelated to employment are divided equitably between the sexes, women may have an even greater need than men to manage time effectively.

ADVANTAGES OF TIME MANAGEMENT

The purpose of time management is not to make people compulsive "do-ers." Rather, it is to allow them to exercise more control of their lives. By controlling time use, people have more time to do what they want and to be with people who are important to them.

Another positive outcome of time management is stress reduction. Those who spend time achieving self-determined, realistic goals feel better about themselves than those frustrated by striving to meet unattainable objectives. Those satisfied with progress toward goals may be less likely to exhibit stress symptoms than dissatisfied peers. The former appear calm while the latter may seem harried.

CURRENT TIME USE ANALYSIS

Before people can try to control time use, they need to analyze the way they currently expend the resource. To do this, experts recommend keeping a time use log for a minimum of three days. It would be preferable to maintain the log for one or two weeks. To some, this might seem like a waste of time, but it is necessary. Without knowing present time use patterns, it is impossible to determine how the resource could be spent more pro-ductively.

Notes in a log can be recorded manually by computer using spreadsheet software. Some recommend entering activities every 15 minutes, but Mac-kenzie (1990) advocates detailed recording of events as they occur. He claims this process makes people more careful about time use. They catch them-selves wasting time, realize what they are doing, and return to more pro-ductive tasks. Thus, logging time use has a self-correcting effect.

Several questions, which apply equally well to a household and a business, should be asked about each listed activity after completing the time log.

Of those queries, the first, and most crucial is, "Does this really need to be done?" Those who fail to question the need for a task face two problems, namely the "activity trap" and the "tyranny of the urgent." Those who fall into an activity trap busily do things but have no idea whether their activities meet their own or the organization's goals (Odiorne, 1975). Such people may or may not be efficient, but they are effective only by chance.

The tyranny of the urgent causes people to respond to the most pressing current problem rather than to the issue most crucial to long-term success (Schwartz and Mackenzie, 1977). Extreme instances of such behavior become crisis management. Then, people must deal with problems under time pressure because of a lack of prior planning. They are too busy fighting fires to plan to avert future crises.

GOALS FOR EFFECTIVE TIME USE

Activities should be continued only if they contribute to individual or organizational goals. Individually, people may set goals relevant to various aspects of their lives such as their career, interpersonal relations, physical or mental wellness, or spirituality. People determine which domains are pertinent to them.

Goal setting is a prerequisite to time management. People without goals have no reason to manage time because they either do not want to achieve anything or have not yet decided what they want to accomplish. Those lacking goals drift. Without an aim, they do whatever comes along.

Goals are what one wants to accomplish. More specific than dreams, they are outcomes. Goals should be concise and indicate a time frame for completion. Challenging yet realistic, goals should be specific rather than vague.

Stating goals does not guarantee that they will be achieved. That is more likely when they are translated into short-run objectives and when plans are developed for their attainment.

DELEGATION OF VITAL TASKS

If a task must be done, do those trying to improve time management have to do it? This is the next question to be addressed. It raises other issues such as the appropriateness of people's skills with respect to a task and the cost-effectiveness of having them complete it. Some organizations, to their detriment, fail to consider such issues. For example, they may place less qualified people on certain projects when those with more suitable credentials are available.

Delegation means assigning a task to others. In this process, people appointed to perform the duty are accountable for its accomplishment. The person who delegated the task still is obligated to his or her superior, however. This means that the delegator must make sure the work gets done. That individual cannot remove his or her obligation by passing the buck.

Even if it is appropriate to delegate a task at the office or home, there may be no one to whom the duty can be assigned. For example, during downsizing, employees and managers are expected to increase productivity by doing more with fewer resources. If managers can quantify productivity gains directly attributable to the addition of an assistant, such a proposal might be considered. Otherwise it is a lost cause.

If hiring a new assistant is not an option, organizations might consider purchasing technology to help managers. For example, word processing, database, and spreadsheet software, if used properly, can perform tasks in minutes that either would have required assistants hours to do manually or would have been less convenient if done on a mainframe computer before the advent of personal computers (PCs).

Before touting the time-saving potential of PCs, a caveat is in order. Computers conserve time only if used by trained individuals to perform needed duties. Many people become so enthralled by the computer's capabilities that they waste time. For example, they may create unnecessary but attractive charts or experiment with new features out of curiosity.

Some organizations have extended the notion of computer-as-assistant. They have purchased *expert systems* that contain all the knowledge on a topic that a human expert could have acquired through a lifetime of study. Such systems can be programmed to make decisions the way a knowledgeable person in the field would. Expert systems still are expensive and time-consuming to develop. They are not yet feasible solutions to most organizations' understaffing problems.

When assigning a task, delegators should abandon unrealistic expectations about how it will be accomplished. If the job is done reasonably well, and the person doing the work is improving, delegators should not interfere. They should praise progress and ignore minor inadequacies if reasonable standards are met.

Delegation can assist time management in the home as well as at work. Those who can afford to do so can hire people to clean their home, perform yard work, and do the laundry. Others should consider sharing those duties with roommates or family members occupying the house.

Regardless of whether people decide to perform a task or delegate it, they should consider completing the activity less often. Sometimes this can be done with minimal consequences. For example, a home or apartment can be cleaned bimonthly instead of weekly, cutting the amount of time spent on that activity in half.

AVOIDING ENVIRONMENTALLY AND SELF-INDUCED TIME WASTERS

If a task must be done, and the individual trying to improve time management skills must do it, then perhaps it can be done more efficiently. To improve efficiency, time wasters must be avoided.

Time wasters have two sources. They can originate from the environment or from oneself. Some believe it is too easy to blame the environment. Instead, people should accept responsibility for their reaction to events seemingly beyond their control.

Environmentally caused and self-induced inefficiencies detract from goal achievement in any relevant sphere of life. Time wasters emanating from the environment include interruptions, unavoidable waiting, meetings called by others, and reverse delegation. Disorganization, procrastination, inability to say no, meetings scheduled by oneself, perfectionism, and excess socializing are self-derived time squanderers. Inefficiencies caused by both the environment and the self and suggestions for dealing with them will be discussed in the following section.

Interruptions

Not all interruptions can be eradicated, but some can be prevented, and others can be managed. One way to avert interruptions at the office is to close the door when working on projects demanding concentration. Another tactic is to arrange one's office so that one's back faces the door while seated at the desk. People passing through a hall are less likely to stop to chat with someone whose back faces them.

Though it is difficult to avoid interruptions at work, minimizing them at home is more of a feat. There is a limit to the number of times a person can ignore a ringing doorbell without being labelled an anti-social recluse.

When the "drop-ins" at home are a person's children, other dependents, or significant others, the situation may call for more judgment and tact than required with individuals at the workplace. Physical or emotional needs of small children must be met. If a parent is trying to work at home on a project that demands concentration, she or he should hire a caregiver or consider working on it only before the children wake up or after they are asleep.

When dealing with children, so-called interruptions may be teachable moments. Parents or caregivers should make the most of such opportunities. Ignoring them could be a mistake.

Adults and older children are more likely to understand one's need to concentrate on a project, but their needs cannot be put off indefinitely. Relationships must be nurtured regularly to survive. Those practicing effective time management should schedule time with significant others and should guard it as carefully as they would time reserved for any other appointment. In chapter 12, dual-career couples were counseled to set aside family time, but scheduling time to spend with significant others applies to anyone who values the maintenance of relationships.

The telephone is another source of interruptions. Managers' administrative assistants can screen calls at the office. Those without such aides or those trying to complete work at home can use an answering machine to screen calls. They can schedule and publicize "quiet time"—several hours dedicated either to major projects or to planning. During this time, the managers or professionals will neither receive visitors nor answer telephone calls.

Quiet time allows managers or professionals to focus on a task without excessive starting and stopping. Repeated starting and stopping wastes time, because it takes 10 to 20 minutes to achieve optimal productivity.

When quiet time is used for planning, it yields benefits. Though it might seem wasteful on the surface, every hour of planning a project produces four hours of time saved during implementation (Schwartz and Mackenzie, 1977).

Those striving to improve time use should avoid playing "telephone tag." If they have an assistant, that person should place the call, because often the other party cannot be reached. If no assistant is available, people unable to reach the party they are telephoning should find out, specifically, when that individual will be available. They should call back only at that time.

Electronic mail (e-mail) may help people avoid telephone tag. If parties have access to e-mail, a sender can transmit a written message at any time, and receivers can view it at their convenience.

Junk Mail

Mail can be another time squanderer. Much incoming mail is worthless to the receiver. Unwanted mail can be discarded quickly, but a better preventative measure is to remove one's name from mailing lists. That approach has drawbacks, however. Since it eliminates an entire class of mail, people may no longer receive valued catalogs or brochures.

Action should be taken on remaining mail after discarding worthless items. Brief but timely notes can be written in response to correspondence and may be appreciated more than a delayed but more lengthy letter. Those who know they will contribute to a favorite charity should write a check the first time they read the solicitation letter rather than the fifth.

Unnecessary Waiting

Waiting for others is another time waster that people must deal with at work and in their personal lives. Some waiting is inevitable, but effective time allocators should either try to minimize it or prepare to use the time productively. They should have an easily accessible file of tasks to work on if telephone calls are put on hold. People can take work with them to appointments in case they have to wait. Short, discrete tasks are most appropriate. For example, correspondence can be answered or the next day's goals set and tasks planned. If they regularly have to wait more than a preset number of minutes for an appointment, those striving to improve time management skills should reschedule the appointment.

Meetings Others Schedule

Compared to meetings they schedule, people have less control over those others call. Regardless of the nature of the meeting, people should ask themselves if they need to attend. Some meetings are scheduled habitually, even if there is little to discuss. If that is the case, people could attend every other meeting and read the minutes of the sessions they skip.

Reverse Delegation

A final environmentally imposed time waster is reverse delegation. This occurs when subordinates try to get their superiors to take responsibility for tasks assigned to the subordinates. Oncken and Wass (1974) refer to the solution to this problem as "keeping other people's monkeys off your back." When a subordinate stops the boss at the water cooler and says, "We have a problem with the XYZ account," and the boss immediately invites the subordinate into her or his office to discuss it, a monkey is ready to jump on the supervisor's back. If the manager listens to the problem and then says, "I'll have to think about this and get back to you," the monkey has taken a leap and landed on the boss's back.

Rather than instinctively assuming responsibility for a subordinate's problems, the boss should make sure the monkey stays where it belongs—on the subordinate's back. To ensure this, the supervisor could direct the subordinate to prepare completed staff work. That person could generate alternatives to the problem, pick a preferred solution, and justify it. Bosses should designate certain times for the "care and feeding of monkeys" (Oncken and Wass, 1974). Subordinates' requests for advice on projects should be limited to those intervals.

Managers should think twice before accepting ownership of other people's problems. By doing so, they will spend their time more effectively.

Disorganization

The first time waster derived from the self is disorganization. At work, this manifests itself through a messy desk or cluttered directory on a personal computer. People supposedly keep important papers on their desks so they can find them, but almost invariably cannot locate the documents when needed. Then they spend precious minutes hunting for the missing papers, often becoming frustrated and exhibiting Type A behaviors, as explained in chapter 13.

Ideally, people should spend the last 10 to 15 minutes of the work day straightening off the top of their desk in preparation for the next day. Similarly, they should organize computerized files and directories regularly.

Organization is also important in the home. Household chores consume about 30 hours per week (Zuker, no date). The gender gap in the performance of household duties, with women completing the lion's share, has been well publicized. Within some relationships, this is changing. The disparity is persistent, however, because it is based on beliefs about gender roles in existence for over 100 years, at least among the white middle class.

Before a home can be organized, some planning must occur. Tasks that must be done daily, weekly, and occasionally should be listed. Everything else should be eliminated.

Grouping related tasks together saves time both at home and at work. At home, people can plan errands so they shop at stores located near one another on the same trip. They can post lists of items to be purchased in an obvious spot like the front of the refrigerator door. Household residents can be asked to add to the lists when they observe that the supply of certain items is dwindling (Zuker, no date).

Until the paperless society becomes reality and bills are paid electronically, those who wish to organize their household need a work center containing slots for incoming and outgoing mail, financial matters, and material to be filed (Zuker, no date). Many kitchen work stations have built-in compartments complementing desk units that can be used for this purpose. Makeshift slots would not be hard to construct either.

Shuffling paper is a sign of disorganization that must be minimized. The A, B, C paperwork sorting system helps people avoid handling paper more than once. In that system, anything labelled "A" has top priority and should be done as soon as feasible. "B" items are less important but still must be done. Tasks relegated to the "C" category are nonessential and can be done if and when people get to them.

Procrastination

Procrastination is another inefficient self-derived use of time. Often procrastinators do low-priority, discrete tasks before starting a major, higher priority project because they want to get the smaller tasks out of the way.

Why do people delay jobs that must be done? Perhaps the tasks are boring. On the other hand, maybe the project is overwhelming, and people are afraid they either lack the skills or perseverance to complete it or that the final product will not measure up to high internal standards. Some might secretly fear doing too well and thus having to live up to others' heightened expectations of them. Others might find themselves trapped in an approach-avoidance syndrome. Part of them wants to forge ahead, yet something holds them back. This sets them up for the activity trap mentioned earlier. They accomplish "busy work" but neglect projects more crucial to long-term success.

A remedy for procrastination is to subdivide large projects. For example, writing a book might seem like a formidable task to some. Approaching that project one chapter at a time makes it seem less overwhelming.

When major projects are subdivided, activities to be completed should be written down and deadlines set for their accomplishment. People should reward themselves for completing identifiable segments of a large project.

Easing into a large assignment by reading articles on a topic or contacting others who have information about it is a good idea. It can whet one's appetite for the project or at least get mundane but necessary tasks out of the way.

Inability to Say No

Inability to say no to activities that do not meet one's goals can create time management problems. The solution here is to learn and apply assertive communication skills, as described in chapter 11.

Self-Scheduled Meetings

People who schedule meetings should question their necessity, particularly if they entail travel. Perhaps a conference call could be substituted for a face-to-face gathering. Advances in telecommunication could make tele-conferences more affordable in the future and provide other options for meetings.

If travel is unavoidable, people should try not to drive, so they can catch up on professional reading en route. Those who have laptop computers can complete other work while traveling.

Even if a meeting does not require travel, those with authority to call one should think twice before doing so. If a memo could accomplish the same thing, it would be more cost-effective. Face-to-face meetings are expensive. When computing costs, prorated salaries and benefits of those attending must be considered along with opportunity costs.

Assuming a meeting must be held, it should be planned in advance. The convener should prepare and distribute an agenda, which should list the topic, the name of the person who will report on it, and the amount of time reserved to discuss that topic. The meeting organizer should make sure the individual reporting on the topic will attend before listing the name on the agenda.

To avoid wasting people's time, meetings should begin promptly. Non-members of the group who are on the agenda should be permitted to arrive just in time for their presentation and should be dismissed immediately after they have discussed relevant questions.

Generally, meetings should be limited to one hour. Some managers believe so strongly that meetings should not drag on that they leave after 60 minutes to emphasize the point.

There are several ways to avoid lengthy meetings. For example, subcommittees can be formed and assigned to work on issues and present alternatives with supporting documentation to the larger group. Or discussion on each topic could be limited. Another way to shorten meetings is to schedule them an hour before quitting time.

Perfectionism

Perfectionism already has been discussed as a reason for reluctance to delegate. Perfectionism also is a self-derived barrier to effective time management. Sometimes the incremental improvement in quality does not justify the time needed to produce it. This is particularly true for correspondence. If a letter communicates a message and is grammatically correct, the extra time required to transform it into a literary work is not worth the effort.

Excess Socializing

Excess socializing consumes time. Some socializing sparks creativity through an exchange of ideas and helps people establish useful contacts. In addition, most people view some contact with others as essential to their mental health.

Too much socializing, however, can detract from other goals. If work piles up at the end of the day due to several idle conversations, corrective action is needed.

Many people find it difficult to escape from office socializers because they do not want to appear rude. Tactics designed to make one's office inaccessible to socializers are similar to those geared to avoid interruptions. To get rid of a socializer who has entered a person's office, that individual can stand during the conversation and move toward the door. A more assertive approach would be to level with the socializer. For example, one could tactfully say, "Jane, I'd like to continue talking to you, but I'm busy right now." If the topic of conversation were work-related, one could schedule an appointment to discuss it later. If not, the person could arrange to have lunch with the socializer at a later date.

ADDITIONAL TIME-SAVING SUGGESTIONS

In the preceding discussion, several techniques were proposed as solutions to time wasters. Other suggestions not yet broached are to match personal and organizational time styles, capitalize on personal productivity peaks, and build a time cushion into daily schedules.

Personal and Organizational Time Congruence

Achieving congruence between personal and organizational time styles averts some miscommunication and resulting conflict. Avoiding unnecessary conflict frees time for more productive use.

Researchers have identified several factors comprising an individual or organizational time style. These include orientation, preferred activity level, a basic approach to time, and the degree to which its use is committed in advance (Felker Kaufman, Lane, and Lindquist, 1991).

Time orientation refers to the past, present, or future. Decision makers geared toward the past usually weigh historical precedent heavily; they respect the status quo. Those oriented to the future expect situations to improve. They also may have relatively long planning horizons (Felker Kaufman, Lane, and Lindquist, 1991).

Preferred activity level can be *monochronic* or *polychronic*. Those who like to finish one task before starting the next have monochronic activity levels. The term polychronic describes those who enjoy doing several tasks simultaneously.

Of the many approaches to time, economic and sociocultural are the only two that will be mentioned. An economic approach views time as a fixed resource that can be budgeted. Sociocultural approaches are learned attitudes associated with time. For example, some families, organizations, or cultures value punctuality more than others.

The degree of time commitment refers to discretionary or nondiscretionary activities that do or do not yield income. This dimension also identifies whether or not tasks must be done at preset times. For example, those working to earn money to provide life's necessities are performing nondiscretionary, income-producing work. Furthermore, they have no leeway regarding when the tasks must be done. On the other hand, those knitting caps to be donated to homeless children as a hobby are engaged in discretionary, non-income-producing activities. They also are free to choose when to pursue their hobby.

Mismatches between an individual's and an organization's time styles can cause conflict. Those who prefer activities to be monochronic and are geared toward the past may be uncomfortable in a future-oriented firm that expects employees to juggle several tasks simultaneously. Similarly, people taught to value time-intensive maintenance of relationships may be ill at ease in organizations stressing economic aspects of time. Such discomfort could provoke conflict. Hours devoted to resolving difficulties induced by time style differences drain time from other endeavors.

Optimization of Personal Productivity Peaks

Those wishing to optimize time use should identify intervals when they are most productive. Some are at their prime early in the morning, while others' productivity peaks occur late at night. People should plan to work on demanding projects during the hours of optimal personal productivity.

Time Cushions

Since most tasks take longer than anticipated, wise time allocators build cushions into their schedules. This gives them flexibility to deal with unexpected problems or opportunities without becoming unglued. They are more relaxed and able to think more clearly than peers with rigid schedules.

SUMMARY

Time management gives people more control over their lives and reduces stress. Keeping a daily activity log can help people assess current time use. Because those without a purpose have no reason to manage time, goal setting is a prerequisite to the effective use of that resource.

Instead of automatically performing tasks, people should question their necessity. If the chores need to be done, perhaps they can be delegated. If that is impossible, tasks can be performed more efficiently by avoiding time wasters.

Time wasters are either environmentally or self-imposed. Interruptions, waiting, meetings others call, and reverse delegation are examples of environmentally induced time squanderers. Disorganization, procrastination, and perfectionism are examples of those that are self-induced.

Besides avoiding time wasters, people should implement other tactics to improve time use. They should ensure a fit between their personal time style and that of the organization employing them, take advantage of personal productivity peaks, and build time cushions into their schedules.

DISCUSSION QUESTIONS

1. On a piece of scratch paper, list everything you have done in the past 24 hours. Answer these questions based on an analysis of the list: What time wasters appear on the list? What, specifically, could you do to manage time more effectively?

2. Is rewarding yourself for reaching your time management goals a form of "mollycoddling" or not? Explain.

3. How are stress and time management related?

4. Explain how new technologies can help managers use time more effectively.

5. Give an example of how a new office technology, designed to be a time saver, can end up wasting a manager's time.

15 Women in International Management

OBJECTIVES

After studying this chapter you should be able to:

1. Define *gaijin*, multinational business, and ethnocentric.
2. Explain why American women are not necessarily treated in a discriminatory way by cultures that generally tend to treat women poorly.
3. Explain steps recommended for citizens of any country who wish to cultivate awareness of and sensitivity to cultures other than their own.
4. Distinguish between "push" and "pull" styles of negotiating.
5. Explain why women are underrepresented in executive positions worldwide.
6. Explain assumptions about women and men underlying the equity and complementary contributions model.

Before proceeding, some terms related to international business need to be defined. An *international business* is based mainly in one nation but interacts with suppliers, customers, or competitors from other countries (Griffin, 1990). Among international businesses, the degree of involvement varies. A simple export/import arrangement would entitle a firm to be called an international business as would a more complex joint venture, in which firms from different countries share ownership in another firm. A *multinational* business transcends national boundaries to a greater degree. It obtains resources and technology from different countries, may have operating facilities in various nations, and also may sell products or services in markets worldwide. Globalization, another common term, refers to the trend toward a world economy composed of interrelated markets (Griffin, 1990).

If multinational corporations have become so prevalent, are there any gender differences in executives of such firms? In a word, yes. In 1989, women represented only 5% of all American expatriate managers. This may change if managers accept ideas proposed by Jelinek and Adler (1988) in the following reading. They suggest that many American women have been socialized in ways that make them particularly suited to negotiate business deals with executives from other countries.

"Women: World-Class Managers for Global Competition" by Mariann Jelinek and Nancy J. Adler

It is no secret that business faces an environment radically different from that of even a few years ago, the result of increasingly global competition. The Commerce Department estimated in 1984 that in U.S. domestic markets some 70% of firms faced "significant foreign competition," up from only 25% a decade previously. By 1987, the chairman of the Foreign Trade Council estimated the figure to be 80%. In 1984, U.S. exports to markets abroad accounted for 12.5% of the GNP; by comparison, Japan's 1984 exports were 16.5% of its GNP.[1] Global competition is serious, it is pervasive, and it is here to stay.

More stringent competition is an important result of this global economy. (See Table 15.1.) Because markets are increasingly interconnected, "world-class standards" are quickly becoming the norm. New products developed in one market are soon visible in markets around the world, as initial producers use their advantage, forcing competitors to meet the challenge or lose market share. Product life-cycle has been reduced by 75%. Product development and worldwide marketing are becoming almost simultaneous. For example, recent developments in superconductivity, initially demonstrated in Zurich, were quickly replicated in the People's Republic of China, the United States, Japan, and in Europe. Similarly, U.S. automobile customers quickly learned to demand improved quality from U.S. automakers, once the Japanese autos had demonstrated it. Standards for price, performance, and quality have been permanently altered worldwide.

NEW COMPETITIVE STRATEGIES

The problem for Americans, who historically have enjoyed the luxury of a large and generally protected domestic market, is how to respond to all these changes. Global competition means much more than sending excess domestic production abroad. Today, many formerly eager markets are contested by well-entrenched locals or by competing foreign companies. The new competition does not involve simply sales abroad, or even foreign competitors here and abroad. Rather, its varied faces are likely to include the following circumstances, none of them typical for most business even a few years ago:

- Extensive on-going operations within foreign countries. This means a vastly increased demand for sophisticated, multiculturally adept managers. Foreign

Table 15.1
Focus of Competition

When Focus of Competition Is:

Local or Regional	National	Export Sales	Sourcing or Manufacturing Abroad	Global Business Arena
Managerial Focus Is: Home Country Focus		————	————	Global Focus
Managerial Relations Tend to: Depend on Own Views Own Resources "Lone Ranger"		————	————	Depend on a Variety of Views, Others' Resources "Team Spirit"
Personnel Policy Emphasizes: Home Country Personnel Policy		Some Expatriates ————	Some Foreign Nationals ————	Multicultural & Multinational Personnel Policy

Thus North American companies in locally oriented competition tend to focus on the home country, with managers generally depending on their own resources and home country personnel. In contrast, a firm sourcing or manufacturing abroad is much more likely to have an international focus and to have moved toward seeing a variety of views and others' resources as essential to team-spirited management, deliberately using multicultural personnel.

operations and markets are neither temporary nor trivial, but essential for long-term survival.

- Strategic management across cultures. Global management necessitates working in numerous countries at once. Yet what works at home, or in one foreign country, may not work in another. Cultural norms and expectations differ. Sensitivity and finesse must be brought to bear on strategic intentions, to transliterate them sensibly. In many cases a straight translation probably will not do, whether of a product name or the more complicated matters of market attack, strategic intent, or mission.

- More foreign personnel throughout the company. Foreign personnel are both necessary and valuable to a firm seeking to penetrate global markets. Even within the United States a broadly pluralistic personnel pool with substantial ethnic identity, most notably Hispanic and Asian, but others as well, belies the mythical "melting pot" image of prior decades. Effectively managing multicultural organization dynamics is a prerequisite for success today and tomorrow, not merely an indulgent gesture or a legal requirement.

- More joint ventures and strategic alliances to gain access to new technology, new markets or processes, and to share costs and lower risk. Indeed, not only are U.S. firms increasingly becoming involved in joint ventures with foreign firms, but more and more the U.S. firm is not the dominant partner. Today, "we" often need "them" as much as or more than "they" need

Table 15.2
Some Alternative Values Orientations

	Culture A	Culture B	Culture C
Individuals seen as:	Good	Both Good & Evil	Evil
World is:	To Be Conquered	Lived With in Harmony	To Be Endured
Human Relations Center on:	Individuals	Extended Groups	Hierarchical Groups
Time orientation:	Future	Present	Past
Action Basis is:	Free Will & Facts	Cultural or Social norms	Biological or Theological

Adapted from ideas in Nancy J. Adler and Mariann Jelinek, "Is "Organizational Culture" Culture Bound?" Human Resource Management 25:1 (Spring 1986), 73-90; as based on F. Kluckhohn and F. L. Strodbeck, Variations in Values Orientations (Evanston, IL: Row, Peterson, 1969)

"us." Thus, cross-cultural management is becoming increasingly critical to success, even survival.

Each of these new competitive strategies demands new skills. Improved ability to communicate across profound differences in approach and expectations, assumptions and beliefs, to say nothing of languages, is key. Because culturally based beliefs, perceptions, expectations, assumptions, and behaviors are deeply held, they are especially sensitive issues, requiring exceptional tact. (See Table 15.2.)

In short, managing globally calls upon an array of cross-cultural skills not readily at hand for most American managers, and not widely taught in most American business schools. To address these nontraditional problems we suggest a nontraditional resource: women managers. Our case is not based on altruism, nor equal opportunity under the law, nor even fairness, although all of these should be mentioned. Our case is based on the pragmatic self-interest of firms facing a challenging global environment.

But can women make it, especially in foreign cultures that presumably do not consider women men's equals? Won't they be ignored, mistreated, or intimidated? Shouldn't we respect foreign countries' cultural norms, even if they appear discriminatory to us? And do American women managers really want to take on this challenge? These are valid concerns, and an emerging body of research suggests some surprising answers. We will look at the special skills women bring to the new global competition and at the results women are achieving abroad, particularly in the fastest growing market in the world, the Pacific Rim. The conclusions may surprise you at first. However, upon reflection, they are utterly comprehensible and point to a powerful resource for a sustainable competitive advantage not readily available or duplicable in other cultures.

A NONTRADITIONAL (BUT INCREASINGLY VALUABLE) RESOURCE

All cultures differentiate male and female roles, expecting males to behave in certain ways, females in others; anticipating that men will fill certain roles, and women others. In many cultures, including America's, the traditional female role supports many attitudes and behaviors contradictory to those defined as managerial. This has been one of the key barriers to women's entry into managerial careers in the U.S. domestic arena: it operates both in terms of self-selection and differential difficulty.

After two decades of women's liberation movements and despite legislation and education, women remain different from men, even in the United States, arguably one of the most assertively egalitarian countries in the world. Men are still typically raised to be more aggressive and independent; women are still typically raised to be social and more communal.[2] Of course, there have been visible changes in sex roles and norms in North America as elsewhere in the world. There is also substantial debate over how much of the difference in behaviors can be attributed to biology and how much to acculturation factors. Nevertheless, in general, men still tend to be more aggressive than women.[3]

Melvin Konner makes a strong argument that male aggression has biological roots in puberty, but that thereafter, greater aggression may be a learned and socially reinforced pattern. He notes that males commit the vast majority of violent crimes in every known society. Women, whose biochemistry does not initially encourage aggression at puberty, according to Konner, tend to evolve behavior patterns that emphasize sensitivity, communication skills, community, inclusion, and relationships.[4]

Research on sex roles and managerial characteristics has tended to reinforce the rather limited view of management skills and leadership most of us have acquired, a view identifying leadership with power and potency with adversarial control. In study after study, undergraduates, MBAs, and managers (male and female) in the United States have tended to identify stereotypically "masculine" (aggressive) characteristics as managerial and stereotypically "feminine" (cooperative and communicative) characteristics as unmanagerial.[5]

Yet American women now make up about half the U.S. workforce, and occupy over a quarter (27.9%) of all managerial and administrative positions,[6] although as late as the mid-1980s they represented only 5% of top executives.[7] In international management, women are rarer still, less than 3%.[8] Yet their achievements call into question some widely held beliefs about women and about management. Their unconventional achievements suggest a resource difficult for others to match.

WOMEN ABROAD

American women have been pursuing graduate education in management in increasing numbers, now accounting for about 50% of the enrollment at some large state schools and about a third of the enrollment at the most prestigious private schools. More and more are developing an interest in international postings. It would be surprising if they did not, as international business is so clearly "where the action is" in many companies today. To investigate the role of North American women as expatriate managers, Adler undertook a four-part study. In the first part, 686 Canadian and American firms were surveyed to identify the number of women sent abroad. Of 13,338 expatriates, 402 or 3% were female.[9] Other parts of the study sought to explain why so few North American women work abroad. The second part of the study surveyed 1,129 graduating MBAs from seven management schools in the United States, Canada, and Europe. Overall, 84% said they would like an international assignment at some point in their career; there were no significant differences between males and females.[10] While there may have been a difference in the past, today's male and female MBAs appear equally interested in international work and expatriate positions.

One need not depend on opinion or assumptions for assessing women's performance internationally; there are documentary research results. In the working world, women are beginning to be assigned abroad. In another part of the study a survey of 60 major North American multinationals revealed that over half (54%) of the companies were hesitant to post women overseas. This is almost four times as many as were hesitant to select women for domestic assignments (14%). Almost three-quarters of the personnel vice-presidents and managers believed that foreigners are prejudiced against female managers (73%), and that prejudice could render women ineffective in international assignments. Seventy percent believed that women in dual-career marriages would be reluctant to accept a foreign assignment, if not totally disinterested. For certain locations, the personnel executives expressed concern about women's physical safety, hazards involved in traveling in underdeveloped countries and, especially for single women, isolation and potential loneliness.[11] These findings agreed with those of a survey of 100 top managers in Fortune 500 firms operating overseas: The majority believed that women face overwhelming resistance when seeking management positions in the international division of U.S. firms.[12]

NO WELCOME MAT?

There is certainly evidence to suggest that women are discriminated against as managers worldwide; women managers in foreign cultures are very rare indeed.[13] In many societies, local women are systematically excluded from managerial roles. Japan offers an excellent case in point; there are almost no Japanese women managers higher than clerical supervisors, especially in large, multinational corporations. In general, Japanese society expects women to work until marriage, quit to raise children, and return, as needed, to low-level and part-time positions after age 40. In Japan, the workplace remains a male domain.[14] Similarly, while women from prominent families in the Philippines can hold influential positions in political and economic life, overall only 2.7% of working women hold administrative or managerial positions in business or government.[15] The picture is similar in India, where women are constitutionally equal to men, but are culturally defined as primarily responsible for the home and children. Women have fared somewhat better in Singapore, where government policy and a booming economy between 1980 and 1983 helped raise women to 17.8% in 1980.[16] Only recently, and as yet rarely, do women fill managerial positions in these countries.[17]

WOMEN IN INTERNATIONAL MANAGEMENT

Clearly, it is the cultures of these foreign countries that perpetuate this scarcity of indigenous female managers in most Asian countries. If so, how can North American companies successfully send female managers to Japan, Korea, Hong Kong, the Philippines, the People's Republic of China, Singapore, Thailand, India, Pakistan, Malaysia, or Indonesia? Is the experience of these countries' women, most specifically their relative absence from managerial ranks, the best predictor of what expatriate women's experiences will be?

Research results suggest that local women's experience is not a good predictor of North American women's reception, experiences or success in Pacific Rim countries.[18] Indeed, it seems that North American predictions confuse the noun "woman" with the adjective "female," as in "female manager." The research disconfirms a set of North American assumptions predicting how Asians would treat North American female managers based on the North Americans' beliefs concerning Asians' treatment of Asian women. Confusing? Yes. Fundamentally important? Also yes. The problem with these assumptions, and the conclusions they lead to, is that they have been proved wrong.

Fifty-two female expatriate managers were interviewed while on assignment in Asia or after returning from Asia to North America as part of the larger study described earlier. Because of multiple foreign points, the 52 women represented 61 Asian assignments. The greatest number were posted in Hong Kong (34%), followed by Japan (25%), Singapore (16%), the Philippines and Australia (5% each), Indonesia and Thailand (4% each), and at least one each in Korea, India, Taiwan, and the People's Republic of China. Since most of the women held regional responsibility, they worked throughout Asia, rather than just in their country of foreign residence. The majority of the women were posted abroad by financial institutions (71%), while the others were sent by publishing, petroleum, advertising, film distribution, retail food, electronic appliances, pharmaceuticals, office equipment, sporting goods, and soaps and cosmetics firms, and service industries (including accounting, law, executive search, and computers).

On average, the women's expatriate assignments lasted two and a half years, ranging from six months to six years. Salaries in 1983, before benefits, varied from US $27,000 to US $54,000 and averaged US $34,500. The women supervised from zero to 25 subordinates, with the average being 4.6. Titles and levels varied considerably; some held very junior positions (such as trainee and assistant account manager), while others held quite senior positions (including one regional vice-president). In no case did a female expatriate hold her company's number-one position in any region or country.

THE EXPATRIATE EXPERIENCE

These expatriates were pioneers. In the majority of cases, the female expatriates were "firsts," with only 10% having followed another women into her international position. Of the 90% who were first, almost a quarter (22%) represented the first female manager the firm had ever expatriated anywhere; 14% were the first women sent by their firms to Asia, 25% were the first sent to the country in question, and 20% were the first women abroad in their specific job. Clearly, neither the women nor their companies had the luxury of role models; there were no previous patterns to follow. With the exception of a few major New York–based financial institutions, both women expatriates and their firms found themselves experimenting, with no ready guides for action or for estimating the likelihood of success.

The companies decided to send women managers to Asia only after a process that might be described as "education." In more than four out of five cases (83%), it was the woman herself who initially introduced the idea of an international assignment to her boss and company. For only six women (11%) had the company first suggested it, while in the remaining three cases (6%) the suggestion was mutual.

The women used a number of strategies to "educate" their companies. Many women explored the possibility of an expatriate assignment during their initial job interview, and simply turned down firms that were totally against the idea. In other cases, women informally introduced the idea to their bosses and continued to mention it "at appropriate moments" until the assignment finally materialized. A few women formally applied for a number of expatriate positions before finally being selected. Some women described themselves as having specifically planned for international careers, primarily by attempting to be in the right place at the right time. For example, one woman predicted that Hong Kong would be her firm's next major business center and arranged to assume responsibility for the Hong Kong desk in New York, leaving the rest of Asia to a male colleague. The strategy paid off: within a year the company sent her, rather than her male colleague, to Hong Kong.

Overall, the women described themselves as having had to encourage their companies and their bosses to consider the possibility of expatriating women in general and themselves in particular. In most cases, they confronted and overcame numerous instances of corporate resistance prior to being sent. For example:

> (Malaysia) Management assumed that women don't have the physical stamina to survive in the tropics. They claimed I couldn't hack it.

> (Thailand) My company didn't want to send a woman to "that horrible part of the world." They think Bangkok is an excellent place to send single men, but not a woman. They said they would have trouble getting a work permit, which wasn't true.

> (Japan and Hong Kong) Everyone was more or less curious if it would work. My American boss tried to advise me, "Don't be upset if it's difficult in Japan and Korea." The American male manager in Tokyo was also hesitant. Finally the Chinese boss in Hong Kong said, "We have to try."

> (Japan) Although I was the best qualified, I was not offered the position in Japan until the senior Japanese manager in Tokyo said, "We are very flexible in Japan"; then they sent me.

In some instances, the women faced severe company resistance. Their companies sent them abroad only after all potential male candidates for the post had turned it down.

> (Thailand) Every advance in responsibility is because the Americans had no choice. I've never been chosen over someone else.

> (Japan) They never would have considered me. But then the financial manager in Tokyo had a heart attack and they had to send someone. So they sent me, on a month's notice, as a temporary until they could find a man to fill the permanent position. It worked out and I stayed.

> (Hong Kong) After offering me the job, they hesitated. "Could a woman work with the Chinese?" So my job was defined as temporary, a one-year position to train a Chinese man to replace me. I succeeded and became permanent.

This cautiousness and reluctance are particularly interesting because they tend to create an unfortunate self-fulfilling prophecy. As a number of women reported, if the company is not convinced you will succeed (and therefore offers you a temporary position rather than a permanent slot, for instance), this will communicate the company's lack of confidence to foreign colleagues and clients as a lack of commitment.

Foreigners will then mirror the home company's behavior, also failing to take the temporary representative seriously. Assignments can become substantially more difficult. As one woman in Indonesia put it, "It is very important to clients that I am permanent. It increases trust, and that's crucial."

OUTCOMES ABROAD: DID IT WORK?

Ninety-seven percent of the North American women described their experiences as successful, despite the difficulties and the reluctance on the part of their firms. While their descriptions were strictly subjective, a number of objective indicators suggest that most assignments did, in fact, succeed. For example, most firms decided to send another woman abroad after experimenting with their first female expatriate. In addition, many companies offered the pioneer women a second international assignment upon completion of the first. In only two cases did women describe failures: one in Australia and one in Singapore. The Australian experience was the woman's second posting abroad, preceded by a successful Latin American assignment and followed by an equally successful post in Singapore. The second woman's failure in Singapore was her only overseas assignment to date.

ADVANTAGES

Perhaps most astonishing was that, above and beyond their descriptions of success, almost half the women (42%) reported that being female served more as an advantage than a disadvantage in their foreign managerial positions. Sixteen percent found being female to have both positive and negative effects, and another 22% saw it as irrelevant or neutral. Only one woman in five found the professional impact of gender to be primarily negative abroad.

The women reported numerous professional advantages to being female. Most frequently, they described the advantage of being highly visible. Foreign clients were curious about them, wanted to meet them, and remembered them after the first meeting. It was therefore somewhat easier for the women than for their male colleagues to gain access to foreign clients' time and attention. Examples of this high visibility included:

(Japan) It's the visibility as an expat, and even more as a woman. I stick in their minds. I know I've gotten more business than my two male colleagues. They are extra interested in me.

(Thailand) Being a woman is never a detriment. They remembered me better. Fantastic for a marketing position. It's better working with Asians than with the Dutch, British, or Americans.

(India and Pakistan) In India and Pakistan, being a woman helps for marketing and client contact. I got in to see customers because they had never seen a female banker before.... Having a female banker adds value for the client.

Visibility was not the only advantage. The women also described the advantages of good interpersonal skills and their observation that men could talk more easily about a wider range of topics with women than with other men. This ease of interchange was especially important in cross-cultural situations, where difficulties of nuance and opportunities for miscommunication abound. The women's ease was unforced and quite sincere, since it springs from fundamental socialization patterns. For example:

(Indonesia) I often take advantage of being a woman. I'm more supportive than my male colleagues.... Clients relax and talk more. And 50% of my effectiveness is based on volunteered information.

(Korea) Women are better at treating men sensitively, and they just like you. One of my Korean clients told me, "I really enjoyed the lunch and working with you."

(Japan) Women are better at putting people at ease. It's easier for a woman to convince a man.... The traditional woman's role ... inspires confidence and trust, there's less suspicion, and I'm not threatening. They assumed I must be good if I was sent. They became friends.

In addition, many of the expatriates described a higher status accorded them in Asia. That status was not denied them as foreign female managers; on the contrary, they often felt that they received special treatment not accorded their male colleagues. Clearly, it was always salient that they were women, but being women did not appear to prohibit them from operating effectively as managers. Moreover, most of the women claimed benefits from a "halo effect." Most of their foreign colleagues and clients had never worked with a female expatriate manager. At the same time, the foreign community was highly aware of how unusual it was for North American firms to send female managers to Asia. Thus, the Asians tended to assume that the women would not have been sent unless they were the best. Therefore, they expected them to be "very, very good."

The problems the women did experience were most often with their home companies rather than their Asian clients. For instance, after obtaining a foreign assignment, some women experienced limits to their opportunities and job scope imposed from back home. More than half the female expatriates described difficulties in persuading their home companies to give them latitude equivalent to that given their male colleagues, especially initially. Some companies, out of concern for the women's safety, limited their travel (and thus their role and often their effectiveness), excluding very remote, rural, and underdeveloped areas.

Other companies made postings temporary, or shorter than the standard male assignment of two to three years. This temporary status was often an important detriment: One Tokyo banker warned potential foreign competitors, "Don't go to Japan unless you're ready to make a long-term commitment in both time and money. It takes many, many years."[19]

Business relationships and the effective development of "comfort levels" center on personal relationships and reliability over the long haul, especially in Japan, but also in many other "slow clock" cultures that focus on the long term.[20] It takes time to build relationships, and time to learn the culture. The contrast to the infamous American emphasis on "fast tracks" and quarterly results could not be more stark.

Managing foreign clients' and colleagues' initial expectations was a key hurdle for many of the women. Since most Asians had previously never met a North American woman in a managerial position, there was considerable curiosity and ambiguity about her status, level of expertise, authority, and responsibility, and therefore the appropriate form of address and demeanor to be used with her. In these situations, male colleagues' reactions were important. Initial client conversations were often directed at male colleagues, rather than at the newly arrived female manager. Senior male colleagues, particularly from the head office, became important in redirecting the focus of early discussions toward the woman. If well done, smooth, on-going work relationships were quickly established.

WOMEN AS *GAIJIN*

Throughout the interviews, one pattern emerged persistently. First and foremost, foreigners are seen as foreigners. Like their male colleagues, the female expatriates are categorized as *gaijin* (foreigners) above all, and not locals. Foreign female managers are not expected to act like local women. Thus, the rules governing the behavior of local women, potentially limiting their access to management and managerial responsibilities, do not apply to the expatriate women. The freedom of action this identification carries is substantial:

(Japan) The Japanese are very smart: they can tell that I am not Japanese, and they do not expect me to act as a Japanese woman. They will allow and condone behavior from foreign women which would be absolutely unacceptable from their own women.

As Ranae Hyer, a Tokyo-based vice-president of personnel of the Bank of America's Asia Division said, "Being a foreigner is so weird to the Japanese that the marginal impact of being a woman is nothing. If I were a Japanese woman, I couldn't be doing what I'm doing here. But they know perfectly well that I'm not."[21]

Ultimately, of course, the firm's product or service and the woman herself must be acceptable in business terms. Simply sending a female will not carry an inadequate product or too-costly services:

(Hong Kong) There are many expat and foreign women in top positions here. If you are good at what you do, they accept you. One Chinese woman told me, "Americans are always watching you. One mistake and you are done. Chinese take a while to accept you and then stop testing you."

(Hong Kong) It doesn't make any difference if you are blue, green, purple, or a frog. If you have the best product at the best price, they'll buy.

Nevertheless, the incremental advantages of easier communication and visibility, greater facility at relationships per se, and greater trust and openness often allow a female expatriate to enjoy significant pluses in a highly competitive atmosphere. Perhaps even more important, women's advantage in succeeding abroad draws on characteristics that have traditionally been a fundamental part of the female role in many cultures—their greater sensitivity, communication skills, and ability to establish rapport. Women need not buy into the competitive game. They can subtly shift the interaction out of the power and dominance modes so typical of business interchange, and so highly dysfunctional in cross-cultural relations, into the sort of co-operative, collaborative modes becoming increasingly important today.

Global competition is a tough game, and "world class" standards are a genuine challenge. Our opponents are worthy foes, strong competitors with numerous advantages. Foreign firms now control state-of-the-art technology, producing top-quality, low-cost products and services that respond quickly and effectively to worldwide clients' rapidly changing needs. Moreover, they often enjoy lower costs for capital and personnel, concerted government support and in some cases, nontariff, cultural barriers to foreign firms' entry into their domestic markets and long-established relationships with other foreign nations. These advantages must be overcome if North

American firms are to prosper in the future. Yet the traditional image of business as warfare and the character of the relationship based on it are increasingly dysfunctional. New modes of "collaborative competition" require traditionally "female" skills. The new competition is so challenging that only the best can stay in the game; we need all the advantages we can muster, including full usage of the best of our resources, male and female.

ALLIANCES AND COOPERATIVE COMPETITION

In businesses from automobiles to semiconductors, insurance and financial services to brokering and steel, competition is very often a matter not only of global enterprise but of collaboration with other firms, foreign as well as domestic. Collaborative competition succeeds by making common cause, by cooperation rather than the independence so typical of North American business behavior. Alliances may be essential to navigating t ie intricacies of, for instance, nontariff barriers to entering the Japanese market; making the connections required to do business in foreign lands; and especially sharing the increasingly substantial investment required to develop new technologies. Global operations require coordinated activities across the whole spectrum of business activity, not merely sales or marketing. Success rests upon relationships, including those at the most senior executive levels, relationships made far more difficult by cultural differences.

Among the more important differences between North America and the cultures of the Pacific Rim, South America, the Middle East, Africa, and most of Europe are the different cultural "clocks" and norms, particularly regarding the depth and strength of relationships per se:

"In Germany, your product is most important to your success; in Japan, it is the human relationships you build. Without them, you will not succeed" (manager of a trading company).[22]

"The Japanese don't want people who do a good job but have a bad attitude" (Japanese CEO, automobile industry).[23] "Strict adherence to personal loyalty is at the core of Japanese concern for people rather than for principles."[24]

THE BOTTOM LINE

In a highly competitive world, especially one generating new norms of business behavior that are counterintuitive to past practice, only the most canny organizations will prosper. Where many competitors form alliances and cooperative ventures, firms that cannot or will not, will operate at a significant disadvantage. They will have to struggle along, "reinventing the wheel" with each new culture.

The sorts of collaborative alliance we have described go far beyond selling or buying abroad. They encompass a broad spectrum of joint activities and common endeavors united by a common thread: the need to negotiate, communicate, cooperate closely over an extended period of time, and build enduring professional relationships are a very serious matter in other cultures, where longevity and trust accrue together and where the nuances of communication can make or break a deal.

Often, simply because so much of "business" is, in the context of other cultures, really a "relationship," it may be invisible to those North Americans most intent on "business, first and last," and most impatient with "socializing." In many other cultures, what we may see as purely social is for them a crucial testing process, to discover whether a relationship can be created that might be the foundation for doing business. Failure to invest the time and energy needed to build the relationship may well doom any attempt to establish a business arrangement.

Without a firm basis of trust, cross-cultural suspicion will find many reasons to feel insulted or challenged by a "rude" foreigner. Failure to comprehend that friendship may have important strategic consequences is equal folly. Within such a context, women represent a significantly underutilized resource. With good management school credentials and business performance, women are a readily trainable, highly useful source of talent, and the international arena suggests a particularly apt new application for the relationship skills still more highly developed among women than among men today. We believe that women are perfect candidates for expatriate positions and international careers both because they perform so well, and because their skills are the skills of the future.

Of course, there are men who are sensitive and skilled in communication; and of course there are women who are insensitive. In general, however, it is women who tend to possess greater sensitivity and relationship skills. Does this mean that these skills cannot be taught to males? On the contrary: the socialization process most women experience is, indeed, a form of "teaching."

Women who are successful abroad can provide role models and coaching for their male colleagues. This means that the women will have to be seen as resources, consulted and relied upon for their special expertise. Business school curricula can also help. Both specialized coursework and cross-cultural elements in all courses can highlight the importance of the international arena. Organizational behavior, organizational development, international management, and cross-cultural experiential activities can all present far broader perspectives than the standard BBA or MBA work focused completely on United States business practices.

American business already faces a global marketplace and global competition. This world is too small and too interconnected for "Lone Ranger" business practices; no single view encompasses all of its reality, and intolerance is a luxury we cannot afford. Traditional U.S. business approaches to competition as battle, which build arm's length business relationships on this basis, seem very risky indeed. Alliances, cooperative efforts, joint ventures, collaborations, and even business more or less as usual but carried out across cultural lines, can be facilitated by skills traditionally thought of as "female."

Global competition is a tough league, so challenging that we must employ all our skills and advantages, and the best of our people. We believe women possess a crucial advantage in social relationship and communication skills. Increasingly, the best of our male managers too will be working to acquire and hone important skills formerly seen as "female," those centering on relationships, communication, and social sensitivity.

DISCUSSION QUESTIONS

1. Do American women really carry "special" skills to global competition, as Jelinek and Adler suggest, or is this a stereotype itself? Explain.

2. Since some cultures still treat women poorly, it seems logical to assume that

American executive women working in those cultures also might be treated poorly. Why doesn't this seem to be true?

It is beyond the scope of this book to address gender issues peculiar to individual countries around the world. Students desiring such information should consult works like Rossman's *The International Business Woman of the 1990s* (1990) or Adler and Izraeli's *Women in Management Worldwide* (1988).

DEVELOPMENT OF A COSMOPOLITAN PERSPECTIVE AND CULTURAL SENSITIVITY

Regardless of whether a person plans to work for a foreign-owned firm in the United States or in another country, two general rules apply. First, most Americans need to develop a cosmopolitan perspective. Through their ideas and behaviors, Americans must show that they are world citizens instead of ethnocentrics who believe in cultural superiority and judge others' cultures according to their standards.

Second, more Americans need to cultivate awareness of and sensitivity to the cultures they will experience. This includes, but is not limited to, knowledge of the culture's:

1. language or dialect;
2. history and customs;
3. expected degree of workplace formality;
4. characteristic view of time and space;
5. view of gift giving as a business practice; and
6. view of the importance of cultivating a personal relationship as a prerequisite to business transactions.

Each of these issues will be discussed in turn.

Generalizations regarding level of formality, and views of time, space, and the importance of developing relationships are just that. Exceptions exist and must be acknowledged to avoid harmful effects of stereotyping, explained in chapter 7. For example, though most people in a given culture stress punctuality, a few individuals may have a relaxed attitude toward time.

Executives must know at least a few phrases of the language spoken in the country where they have been assigned. Fluency is preferable. Executives who travel to another country unable to speak a word of the native tongue risk being considered ethnocentric or unprepared. Familiarity with the nation's history and customs is as basic as language facility. Knowledge of customs and language can prevent major business blunders, a classic example of which was the Chevrolet car named Nova. Spanish-speaking people avoided buying the car because in that language *No va* means "doesn't go."

Colors also have different meanings in various cultures. In the United States, for example, pink has been associated with femininity, but in other cultures, yellow is considered the most feminine color.

Within one country, corporate norms regarding the degree of formality expected may vary widely. Americans tolerate and sometimes encourage a relaxed atmosphere. In Germany, on the other hand, formality extends to language. A different form of address is used for acquaintances and co-workers or supervisors than for family or close personal friends. It would be inappropriate to use the personal pronoun, *du*, meaning "you," when speaking to associates with whom one had not developed a close, personal relationship. For those individuals, the more formal *Sie* would be the preferred word.

Other cultures have different views of time in terms of the amount required for business negotiations and punctuality. According to Rossman (1990), "few deals are closed on the first meeting anywhere in the world." It may take several meetings to develop a relationship of trust. Without that, in many countries, no business transactions will occur.

It is common for some Latin American and Middle Eastern executives to arrive at meetings extremely late. Americans should be aware that this might happen and should try not to become upset by it. American women should not assume they are being discriminated against because their foreign counterparts make them wait. They would treat men the same way.

Neither should American women automatically assume they are being sexually harassed if a male Latin American or Arab stands only a few inches away from them. Rossman (1990) recommends not backing away because that action would be "perceived in Latin America and the Middle East as the proof of the U.S. coldness that they have heard about." Most Arabs and Latin Americans are comfortable with less personal space than most Scandinavians, British, and Americans.

Another cultural variation is the practice of gift giving as part of doing business. In most countries, small, "token" gifts are appropriate, though care must be taken in selecting the specific item. For example, Rossman (1990) mentions that cheese is an inappropriate gift for the Chinese, who consider it spoiled milk.

Executives must be careful when giving larger gifts to avoid violating United States or foreign laws against bribery. The Foreign Corrupt Practices Act, a U.S. law passed in 1977 and amended in 1988, has not been enforced vigorously, but remains in effect. The law bans the exchanging of money or other valuables to obtain or retain business. Minor mementos are excluded from this prohibition, and to be illegal, an official of a foreign political party or government must be bribed (Rossman, 1990).

As stated earlier, developing a personal relationship with foreign business executives is crucial. American executives can start this process using various communications media, but eventually, personal meetings will have to take place. Rossman contends that, due to socialization, many American women have developed a more successful style of negotiating with foreign executives than have American men. She says that many women use a "pull" style in which all affected thoroughly discuss issues before making a decision. The "pull" style also is characterized by the expression of feelings and an attempt to find common ground. Tentative speech, deemed a weakness in the United States, is more acceptable to some foreign nationals than a direct, terse communication style, which may be considered rude.

Many American males supposedly have been socialized to use a "push" negotiations style. They present facts, promote their opinions based on reason and logic, and act as vises to force a solution. A common belief is that they want results in the present (Rossman, 1990).

Women in the United States supposedly see themselves as "bridges" in negotiations. Concerned with the process as well as the outcome, they are future-oriented.

There is nothing innately sex-linked about a "push" or "pull" negotiating style. Both can be learned. It would be a mistake to presume that women are more comfortable with a "pull" style or men with the opposite style, because not all individuals of one sex are socialized identically. Nevertheless, Rossman (1990) concludes that a "pull" negotiating style is preferable in the Far East, Latin America, Middle East, and in some European nations.

So far, this discussion has centered on Americans doing business in other countries. It is possible to experience various cultures without travelling to other nations by working for a foreign-owned firm. That poses challenges, because some nations' executives export discriminatory attitudes to U.S. facilities. Some Japanese-owned companies in the United States have discriminated not only against females but also against non-Asian males.

Foreign firms may not be aware of the importance of U.S. equal employment opportunity laws until they experience discrimination lawsuits. This may have been the case for Honda of America, a Japanese-owned firm that agreed to an out-of-court-settlement of a sex discrimination suit (Rossman, 1990).

To reduce ethnocentrism, it is appropriate to examine briefly the status of women in executive or leadership roles in other parts of the world. When thinking of political leaders, names of former heads of state like Margaret Thatcher, Golda Meir, and Indira Gandhi come to mind immediately. Some of these women achieved their posts through association with powerful male relatives or mates, but they were recognized world leaders in their own right, nonetheless.

REASONS FOR THE UNDERREPRESENTATION OF WOMEN IN EXECUTIVE POSITIONS WORLDWIDE

Reasons for women's worldwide underrepresentation as business executives vary, but Adler and Izraeli (1988) identify the "masculinization" of management, social policy, the role of higher education, level of economic development, and the domestic sphere as factors affecting women's participation as executives.

Regarding the first factor, "everywhere leadership in general and management in particular are masculine domains" (Adler and Izraeli, 1988). Depending on one's perspective, this statement could be considered discouraging or challenging. However, as Adler and Izraeli (1988) acknowledge, "there is considerable variance from place to place in the proportion of women in management and in their prospects for entry and promotion."

Social policy can help or hinder women's progress through legislation and methods of resource allocation. In South Africa, for example, women's progress was hindered by a law that gave husbands control over their wives' right to negotiate contracts. That law was rescinded in 1984 for white women; at that time, it still applied to black women.

It might be surprising that access to higher education is a prerequisite to a successful management career only in nations such as Israel, Canada, and the United States. In those countries, firms recruit prospective managers from universities directly. In other nations, such as England, in-house training programs are the usual sources of managerial candidates. Thus, aspiring executive women in those nations face two hurdles: they must be hired, and then they must be chosen for management training (Adler and Izraeli, 1988). In expanding economies, there is greater demand for labor. More women may join the workforce. Once there, some women gravitate toward typically higher paying management positions.

Finally, the domestic sphere cannot be ignored. If parenting is gender-specific in a culture, and that culture insists on a mother's physical presence with her children throughout the day, the social costs of pursuing time-intensive careers like management may be considered too high (Adler and Izraeli, 1988).

ASSUMPTIONS ABOUT WOMEN'S ROLES IN MANAGEMENT: EQUITY VERSUS COMPLEMENTARY CONTRIBUTIONS

Various cultures can be categorized according to

assumptions they make about women's roles in management. Countries like the United States subscribe to an *equity model* in which women are assumed to be identical, as professionals, with men, and therefore equally capable of contributing in ways similar to those of men.... The primary question is one of access. Are women given the opportunity to demonstrate their competence? Primary change variables include legal requirements... and structural change. (Adler and Izraeli, 1988)

In the *complementary contribution model*, more characteristic of Sweden and some European countries, men and women are assumed to differ and therefore to be capable of making different, but equally valuable, contributions to the organization.

From this second perspective, change strategies revolve around (1) identifying the unique contributions of men and women, (2) creating enabling conditions for both types of contribution to be made and rewarded... and (3) looking for synergy— ways in which men's and women's contributions can be combined to form new and more powerful managerial processes and solutions to the organization's problems. (Adler and Izraeli, 1988)

Equity model supporters dislike the complementary contribution theory. To them, seeing women or minorities as different is similar to labelling them as inferior. According to the complementary model,

there are many equally valid, yet different, ways to manage, the best way being based on recognizing, valuing, and combining the differences. From this second point of view, not to see women's uniqueness is to negate their identity and... contribution to the organization. (Adler and Izraeli, 1988)

SUMMARY

This chapter examined gender differences in global management. It advocated greater cultural awareness and suggested general cultural variations with which the astute multinational executive should become familiar. The chapter briefly summarized the status of executive women worldwide without exploring conditions unique to any one country. Finally, the equity and complementary contribution models were presented as two sets of assumptions underlying different cultures' views of women in management.

DISCUSSION QUESTIONS

1. What type of management approach, discussed in an earlier chapter of this book, is similar to the "pull" style described by Rossman? Explain.
2. Is the trend toward "valuing diversity," discussed in an earlier chapter, more consistent with the equity or complementary contribution model? Explain.
3. Do you agree or disagree with Rossman's statement that American women may be more successful at negotiating with foreign executives than American men? Explain.

16   Case Studies

Each case study in this chapter focuses on several issues that have been presented throughout this book. The following comments are intended to help students analyze the cases effectively.

1. Do not list lack of communication as the most important underlying problem. Communication is nearly always a critical issue and can be considered a "given."
2. Do not use the excuse that there is insufficient information to make a decision. Managers must make decisions with imperfect knowledge. A lack of relevant data is typical even in this era of information overload.
3. Criteria are factors based on which you evaluate alternatives. For example, if you were building a new home, cost would probably be one factor to consider when selecting a contractor. Another factor might be an estimate of the quality of finished homes built by that contractor. In this simplified example, *quality* and *cost* would be two (of many) criteria used to evaluate alternative contractors.

Use these questions to analyze each case:

1. List the issues involved in the case that are relevant to the study of gender issues in management.
2a. Of the issues identified in item 1, what is the most important underlying problem?
2b. What is the most pressing problem currently?
3. Identify three alternatives to the problems listed in items 2a and 2b.
4. List at least two criteria on which the alternatives should be evaluated.
5. Evaluate the alternatives based on your criteria. Pick a solution to each problem. Justify your decision.

"Joyce Woo and NT & C"
by James Kirkpatrick

NT & C Network Systems is a relatively new division of the National Telephone and Communication Corporation. It has supplied data communication products for a diverse customer base in the Washington, D.C. area since the mid-1980s. The Fairfax, Virginia office has undergone several changes from 1989 to 1991. Top management has been shifted to other regions and this office has recently received a new general sales manager. Alex Bracewell has been promoted to this position because he has more business marketing background and less of the technical proficiency required of his subordinates.

The consent decree negotiated by the Equal Employment Opportunity Commission and signed by NT & C in the early 1970s influenced an affirmative action plan which now more actively solicits women for management training programs. The NT & C Equal Opportunity Policy Statement reads as follows:

Equal opportunity is the lifeline of our business. It has been NT & C's longstanding tradition as well as our corporate policy to treat each individual with dignity and respect. Furthermore, it is critical that our workforce reflect the marketplace to ensure our leadership position. To guarantee this, we will effectively utilize all of our human resource talent and continue to pursue this effort. NT & C will:

- comply with both the letter and the spirit of all applicable laws and regulations governing employment;
- provide equal opportunity to all employees and to all applicants for employment;
- take appropriate affirmative action to make opportunity a reality;
- prohibit unlawful discrimination or harassment because of race, color, religion, national origin, sex, age, physical or mental disability, or because of one's status as a special disabled veteran or veteran of the Vietnam era, in any employment decision or in the administration of any personnel policy;
- make reasonable accommodations to the physical and/or mental limitations of otherwise qualified employees or applicants with disabilities;
- prohibit the use of a person's sexual orientation or marital status as a criterion in personnel decisions;
- ensure that maximum opportunity is afforded to all minority and women-owned businesses to participate as suppliers, contractors, and subcontractors of goods and services to NT & C; and comply with regulatory agency requirements and with federal, state and local procurement regulations and programs;
- advise employees of the rights to refer violations of this policy to their supervision, or to the appropriate NT & C organization charged with administration of the Equal Opportunity/Affirmative Action policy, without intimidation or retaliation of any form for exercising such rights.

I want to reaffirm NT & C's commitment of providing equal opportunity to all employees and applicants for employment in accordance with all applicable laws, directives, and regulations of federal, state, and local governing bodies and agencies thereof.

I expect all managers throughout NT & C to comply fully with all aspects of this policy, and to conduct themselves in accordance with equal opportunity principles.

Demonstrated commitment to equal opportunity is an investment in our people and our future growth. Consequently, a company that attracts, selects, develops, and retains the best will remain the industry leader. NT & C's ongoing efforts in this direction will provide us with critical, competitive advantage in the marketplace.

—James P. Evans, Chief Executive Officer, January, 1990

In reference to the section of the policy statement concerning NT & C's policy to "prohibit unlawful discrimination or harassment because of race, color, religion, national origin, sex, age, physical or mental disability, or because of one's status as a special disabled veteran or veteran of the Vietnam era, in any employment decision or in the administration of any personnel policy," Joyce Woo contends that Alex has discriminated against her based on her sex and Korean ancestry. She has not filed a complaint because of a fear of discharge. Bracewell's view adversely affects her personal and professional effectiveness. Joyce feels she has been ignored regarding promotions that were available and given to white males with less experience, education, and enthusiasm.

Joyce's background must be explored to better understand the situation. Joyce Woo is a Regional Accounts Manager for NT & C Network Systems in the Fairfax, Virginia, office. She was born in Washington, D.C. to Korean parents. Her father is an attorney for the U.S. Patent Office in Washington, D.C., and has a Ph.D. in patent law from Georgetown University. Her mother is a nutritionist at the Walter Reed Army Medical Center, which is in Washington, D.C. She has an M.S. in nutrition, also from Georgetown University. Joyce's three brothers have bachelor's degrees in various business fields, and she has no sisters.

In 1984, Joyce earned an M.S. in Finance and Marketing from Georgetown University. Her first job was as a sales representative for Tandy Corporation where she was immediately promoted to the district manager. Joyce remained in that position for two years. Perceiving no remaining promotion potential, she left Tandy in 1986 to work for NT & C as a programming staff systems analyst. In 1987, Joyce was promoted to staff manager at NT & C headquarters. There she supervised six accountants who were responsible for auditing corporate financial reports. She stayed until she was offered her present position.

Joyce's current position, offered to her in January 1989, involved both a promotion and relocation. Jeff Josephson, who had originally hired Joyce, arranged for NT & C to pay her relocation expenses. She purchased a house in Clifton, Virginia, less than ten miles from her new office. Joyce and Jeff had a unique relationship during the time they worked together. Joyce was very pleased to have such a competent supervisor. Their cooperative efforts significantly improved 1990 sales. Jeff saw that Joyce had generated so much business that he hired a personal assistant to help continue her progress. Joyce and Jeff worked together effectively for 12 months before he was replaced by Alex. Jeff prepared Joyce's 1990 performance evaluation.

Joyce's performance evaluation stated that she had far exceeded goals set for her by management. She had achieved 123% of her sales objective. Her efforts led the sales team for the Maryland, Washington, D.C., and Northern Virginia area and mitigated the overall sales decline caused by low sales posted by other co-workers on the team, all of whom were men.

A major problem started when Joyce's co-workers became resentful of the way her 1990 performance reflected on them. Joyce continued her sales promotion efforts though they were discouraged by ongoing conflict with her male peers. They consistently treated her as if she were a subordinate though she had a higher salary than most of the team. During meetings between the team and clients, Joyce's co-workers tried to humiliate her.

Based on her outstanding sales performance in 1990, Joyce's 1991 sales objective was set unrealistically high. Her sales objective, set by Alex, was expanded $4.2 million to total $8 million in 1991. Even if there had been a potential for $8 million in sales, an economic recession absolutely devastated it. This was demonstrated by sales which dropped 65% in comparison to sales through the same period in 1990.

These incidents may have fueled Joyce's current dilemma. Knowing her objective had been increased, many customers offered to make additional purchases from Joyce in return for special favors. Among these favors are lower prices for products to increase customer profit margins, special buy-back agreements to return products that are purchased but unprofitable to use, and agreements to reduce service to accounts of the customer's competitors. Perhaps the most offensive favor which was asked of Joyce was when a customer, who had a large account with her, began to request sexual favors. At first she ignored the requests. The customer did not stop the harassment and became more forceful in his attempts to gain sexual favors from her. She informed Alex Bracewell, who said he didn't think the customer, who was a white male, could like Asian women and if he did, she should take it as a compliment.

Joyce decided to seek another position within NT & C so she could transfer out of the Fairfax location and away from the problems associated with it. She informed Alex Bracewell of her intentions. He said he would not release her for transfer to another position because he did not view any of these issues as relevant to her ability to perform her job.

"General Computer Inc."
by Barbara Lyons

General Computer Inc. (GCI), was founded in 1972 by Edson Decker, a brilliant Engineer, and now the Corporate President. Edson began GCI after resigning from a well-established computer firm. He started from his garage with some innovative ideas, which were an almost overnight success story. The Corporation has since grown into multinational status, employing almost 10,000 people. GCI is headquartered in the Boston, Massachusetts, area, with branch offices in every state, as well as production facilities overseas.

Facilities for Sales, Service and Systems Support are colocated and are expected to share equipment and supplies, and to provide each other with unlimited support. The only real division between departments occurs in year-end accounting for profits and losses. GCI has contracts with the U.S. Department of Defense and is required to submit affirmative action plans regularly.

Though GCI has developed into a major corporation within the computer industry, its human resources policies and affirmative action program are currently immature at best. This situation was recently identified, and the human resources staff was increased significantly. To date, affirmative action has served to benefit mainly minorities, with little progress for women. Women in the organization continue to be concentrated in clerical and secretarial positions.

Carol Brown, a two-year community college graduate with a Secretarial Science degree hired on at GCI a little over two years ago, as a Customer Service Secretary. Her responsibilities had been to the Customer Service Branch Manager, Jim Stone. Jim and Carol had an instant friendship and developed an excellent working relationship. Jim immediately recognized Carol's potential. He encouraged her to accept increasingly more responsibilities that were not requirements of her secretarial position. Jim's intent was to provide Carol with as much exposure and visibility as possible. Jim provided Carol with unwavering support and it was his persuasion that led Carol to return to college part-time. Carol is currently pursing her bachelor's degree in Business Administration.

It was also Jim's influence and active campaigning that landed Carol a promotion to the newly created position of Assistant Service Manager. This position was originally intended for someone already possessing a bachelor's degree. However, Jim was able to convince the Human Resources Manager to give Carol an opportunity since she was already familiar with the customer base and was actively attending college in the evenings.

As Assistant Manager, Carol's primary responsibility is to handle all customer complaints and to prioritize Customer Service Representative (CSR) activities, including installations, and parts and service scheduling. Carol also provides direct interface between the Sales and Systems Departments and branch service personnel, as well as Service Support groups at headquarters. This position was created to relieve Jim of these responsibilities to free up his time for contract negotiations and personnel issues.

Carol is one of only three women working at this branch office, which has a total staff of 18. She is also the only woman in a management position outside of headquarters. The other two women are Pat, the Secretary for Sales and Systems, and Sheila, the secretary hired to replace Carol. Additional personnel Carol deals with on a daily basis are her subordinates, the CSRs, the Sales Manager, Dave Cummings, and the Systems Manager, Lou Hardy. When necessary, Carol also deals with Phil Bayly, Jim's manager at headquarters.

Carol, who is exceptionally bright and capable, was well liked as the secretary. She has, however, begun to feel strain in her relationships with both the CSRs and the other managers since accepting the position of Assistant Manager four months ago. The only relationship that has remained relatively stable is Carol's with Jim.

As Carol fought back frustration one evening at the dinner table, she decided to enlist her husband's support. Their conversation went as follows.

Carol: Bob, I just don't understand why my interactions with everyone are so tense. It's as if no one believes I am capable of handling my job. Everything I suggest is both suspect and scrutinized.

Bob: What do you mean Carol? I thought you got along so well with the CSRs?

Carol: I did before! That's just it! When I ask them to do anything, I have to insist and actually pull rank before they take me seriously. Then they go away in a huff, as if every decision I make could have been made better by someone else. Not only that, but they get angry when I tell them to ask the secretary to make their copies and handle their reservations.

Bob: I bet they wouldn't ask you to do those things if your name were Carl and not Carol.

Carol: No kidding! I knew this transition from a peer to a supervisor-subordinate situation wasn't going to be easy, but this is much worse than I ever expected. I just don't receive the same respect as the other managers do.

Bob: Well, hang in there Carol, it's got to improve. What about the managers? Are you still having problems with them too?

Carol: Oh that's another story. Today was typical. One of our customers called his salesperson to complain about what he perceived as a service problem. So he and Dave came to discuss it with Jim and me. When Jim was out, it was clear they felt I could not handle it alone. So I thought, "Here is my real opportunity to show them I can do it." But by the time I could call headquarters for some parts updates on this customer, Dave has already called Phil Bayly in Boston, and he was calling me on the other line to find out why I wasn't handling the problem for Dave. This kind of situation really makes me look bad, as if I'm not doing my job. You know even when I do get the job done, they thank Jim.

Bob: I really don't know what to say, other than to talk to Jim. Maybe he can help; he's always been supportive in the past.

Carol sat down with Jim the next morning. As they were discussing Carol's concerns, Dave came into Jim's office with some customer representatives from a newly established account. Dave was quick to introduce them to Jim and to make arrangements for Jim to join them at lunch. As Dave and the customers were about to leave, Jim asked the customers if they had met his Assistant Manager, Carol. He then expressed his utmost confidence that she would handle any of their problems both quickly and professionally. When they were safely down the hall, Carol exclaimed to Jim, "You see? This is just the kind of thing I have been telling you about. If you hadn't introduced me to that customer, no one would have. Not only that, but Dave did not include me in the lunch plans. This is going to be an important customer for us and I could have started to establish rapport with them over lunch." Jim responded, "Oh Carol, you sometimes take things too personally. Just give it a chance and things will work out!"

Later that week, Carol asked her old lunch mate and confidante, Pat, to dinner. Carol wanted to discuss her ongoing concerns. She had tried to conceal these feelings up until now because she did not want to appear weak or petty. But now the situation had come to a point where Carol was seriously contemplating a career move. At dinner, Pat confirmed Carol's suspicions. For months the office grapevine had been buzzing with rumors that she and Jim were sleeping together. Her alleged affair was supposedly the reason why she received the promotion. There had even been absurd rumors that Carol and Jim were leaving their respective spouses to be with each other. Pat told Carol that she had heard conversations like "Where do you think those two go together at lunch time? They sure are gone a long time."

Carol had put up with innuendos and derogatory comments directed both at her personally and at women's capabilities in general, during her entire tenure at GCI. Most of these comments were made jokingly, but some had definite serious undertones. Most of the comments came from Lou, whom everyone simply overlooked and wrote off as a "chauvinist." These rumors were so unfounded and degrading that Carol decided she could no longer sit back and accept this situation passively. Carol was aware that her actions would probably evoke serious repercussions in her relationship with Jim, whose stand had always been one of not wanting to "rock the boat."

"Monica Garcia and the Colonial Bank of Chicago" by Jill Geurink Cain

The Colonial Bank of Chicago was founded in 1940 by Alex Edwards. Its success has centered around a conservative approach to banking. The vice-president, Eric Leland, has masterminded the recent growth and national expansion of the bank.

Monica Garcia started as a teller at Colonial Bank of Chicago, at age 20, while putting herself through college. She was very motivated and excelled in her position. Monica enjoyed her job as a teller and quickly demonstrated a desire to learn more about banking business. After receiving her college degree at age 22, she was offered a position in personal banking.

Monica loved her new job. She performed remarkably in the challenging new tasks of the position. In the several years which followed, Monica was put in charge of specialized services, such as retirement services and managing the clerical staff. She demonstrated superior leadership and was soon promoted to an officer position.

Memo # 1
Colonial Bank of Chicago
To: Monica Garcia
From: Eric Leland
Congratulations, Monica! Your reviews have been superior and have proved your dedication to the bank and to your position as personal banker. I am pleased to inform you that due to your excellent performance, you have been chosen to fill the new position as personal banking officer. Congratulations on your promotion!

Monica was thrilled about the promotion. She had begun to wonder if her efforts were being recognized. Obviously, they were. Finally her hard work and long hours had paid off. With her promotion came a 10% salary increase and full benefits.

At the age of 27, Monica's personal life was going just as well as her professional life. In the preceding year, she had gotten married, and she and her husband bought a new home. The promotion could not have occurred at a better time! After four months in her new position, Monica discovered she was pregnant. She and her husband were delighted.

During the first three months, Monica's pregnancy was normal, but then major complications developed. Her doctor prescribed bed rest for the remaining six months of the pregnancy. Monica was devastated at the thought of having to leave her new job which meant so much to her; she felt there was really no alternative in the matter. She soon realized that it was a matter of saving her baby or her job.

Memo # 2
Colonial Bank of Chicago
To: Eric Leland
From: Monica Garcia
Due to recent complications in my pregnancy, I must spend the next six months preceding the birth of my baby at home. I highly regret leaving my new position, which I have so thoroughly enjoyed. I fully intend to return to work six weeks after the baby is born. I hope you will accept my seven and one half month leave of absence. I feel that I will be able to return to my job at full capacity. Thank you for your understanding.

Memo # 3
Colonial Bank of Chicago
To: Monica Garcia
From: Eric Leland
After reviewing your request, I have decided to grant you the leave of absence for the desired duration. The time request extends beyond what we normally implement, but because of your exemplary past performance, an exception will be made.

I wish I could offer you an officer position upon your return, but business must continue. Therefore, I will replace you ASAP. I can promise you an equivalent position when you return. I trust that you will find this acceptable. My best wishes for the remaining months of your pregnancy.

Though she regretted having to give up her job as personal banking officer, Monica agreed to the terms of her leave set forth by Mr. Leland. The next six months passed quickly and she gave birth to a baby girl. After six additional weeks, she returned to the bank. Monica was not surprised that upon her return, she was transferred to a different department.

Monica was placed in public relations, a department about which she knew little, but she was eager to learn. After eight weeks of training, observing, and attending seminars on public relations in banking, she was finally given a chance to "show her stuff."

Monica quickly found herself working on all-male teams. This did not bother her until she began to sense a dysfunctional, competitive attitude on the part of some of the men. Sam and Fred were very helpful, and she enjoyed working with them. But Jerry, Frank, Todd, and George were often quick to shoot down Monica's ideas and frequently talked among themselves leaving her out of the team.

Monica was up for her six-month review. She received the following memo:

Memo # 4
Colonial Bank of Chicago
To: Monica Garcia
From: Eric Leland
I am concerned about the observed performance in your new public relations position. Your contributions to the public relations team have been less than adequate. I expect to see notable improvement in your work by the next review. If you feel you need more training, please let me know.

Monica was very distraught by the memo and immediately requested a personal conference with the vice-president, Eric Leland. The conversation went as follows:

Eric: I assume you came here to inquire about additional training.

Monica: On the contrary—I was shocked by the comments on my last review. I want to have the chance to give you my side of the story. I have tried to aggressively work with the public relations team, but some of the men are convinced that they are not going to let me get in the way of their ideas. I would like to suggest that you add another woman to the team so that the new ideas will have more power behind them. Maybe then the others will listen.

Eric: I respect what you are saying, but I can not let someone within the team make an administrative decision. I am an objective observer, and what I have observed is decreased performance relative to your previous job as personal banking officer. My suggestion is that you should not let your changing family life change your performance at work. You must learn to make this distinction.

Monica: Thank you for sharing your opinions, Mr. Leland. I now see where you are coming from, and I will follow up on the subject after having some time to think.

"Moving into Management in Switzerland: The Case of Celine Michellod" by Linda Salamin

Celine Michellod is a woman in her late 40s presently working as general manager of a supermarket. This store is part of a chain called Denner, which allows all capable employees to reach the position of general manager. For women, however, that is where it ends. Denner hires 90% females for its entry level positions and 100% males for middle and upper management positions. Being a Swiss chain, Denner has not met with any problems regarding this practice; in Switzerland companies are allowed to specify in newspaper ads age, sex and nationality.*

Some background about Switzerland is necessary to fully comprehend Celine's situation. There are still three cantons (states) where women do not have the right to vote. In Lichtenstein, a Swiss principality, women cannot vote. The "women's movement" is starting to come to life—but very slowly. The women in Switzerland who cannot vote have asked the federal government to investigate the situation. In these autonomous cantons the male electorate has decided year after year that women do not need voting rights. (Yes, this is still true today in even a rich and industrialized country such as Switzerland.)

Unlike Americans, who view the Constitution as the legal basis for all, the Swiss believe that the citizens' opinions now are more important than a dusty constitution.

*Nullis (1991) reports that "sexual equality became law" in 1981 and that Swiss women have generally had the right to vote since 1971. In June 1991, Swiss women went on strike to demand equal pay and employment opportunity, but the strike had limited effect.

Therefore, even though the Swiss Constitution calls for "egality" between the sexes, if the current voters continue to refuse to extend voting rights to women, their actions take priority over the Constitution.

Celine is Spanish born; she moved to Switzerland when she was 16 years old to find work. She was brought up in a typical lower middle class Spanish family where the father was considered the patriarch and the mother usually stayed at home with the couple's children.

Celine was the eldest of eight. Her father was a factory worker. Neither parent was very well educated. Celine led a typical Spanish childhood; she graduated from high school and ended her formal education there. She grew up viewing men as more educated, stronger and more capable in most things than women.

Since there was high unemployment and poverty in her country, she decided to go to Switzerland to find work. Once in Switzerland, Celine worked as a waitress for seven years before meeting her husband, who was Swiss. They married and soon started a business—a bar and restaurant. This business was managed like all others where Swiss couples work together. The husband handled all financial and administrative duties, ordering, hiring and firing of employees, while the wife cleaned and waited on tables.

Celine had little notion of how the business was going, until one day, 10 years later, it went bankrupt. Celine and her husband got a divorce, and Celine lived with her daughter.

At this point, she started working for Denner, a supermarket chain, as a salesperson, stocking shelves and occasionally working the registers. For four years Celine worked conscientiously at her menial tasks, barely making ends meet, until one day, the store was having personnel problems. The general manager had quit. Since Denner has a policy of hiring from within whenever possible, and Celine was the employee with greatest seniority in the store, she was asked to fill the position. She accepted with hesitation.

She went through a three-month management training program for Denner, where she learned the mechanics of a general manager's position. Ideas about how to manage people were not mentioned. Therefore Celine was more or less left to herself as to how to actually get people to do things; she was instructed regarding all paperwork, deadlines, ordering, etc.

So Celine started her new management position. She was in charge of 35 employees, eight of them men. In this grocery store there was a butcher shop, which Celine also managed. The head butcher reported to her.

Celine was generally very sociable and agreeable. As a manager, however, she demanded that the employees abide by the rules and regulations without exception. Without this set of rules she would have been lost as this was formal; the employees had to do what was indicated.

A change in breaktime procedure illustrates Celine's approach to management. The previous manager had allowed employees to leave the store to take their break at a coffee shop in the mall in which the supermarket was located. Celine would no longer allow this. She was afraid that employees would leave the store with unpurchased items and would take longer than the 15-minute break to which they were entitled.

Celine had no real way of knowing how to manage and she could only abide by written rules. She had no authority or power with her superiors; she was new. To her credit, Celine was an extremely hard worker and was an example to all who saw her work. Nevertheless, the store that Celine managed began to lose business.

"Jane Doe's Promotion"
by Sandra Kotinek

Valley College, since its inception in 1954, specialized in post-secondary education and training. It had a respectable reputation within its immediate service area. The college's mission was to provide adult education and training for entry level jobs within a classroom setting. The administration was headed by a male director and deputy-director, who answered to a board made up of local business executives and residents. Its mission and structure remained unchanged until the early 1960s, when two factors disrupted the status quo: the large number of "baby boomers" reaching adulthood and needing training and the radical changes American society was undergoing, i.e., the questioning of traditional institutions—including education—and of male and female roles.

In response to these changes, Valley College expanded its physical facilities to handle increased enrollments and hired more female instructors and support staff. Due to the rapid expansion, the administrative structure was broadened horizontally by establishing divisions, each headed by male managers. In mid-1960, the first female was hired as a manager. Each manager had much autonomy, but organizational decisions were still made by the top two administrators.

During the latter 1960s, female facility and support staff constituted a slight majority of the employees. The number of female students also increased. At this time, the administrative structure was expanded. Male managers were promoted to vice-president positions and were included in the decision-making process. In filling the vacancies, one female was hired as a manager. At the same time, Valley College initiated many innovative training programs. The school developed expertise in the computer field; began aggressively promoting linkage with business and industry; encouraged recruitment of female students for traditional and nontraditional training; established a support network for women students; and moved more women into supervisory positions. Valley College had an image of being a progressive and responsive institution providing quality training.

JANE DOE: INDIVIDUAL AND PROFESSIONAL DESCRIPTION

Jane Doe had graduated from a state university with an undergraduate degree in English, and a master's degree in Marketing. Her first position was that of promotional manager for a medium-sized book publishing company. In this capacity, she worked with the printing and marketing staff to develop publicity sales campaigns and to promote the organization. Within a few years, Jane had established an extensive network among media staff and the area business community. However, since the company was family-owned and Jane saw no possibility for advancement, she applied and was hired as promotional manager at Valley College.

In her first few months at Valley College, Jane met with staff at all levels to find out their concerns and thereby determine how her department could help staff do their jobs better. She then established a committee, made up of a cross-section of employees, to develop goals and guidelines to achieve them.

Jane's enthusiasm and "can-do" attitude was contagious. For the first time, the staff believed that they could have meaningful input that would produce concrete results. It was particularly rewarding to work with Jane because she had expertise in marketing and promotion, was conscientious, had excellent problem-solving skills, shared authority, and was an effective manager.

While she preferred to operate with little oversight from the administrative cabinet, she informed the cabinet of her activities with reports listing current or future objectives with timelines. When listing department achievements, she made a point of giving credit to the individual or staff members responsible. Jane was known for always being prepared or knowledgeable, and this occasionally created some difficulties with the administration or board. It was not unusual for Jane to question an action or proposal, in her soft-spoken way, and have the facts to support her position at hand.

It was no secret that Jane had her sights on a higher level position, and her hard work was one means to that end. She also was working toward her doctorate and had volunteered to write several promotional publications for the college. Her contacts with the media assured her of attention and accessibility, and she became the public spokesperson with increasingly higher visibility internally and externally.

JANE DOE: PROMOTION TO THE ADMINISTRATIVE HIERARCHY

With the influx of females into Valley College as employees and students, the increased emphasis on training and support programs for females, and the advent of equal employment opportunity legislation, the male administration decided a female should be added to the hierarchy. Since there was no current opening, this would involve creating a special area of responsibility. Whether the administration already had decided to promote Jane and created a new position for her or whether they created the position and then filled it with Jane is unknown. However, it was announced that a vice-president of public relations position would be added to the administrative cabinet. To no one's surprise and most co-workers' happiness, Jane Doe was selected.

The administration indicated that Jane was chosen for this position because of her high visibility doing presentations for the college and her organizational and planning skills, which had resulted in successful promotion of the school. Her new duties would give her the formal authority to continue and expand her role as spokesperson; act as liaison among the school, the business community, the general public, and state and local governmental units; increase her involvement in writing professional articles and publications relating to the college; and serve as supervisor of the promotional department.

The expectations of the other male administrators appeared to be the obvious: having a female cabinet member would be good for the school's image. Jane would formally take over the bothersome duties of dealing with the media and would act as figurehead at formal functions; she would also free up other administrators by replacing them as representatives on various committees involving educational, business, and government issues or projects. Her strong writing abilities would be available to assist other cabinet members in producing documents for publication; and Jane would still have oversight responsibility for continuing the success of the promotional department as supervisor.

JANE DOE: EFFECT OF PROMOTION

In essence, Jane's promotion was actually job expansion, as she basically retained her prior responsibilities and was given an increased workload in the same task areas. However, this was not obvious at the time to anyone, including Jane.

Jane was very happy with her promotion, and at the department celebration party, talked at length about what she hoped to accomplish and how. Shortly after her appointment, she reorganized the department into various levels and responsibilities, so that there was a clear channel of reporting and delegation of authority. The system worked well during the first few months. As Jane became increasingly involved in her new role as official spokesperson and representative of the college administration, she was rarely on campus, and it became more difficult to communicate with her.

Her isolation from her own staff and other co-workers increased as she began to work with the college director on an ambitious writing project on the history of the college. She also wrote many professional articles to enhance her image and that of the school.

Without a responsive supervisor, problems began to occur in the promotional department. There was no longer any direction from Jane, only directives. Jane had no time to address issues or new goals. Her reaction to those in mid-management levels under her supervision was to order them to follow the system. Instead of her usual method of encouraging and rewarding, she began to be accusatory and punitive. When infrequent department meetings were held, Jane would invariably arrive late from some other commitment and have to leave early to make another commitment. She no longer was well-prepared and knowledgeable about the functional activities, but talked about "our mission." Jane rarely socialized any longer with department co-workers, most often taking coffee with other administrative cabinet members. Her attitude toward other staff became increasingly autocratic. Such changes in Jane's behavior resulted in estrangement from several of her close female friends in mid-management. The last straw in the alienation of Jane from her co-workers occurred when she finally earned her doctorate. She sent out a memo instructing all staff to address her as "Dr. Doe." In the eyes of her co-workers Jane had become one of "them."

Within a year or two, the supervision of the promotional department was transferred to a mid-manager. While Jane continued to run here and there as the college representative, she no longer appeared at public gatherings of important outside officials or business people. She continued to crank out massive amounts of printed matter under her name or as co-author with other administrative cabinet members.

After four years of serving in the administrative hierarchy, Jane resigned to establish her own consulting business.

Reference Lists and Article Endnotes

CHAPTER 1

Burns, T., & Stalker, G. (1961). *The Management of Innovation*. London: Tavistock.

Davis, S. (1984). Political methodology and social change: Issue development in a women's studies course. In D. Hai (Ed.), *Women and men in organizations: Teaching strategies* (pp. 33–41). Washington, DC: George Washington University.

Deckard, B. (1983). *The women's movement*. New York: Harper and Row.

Ferguson, K. (1984). *The feminist case against bureaucracy*. Philadelphia: Temple University Press.

Harari, O., & Mukai, L. (1990). A new decade demands a new breed of manager. *Management Review, 79*(8), 20–24.

Kanter, R. (1987, Jan.). From status to contribution: Some organizational implications of the changing basis for pay. *Personnel*, pp. 12–37.

Kanter, R. (1989, Nov./Dec.). The new managerial work. *Harvard Business Review*, pp. 85–92.

Mintzberg, H. (1975, July/Aug.). The manager's job: Folklore and fact. *Harvard Business Review*, pp. 49–61.

Pinchot, G. (1985). *Intrapreneuring*. New York: Harper & Row.

Ruth, S. (1980). *Issues in women's studies*. Geneva, IL: Houghton Mifflin.

Sayles, L. (1964). *Managerial behavior*. New York: McGraw-Hill.

Snyder, Neil, & Glueck, W. (1980). How managers plan—the analysis of managers' activities. *Long Range Planning, 13*, 75.

CHAPTER 2

Abarbanel, K. (1987). The drop-out myth. *Executive Female, 10*(3), 6.

Baumeister, R. (1986). *Identity, cultural change, and the struggle for self*. New York: Oxford University Press.

Bell, E. (1990). The bicultural life experience of career-oriented black women. *Journal of Organizational Behavior, 11*, 459–477.

Billard, M. (1990, Apr.). Women on the verge of being CEO. *Business Month*, pp. 26–47.

Boone, L., & Johnson, J. (1980). Profiles of the 801 men and 1 woman at the top. *Business Horizons, 23*(1), 47–48.

Cannings, K., & Montmarquette, C. (1991). Managerial momentum: A simultaneous model of the career progress of male and female managers. *Industrial and Labor Relations Review, 44*(2), 213–228.

Colwill, N. (1982). *The new partnership: Women and men in organizations*. Palo Alto, CA: Mayfield Publishing.

Donnell, S., & Hall, J. (1980, Spring). Men and women as managers: A significant case of no significant difference. *Organizational Dynamics, 8*, 60–77.

Doyle, K. (1989, Mar.). Madam C. J. Walker: First black woman millionaire. *American History Illustrated*, pp. 24–25.

Dusky, L., & Zeitz, B. (1988). *The best companies for women*. New York: Simon & Schuster.

Fierman, J. (1990, July 30). Why women still don't hit the top. *Fortune*, pp. 40, 42, 46, 50, 54, 58, 62.

Filipowski, D. (1991, June). Life after HR. *Personnel Journal*, p. 64.

Fisher, A. (1992, Sept. 21). When will women get to the top? *Fortune*, pp. 44–48, 52, 56.

Forbes, J., & Piercy, J. (1983, Sept./Oct.). Rising to the top: Executive women in 1983 and beyond. *Business Horizons*, pp. 38–48.

Forbes, J., Piercy, J., & Hayes, T. (1988, Nov./Dec.). Women executives: Breaking down barriers? *Business Horizons*, pp. 6–9.

Garland, S. (1991, Sept. 2). Commentary: How to keep women managers on the corporate ladder. *Business Week*, p. 64.

Gilson, E., & Kane, S. (1987). *Unnecessary choices*. New York: William Morrow.

Gordus, J., & Oshiro, M. (1986). Ethnic-minority women in the private corporation: The case of officials and managers. In W. Van Horne (Ed.), *Ethnicity and women* (pp. 157–183). Madison: Board of Regents of the University of Wisconsin.

Hamill, K. (1956). Women as bosses. *Fortune, 53*(6), 104–108, 214–216, 219–220.

Hammonds, K., & Symonds, W. (1991, Apr. 15.). Taking baby steps toward a daddy track. *Business Week*, pp. 90–92.

Hatcher, M. (1991). The corporate woman of the 1990s. *Psychology of Women Quarterly, 15*, 251–259.

Hellwig, B. (1985, Apr.). 73 women ready to run corporate America. *Working Woman*, pp. 98–101, 146, 148, 150.

Hellwig, B. (1992, Sept./Oct.). Executive female's breakthrough 50. *Executive Female*, pp. 43–46.

Hennig, M., & Jardim, A. (1977). *The managerial woman.* New York: Pocket Books.

Hilton/Sucherman Productions and The Leigh Bureau. (1990). *Meeting the Challenge.* Irwindale, CA: Barr Films.

Hurtado, A. (1989, Summer). Relating to privilege: Seduction and rejection in the subordination of white women and women of color. *Signs,* pp. 833–856.

Insel, B. (1987, May). The making of a top manager. *Working Woman,* pp. 105–109, 191.

Jacobs, N., & Hardesty, S. (1987, June). Why some women are dropping out. *Management Review,* pp. 61–63.

Jenkins, M. (1988). She issued the call: Josephine St. Pierre Ruffin 1842–1924. *Sage,* 5, 74–76.

Kaledin, E. (1984). *American women in the 1950s: Mothers and more.* Boston: Twayne.

Karsten, M., & Kleisath, S. (1986). Team sports as a predictor of business success. *Central State Business Review,* 5, 2–4.

Karsten, M., & Kleisath, S. (1987). Extracurricular activities and management success: A comparison between the sexes. *Central State Business Review,* 6, 26–27.

Konrad, W. (1990, Aug. 6). Welcome to the women-friendly company. *Business Week,* pp. 48–55.

Labor agency sees progress in breaking firms' "glass ceilings." (1992, Aug. 12). *The Wall Street Journal,* pp. B1, B4.

Larkin, M. (1984). Female and male executives compared. *The Executive Female,* 7, 46.

Lemkau, J. (1979). Personality and background characteristics of women in male-dominated occupations. *Psychology of Women Quarterly,* 4(2), 221–239.

Moore, L., & Rickel, A. (1980). Characteristics of women in traditional and non-traditional managerial roles. *Personnel Psychology,* 33, 317–333.

Morrison, A. (1992). Leadership diversity and leadership challenge. *Issues & Observations,* 12(3), 1–4.

Morrison, A., & Von Glinow. (1990). Women and minorities in management. *American Psychologist,* 5(2), 200–207.

Morrison, A., White, R., Van Velsor, E., & the Center for Creative Leadership. (1987). *Breaking the glass ceiling.* Reading, MA: Addison-Wesley.

Nelson, S. (1987). *Two Dollars and a dream.* New York: Filmakers Library.

Nkomo, S. (1988). Race and sex: The forgotten case of the black female manager. In S. Rose & L. Larwood (Eds.), *Women's careers: Pathways and pitfalls* (pp. 133–150). New York: Praeger.

Ray, E. (1988). The concrete ceiling. *Executive Female,* 11(6), 34-38.

Raynolds, E. (1987). Management women in the corporate workplace: Possibilities for the year 2000. *Human Resource Management,* 26(2), 265-276.

Roman, M. (1990, Oct.). Women, beware: An MBA doesn't mean equal pay. *Business Week,* p. 57.

Samon, K. (1991, July). Great expectations: An update on the Wharton women of '80. *Working Woman,* pp. 66–72.

Schwartz, F. (1989, Jan./Feb.). Management women and the new facts of life. *Harvard Business Review,* pp. 65–76.

Taylor, A. (1986, Aug. 18). Why women managers are bailing out. *Fortune*, pp. 16–23.

U.S. Bureau of the Census. (1992). *Statistical Abstract of the United States*. Washington, D.C.: U.S. Department of Commerce. Table 220, p. 144.

Van Horne, W. (1986). *Ethnicity and women*. Madison: Board of Regents of the University of Wisconsin.

Vaudrin, D. (1984). Factors contributing to the upward mobility of women managers and an exploratory study of mentoring and other influential relationships. Ph.D. Diss., Seattle University. (From *Dissertation Abstracts International*, 1983, *44*, University Microfilms No. 8328367)

Wentling, R. (1992). Women in middle management: Their career development and aspirations. *Business Horizons*, *35*(1), 47–54.

Women on boards. (1992, June 16). *The Wall Street Journal*, p. B1.

CHAPTER 3

Bird, C. (1976). *Enterprising women*. New York: W. W. Norton.

Deckard, B. (1983). *The women's movement*. New York: Harper and Row.

Famous firsts: Sibyl of a modern science. (1964, Nov. 21). *Business Week*, pp. 196, 198, 200.

Fiedler, F. (1967). *A theory of leadership effectiveness*. New York: McGraw-Hill.

Follett, M. (1924). *Creative experience*. New York: Longmans, Green.

Fox, E. (1968, Nov./Dec.). Mary Parker Follett: The enduring contribution. *Public Administration Review*, pp. 520–529.

Goodmeasure, Inc. (1979). *Tale of O: On being different in organizations*. Cambridge: Author.

Greenwood, R. (1985, Summer). Lecture in administrative theory and practice course. NOVA University. Ft. Lauderdale, FL.

Kanter, R. (1983). *The change masters*. New York: Simon & Schuster.

Kanter, R. (1989). *When giants learn to dance*. New York: Simon & Schuster.

Kanter, R., Stein, B., & Jick, T. (1992). *The challenge of organizational change: How companies experience it and leaders guide it*. New York: The Free Press.

The professional woman. (1906). *The Spectator*, pp. 250–251.

Schlagenhaft, S. (1988). *Popular opinions and legal status of working women from the late 19th and early 20th centuries*. Unpublished paper.

Yost, E. (1949). *Frank and Lillian Gilbreth: Partners for life*. New Brunswick, NJ: Rutgers University Press.

CHAPTER 4

Ansberry, C., & Adler, S. (1991, Feb. 27). USX will settle bias case, is sued. *The Wall Street Journal*, p. B6.

Deckard, B. (1983). *The women's movement*. New York: Harper and Row.

Equal Employment Advisory Council. (1981). *Comparable worth: A symposium on the issues and alternatives*. Washington, DC: Author.

Gleckman, H., Smart, T., Dwyer, P., Segal, T., & Weber, J. (1991, July 8). Race in the workplace: Is affirmative action working? *Business Week*, pp. 50–62.

Holleran, P., & Schwarz, M. (1988, Winter). Another look at comparable worth's impact on black women. *The Review of Black Political Economy*, pp. 97–102.

Jones, J. (1980, Fall). Lecture in equal employment law course. University of Wisconsin-Madison.

Justices adopt fetal position. (1991, Mar. 22). *The Wall Street Journal*, p. A8.

Kilpatrick, L. (1990, Mar. 9). In Ontario, "equal pay for equal work" becomes a reality, but not very easily. *The Wall Street Journal*, p. B1.

Ledbetter, B. (1985, Jan.). Women in higher education: Traditions, transitions, and (a few) revolutions. Keynote address at conference, Saint Louis University, Metropolitan College, Division of Continuing Education.

Malveaux, J. (1985–86). Comparable worth and its impact on black women. *The Review of Black Political Economy*, 14(2–3), 49–58.

Roman, M. (1990, Oct. 29). Women, beware: An MBA doesn't mean equal pay. *Business Week*, p. 57.

Twomey, D. (1990). *Equal employment opportunity law*. Chicago: South-Western Publishing.

CHAPTER 5

Alexander, K. (1990, July 25). Both racism and sexism block the path to management for minority women. *The Wall Street Journal*, pp. B1, B5.

Anderson, C., & Hunsaker, P. (1985, Feb.). Why there's romancing at the office and why it's everybody's problem. *Personnel*, pp. 57–63.

Biles, G. (1981, June). A program guide for preventing sexual harassment in the workplace. *Personnel Administrator*, pp. 49–56.

Chrysler takes harassment firing to Supreme Court. (1992, Sept. 23). *The Wisconsin State Journal*, p. 1.

Clarke, L. (1986, Apr.). Women supervisors experience sexual harassment too. *Supervisory Management*, pp. 35–36.

Denis, M. (1984–85, Winter). Race harassment discrimination: A problem that won't go away? *Employee Relations Law Journal*, pp. 415–434.

Deutschman, A. (1991, Nov. 4). Dealing with sexual harassment. *Fortune*, pp. 145, 148.

Ford, R., & McLaughlin, F. (1988). Sexual harassment at work. *Business Horizons* 31(6), 14–19.

Fritz, N. (1989, Feb.). In focus: Sexual harassment and the working woman. *Personnel*, pp. 4–8.

Galen, M., Weber, J., & Cuneo, A. (1991, Oct. 18). Sexual harassment: Out of the shadows. *Business Week*, pp. 30–31.

Greene, R. (1986, June 16). A pattern of fornication. *Forbes*, p. 66.

Hayes, A. (1991, Oct. 11). How the courts define harassment. *The Wall Street Journal*, p. B1.

Ingrassia, L. (1991, Oct. 18). Thomas battle creates wariness, uncertainty about office humor. *The Wall Street Journal*, p. B2.

In many small businesses, harassment is big worry. (1991, Oct. 18). *The Wall Street Journal*, p. B3.

Lublin, J. S. (1991, Oct. 18). As harassment charges rise, more firms fight back. *The Wall Street Journal*, p. B3.

Lublin, J. S. (1991, Dec. 2). Sexual harassment moves atop agenda in many executive education programs. *The Wall Street Journal*, p. B1.

MacKinnon, C. (1992). Sexual harassment: the experience. In M. Eskenazi & D. Gallen (Eds.), *Sexual harassment: Know your rights!* (pp. 23–60). New York: Carroll & Graf.

Meyer, A. (1992). Getting to the heart of sexual harassment. *HRMagazine*, 37(7), 82–84.

Moskal, B. (1991, Nov. 18). Sexual harassment: An update. *Industry Week*, pp. 37–38, 40–41.

Pereira, J. (1988, Feb. 10). Women allege sexist atmosphere in offices constitutes harassment. *The Wall Street Journal*, p. 21.

The power pinch: Sexual harassment in the workplace. (1981). Northbrook, IL: MTI Teleprograms Inc. [Film].

Riddle, J. (1992, Mar. 8). Motel room humor leaves Blang's listeners cringing. *Wisconsin State Journal*, p. 6C.

Sandroff, R. (1992, June). Sexual harassment: The inside story. *Working Woman*, pp. 47–51.

Schmitt, E. (1990, Sept. 12). 2 in 3 military women report harassment. *Wisconsin State Journal*, p. 2A.

Segal, T., & Schiller, Z. (1991, Oct. 28). Six experts suggest ways to negotiate the minefield. *Business Week*, p. 33.

Solomon, C. (1991). Sexual harassment after the Thomas hearings. *Personnel Journal*, 70(12), 32, 34–36.

Solomon, J. (1990, Aug. 22). Love at the workplace, but no labor's lost. *The Wall Street Journal*, p. B1.

Stuart, P. (1991). Prevent sexual harassment in your work force. *Personnel Journal*, 70(12), 34.

Templin, N. (1991, Oct. 18). As women assume more power, charges filed by men may rise. *The Wall Street Journal*, p. B3.

Wagner, E. (1992). *Sexual harassment in the workplace.* New York: Creative Solutions, Inc.

Westhoff, L. (1986, Feb.). What to do about corporate romance. *Management Review*, pp. 50–55.

Who's hurt and who's liable: Sexual harassment in the schools—A curriculum guide for school personnel. (1986). Boston: Massachusetts Department of Education.

CHAPTER 6

Adler, N. (1991). *International dimensions of organizational behavior* (2nd ed.). Boston: PWS Kent.

Cohen, J. (1991, Jan.). Managing tomorrow's workforce today. *Management Review*, pp. 17–21.

Cox, T. (1991). The multicultural organization. *Academy of Management Executive*, 5(2), 34–47.

Fine, M., Johnson, F., & Ryan, M. (1990). Cultural diversity in the workplace. *Public Personnel Management, 19*(3), 305–319.

Hanamura, S. (1989). Working with people who are different. *Training & Development Journal, 43*(6), 110–114.

Kennedy, J., & Everest, A. (1991). Put diversity in context. *Personnel Journal, 70*(9), 50–54.

Leonard, W. (1991). Ways to make diversity programs work. *HRMagazine, 36*(4), 37–39, 98.

Livingston, A. (1991, Jan.). 12 companies that do the right thing. *Working Woman,* pp. 57, 59, 61.

Mandell, B., & Kohler-Gray, S. (1990, Mar.). Management development that values diversity. *Personnel,* pp. 41–47.

Overman, S. (1991). Managing the diverse workforce. *HRMagazine, 36*(4), 32–36.

Piturro, M., & Mahoney, S. (1991, May/June). Managing diversity. *Executive Female,* pp. 45–48.

Solomon, J. (1989, Feb. 10). Firms address workers' cultural variety. *The Wall Street Journal,* p. B1.

Songer, N. (1991). Work force diversity. *Business and Economic Review, 37*(3), 3–6.

Thomas, R. (1991). *Beyond race and gender.* New York: AMACOM.

CHAPTER 7

Text References

Andersen, M. (1988). *Thinking about women: Sociological perspectives on sex and gender* (2nd ed.). New York: Macmillan.

Astrachan, A. (1986). *How men feel: Their response to women's demands for equality and power.* Garden City, NY: Anchor Press/Doubleday.

Baron, A. (1984). The achieving woman manager: So where are the rewards? *Business Quarterly, 49*(2), 70–73.

Bem, S. (1975). *Androgyny and mental health.* Paper presented to meeting of the American Psychological Association.

Blaun, R. (1988). Plugging into the power source. *Executive Female, 11,* 18–22, 76.

Bly, R. (1992). *Iron John: A book about men.* New York: Random House.

Bowman, G., Worthy, N., & Greyser, S. (1965, July/Aug.). Are women executives people? *Harvard Business Review,* pp. 15–28, 164–178.

Brenner, O., Tomkiewicz, J., & Schein, V. (1989). The relationship between sex role stereotypes and requisite management characteristics. *Academy of Management Journal 32,* 662–669.

Doering, C., Brodie, R., Kraemer, T., Becker, H., & Hamburg, D. (1974). Plasma testosterone levels and psychologic measures in men over a two-month period. In R. Friedman & R. Richert (Eds.), *Sex differences in behavior* (pp. 413–431). New York: Wiley.

Ferguson, H. (1985). *A study of the characteristics of American Indian professional women in Oklahoma.* Columbus: Ohio State University.

Hall, R., & Sandler, B. (1984). *Out of the classroom: A chilly campus climate for women?* Washington, DC: Project on the Status and Education of Women of the Association of American Colleges.

Heilman, M., Block, C., Simon, M., & Martell, R. (1989). Has anything changed? Current characterizations of men, women, and managers. *Journal of Applied Psychology, 74,* 935–942.

Henderson, J., & Marples, B. (1986). When older women work for younger women. In L. Moore (Ed.), *Not as far as you think: The realities of working women* (pp. 107–120). Lexington, MA: Lexington Books.

How men adjust to a female boss. (1977, Sept. 5). *Business Week,* pp. 90, 94.

Hyde, J., & Linn, M. (1988). Are there sex differences in verbal abilities? A meta-analysis. *Psychological Bulletin, 10*(4), 53–69.

Jacklin, C. (1989). Female and male: Issues of gender. *American Psychologist, 64,* 127–133.

Kagan, J., & Malveaux, J. (1986, May). The uneasy alliance of the boss and the secretary. *Working Woman,* pp. 105–109.

Kanter, R. (1977). *Men and women of the corporation.* New York: Basic Books.

Konrad, W. (1990, Aug. 6). Welcome to the women-friendly company. *Business Week,* pp. 48–55.

Kruser, P. (1993, June). What women think of women bosses. *Working Woman,* pp. 40–43, 84, 86.

Maccoby, E., & Jacklin, C. (1975). Sex differences and their implications for management. In F. Gordon and M. Strober (Eds.), *Bringing women into management* (pp. 23–38). St. Louis: McGraw-Hill.

Massengill, D., & DiMarco, N. (1979). Sex role stereotypes and requisite management characteristics: A current replication. *Sex Roles, 5,* 561–570.

Powell, G. (1988). *Women and men in management.* Newbury Park, CA: Sage Publications.

Powell, G. (1990). One more time: Do female and male managers differ? *Academy of Management Executive, 4*(3), 68–75.

Powell, G., & Butterfield, D. (1979). The "good manager": masculine or androgynous? *Academy of Management Journal, 22,* 395–403.

Ragins, B., & Sundstrom, E. (1990). Gender and perceived power in management-subordinate relations. *Journal of Occupational Psychology, 63,* 273–287.

Ramos, M. (1981). *A study of black women in management.* Ph. D. diss., University of Massachusetts.

Rigdon, J. (1991, July 10). Exploding the myth: Asian-Americans increasingly suffer emotional toll. *The Wall Street Journal,* p. A1.

Sargent, A. (1981). *The androgynous manager.* New York: AMACOM.

Schein, V. (1973). The relationship between sex role stereotypes and requisite management characteristics. *Journal of Applied Psychology, 57,* 95–100.

Sutton, C., & Moore, K. (1985, Sept./Oct.). Executive women 20 years later. *Harvard Business Review,* pp. 43–66.

Wade, T. Joel, Thompson, V., Tashakkori, A., & Valenti, E. (1989). A longitudinal analysis of sex by race differences in predictors of adolescent self-esteem. *Personality & Individual Differences, 10*(7), 717–729.

Endnotes, Gary Powell, "One More Time: Do Female and Male Managers Differ?"

1. J. Grant, Women as Managers: What They Can Offer to Organizations, *Organizational Dynamics*, Winter 1988, 56–63.

2. F. N. Schwartz, Management Women and the New Facts of Life, *Harvard Business Review*, January-February 1989, 65–76.

3. U.S. Department of Labor, Bureau of Labor Statistics, Employment and Earnings, October 1989, Table A-22, 29; *Handbook of Labor Statistics*, Bulletin 2175, December 1983, Table 16, 44–46; J. B. Forbes, J. E. Piercy, & T. L. Hayes, Women Executives: Breaking Down Barriers?, *Business Horizons*, November-December 1988, 6–9.

4. For a review of research on sex role stereotypes, see D. M. Ruble & T. N. Ruble, Sex Stereotypes, in A. G. Miller (Ed.), *In the Eye of the Beholder* (New York: Praeger, 1982).

5. For a full report of this review with complete references, see G. N. Powell, Chapter 5, Managing People, in *Women and Men in Management* (Newbury Park, CA: Sage, 1988).

6. The technical terms used by researchers for these types of behavior are initiating structure behavior and consideration behavior.

7. G. H. Dobbins & S. J. Platz, Sex Differences in Leadership: How Real Are They? *Academy of Management Review*, 1986, 11, 118–127.

8. G. H. Dobbins, Effects of Gender on Leaders' Responses to Poor Performers: An Attributional Interpretation, *Academy of Management Journal*, 1985, 28, 587–598.

9. D. Instone, B. Major, & B. B. Bunker, Gender, Self Confidence, and Social Influence Strategies: An Organizational Simulation, *Journal of Personality and Social Psychology*, 1983, 44, 322–333.

10. S. M. Donnell & J. Hall, Men and Women as Managers: A Significant Case of No Significant Difference, *Organizational Dynamics*, Spring 1980, 71.

11. Commitment to work, job, career, and organizations have all been examined in different streams of research. This article simply refers to commitment in general, since each type of commitment suggests a greater degree of involvement in work in spite of fine differences among them.

12. L. H. Chusmir, Job Commitment and the Organizational Woman, *Academy of Management Review*, 1982, 7, 595–602.

13. K. M. Bartol & D. A. Butterfield, Sex Effects in Evaluating Leaders, *Journal of Applied Psychology* 1976, 61, 446–454; J. Adams, R. W. Rice, & J. Instone, Follower Attitudes toward Women and Judgments concerning Performance by Female and Male Leaders, *Academy of Management Journal*, 1984, 27, 636–643.

14. Grant, 62.

15. G. N. Powell, Career Development and the Woman Manager: A Social Power Perspective, *Personnel*, May-June 1980, 22–32.

16. P. Watts, Bias Busting: Diversity Training in the Workplace, *Management Review*, December 1987, 51–54; B. Zeitz & L. Dusky, Levi Strauss, in *The Best Companies for Women* (New York: Simon and Schuster, 1988).

17. L. Festinger, *A Theory of Cognitive Dissonance* (Evanston, IL: Row, Peterson, 1957).

18. *The Corporate Woman Officer* (New York: Heidrich & Struggles, 1986); G. R. Roche, Much Ado about Mentors, *Harvard Business Review*, January-February 1979, 14–28; D. M. Hunt & C. Michael, Mentorship: A Career Training and Development Tool, *Academy of Management Review*, 1983, 8, 475–485; R. N. Noe, Women and Mentoring: A Review and Research Agenda, *Academy of Management Review*, 1988, 13, 65–78.

19. Women and Minority Workers in Business Find a Mentor Can Be a Rare Commodity, *Wall Street Journal*, November 11, 1987, 39.

20. K. E. Kram, Chapter 7, Creating Conditions That Encourage Mentoring, in *Mentoring at Work* (Glenview, IL: Scott, Foresman, 1985).

21. M. H. Brenner, Management Development for Women, *Personnel Journal*, March 1972, 166.

22. Programs: Center for Creative Leadership, Greensboro, NC, July 1988-June 1989, 15.

23. Zeitz & Dusky.

CHAPTER 8

Text References

Hennig, M., & Jardim, A. (1977). *The managerial woman.* New York: Pocket Books.

Karsten, M., & Kleisath, S. (1986). Team sports as a predictor of business success. *Central State Business Review, 5,* 2–4.

Karsten, M., & Kleisath, S. (1987). Extracurricular activities and management success: A comparison between the sexes. *Central State Business Review 6,* 26–27.

Maccoby, E., & Jacklin, C. (1974). *The Psychology of Sex Differences.* Stanford, CA: Stanford.

Maccoby, E., & Jacklin, C. (1975). Sex differences and their implications for management. In F. Gordon and M. Strober (Eds.), *Bringing women into management* (pp. 23–38). St. Louis: McGraw-Hill.

References, Joan E. Riedle, "A Brief Look at Gender Role Socialization"

Bem, S. L. (1981). Gender schema theory: A cognitive account of sex-typing. *Psychological Review, 88:* 354–364.

Bem, S. L. (1983). Gender schema theory and its implications for child development: Raising gender-aschematic children in a gender-schematic society. *Signs, 8:* 598–616.

Bem, S. L., & Bem, D. J. (1970). Case study of a nonconscious ideology: Training the woman to know her place. In D. J. Bem (Ed.), *Beliefs, attitudes, and human affairs* (pp. 89–99). Belmont, CA: Brooks/Cole.

Condry, J., & Condry, S. (1976). Sex differences: A study of the eye of the beholder. *Child Development, 47:* 812–819.

Gettys, L. D., & Cann, A. (1981). Children's perceptions of occupational sex stereotypes. *Sex Roles, 7:* 301–308.

Hyde, J. S. (1985). *Half the human experience: The psychology of women* (3rd ed.). Lexington, MA: D.C. Heath & Co.

Mead, M. (1935; 1963). *Sex and temperament in three primitive societies.* New York: William Morrow & Co.

Mischel, W. (1966). A social-learning view of sex differences in behavior. In E. E. Maccoby (Ed.), *The development of sex differences* (pp. 56–81). Stanford: Stanford University Press.

Mischel, W. (1970). Sex-typing and socialization. In P. H. Mussen (Ed.), *Carmichael's manual of child psychology* (Vol. 2, 3rd ed., pp. 3–72). New York: Wiley.

Reis, H. T., & Wright, S. (1982). Knowledge of sex-role stereotypes in children aged 3 to 5. *Sex Roles*, 8:1049–1056.

Secord, P. F., Bevan, W., & Katz, B. (1956). The Negro stereotype and perceptual accentuation. *Journal of Abnormal and Social Psychology*, 53:78–83.

Smith, P. A., & Midlarsky, E. (1985). Empirically derived conceptions of femaleness and maleness: A current view. *Sex Roles*, 12:313–328.

Tajfel, H. (1981). *Human groups and social categories: Studies in social psychology.* Cambridge: Cambridge University Press.

Tavris, C., & Wade, C. (1984). *The longest war: Sex differences in perspective* (2nd ed.). San Diego: Harcourt Brace Jovanovich.

Unger, R., & Crawford, M. (1992). *Women and gender: A feminist psychology.* New York: McGraw-Hill.

Weitzman, L. J. (1979). *Sex role socialization: A focus on women.* Palo Alto, CA: Mayfield.

Will, J. A., Self, P. A., & Datan, N. (1976). Maternal behavior and perceived sex of infant. *American Journal of Orthopsychiatry*, 46:135–139.

CHAPTER 9

Burke, R., & McKeen, C. (1990). Mentoring in organizations: Implications for women. *Journal of Business Ethics*, 9, 317–332.

Dunbar, D. (1990, Mar.). Desperately seeking mentors. *Black Enterprise*, pp. 53–56.

Garrison, C., & Comer, K. (1984). Professional advancement: Is mentoring the key to success? In M. Swoboda (Ed.), *Is mentoring the key to success?* (pp. 4–13). Madison, WI: Office of Women and Equal Opportunity Programs for the University of Wisconsin System. (Proceedings from conference, Wisconsin Planning Committee, National Identification Program, American Council of Education, Madison, WI.)

Hennefrund, W. (1986). Taking the measure of mentoring. *Association Management*, 38, 78–83.

Holland, J. (1978). *The occupations finder.* Palo Alto, CA: Consulting Psychologists Press.

Josefowitz, N. (1980). *Paths to power.* Reading, MA: Addison-Wesley.

Kizelos, P. (1990, Apr.). Take my mentor, please! *Training*, pp. 49–55.

Lawrie, J. (1987, Mar.). How to establish a mentoring program. *Training and Development Journal*, pp. 25–27.

Missirian, A. (1982). *The corporate connection: Why executive women need mentors to reach the top.* Englewood Cliffs, NJ: Prentice-Hall.

Myers, I. (1987). *Introduction to type.* Palo Alto, CA: Consulting Psychologists Press.

Nkomo, S. (1988). *Race and sex: The forgotten case of the black female manager.* In S. Rose & L. Larwood (Eds.), *Women's careers: Pathways and pitfalls* (pp. 133–150). New York: Praeger.

Nussbaum, B. (1991, Oct. 7). A career survival kit. *Business Week,* pp. 98–100.

Pell, A., & Furbay, A. (1975). *College student guide to career planning.* New York: Simon & Schuster.

Thomas, D. (1989). Mentoring and irrationality: The role of racial taboos. *Human Resource Management, 28,* 279–290.

Zey, M. (1985, Feb.). Mentor programs: Making the right moves. *Personnel Journal,* pp. 53–55.

CHAPTER 10

Bhatnagar, D. (1988). Professional women in organizations: New paradigms for research and action. *Sex Roles, 18*(5–6), 343–354.

Brass, D. (1985). Men's and women's networks: A study of interaction patterns and influence in an organization. *Academy of Management Journal, 28,* 327–343.

Crossen, C. (1990). Pssst! The new way to network is... *Working Woman, 15*(9), 154, 156.

Denton, T. (1990). Bonding and supportive relationships among black professional women: Rituals of restoration. *Journal of Organizational Behavior, 11,* 447–457.

Dunbar, D. (1991, Mar.). Back-to-school daze. *Black Enterprise,* p. 17.

Editors of *Working Woman.* (1984). *Who you know: The Working Woman report.* New York: Simon & Schuster.

Farish, P. (1987, Sept.). Aspiring women. *Personnel Administrator,* p. 14.

Feiring, C., & Coates, D. (1987). Social networks and gender differences in the life space of opportunity: Introduction. *Sex Roles, 17,* 611–619.

George, K. (1988, Mar.). Women on management, excellence, networking, how to make it happen. *Association Management,* pp. 42–47.

Kleiman, C. (1980). *Women's networks.* New York: Lippincott & Crowell.

Michaelson, G. (1988, Aug.). It's a small world if you've got a big network. *Sales & Marketing Management,* p. 74.

Mueller, R. (1987, Sept./Oct.). Social networks and corporate culture. *The Corporate Board,* pp. 10–13.

The old school ties that bond. (1986, Aug. 25). *U.S. News & World Report,* pp. 53–55.

Olson, M., & Lippitt, R. (1985). Networking for support, growth, and gain. *Training, 22,* 65–67.

Pearson, J. (1989, May). Network your way to the top! *The Toast Master,* pp. 8–11.

Salzman, M. (1986, Oct. 6). The lacrosse connection. *Forbes*, pp. 172–173.

Smith, L. (1991, July/Aug.). Networking: Breaking in. *Executive Female*, p. 19.

Solomon, C. (1991, Oct.). Networks empower employees. *Personnel Journal*, p. 51.

Sonnenberg, F. (1990, Sept.). The professional (and personal) profits of networking. *Training and Development Journal*, pp. 55–57.

Women's job contacts may hold them back. (1991, Apr. 4). *The Wall Street Journal*, p. B1.

CHAPTER 11

Agee, M. C. (1984). *Powerplay: What really happened at Bendix*. New York: Simon & Schuster.

Baron, A. (1979). Assertiveness quotient and scoring assertiveness quotient. In *Study Guide for Business C216-A46 Assertiveness in the Business Environment* (pp. 45–47). Madison: University of Wisconsin-Extension, 1979.

Bower, G., & Bower, S. (1976). *Asserting yourself*. Reading, MA: Addison-Wesley.

Cammaert, L., & Larsen, C. (1979). *A woman's choice: A guide to decision making*. Champaign, IL: Research Press.

Duke, B., & Sitterly, C. (1988). *A woman's place: Management*. Englewood Cliffs, NJ: Prentice-Hall.

Fairhurst, G., & Snavely, B. (1983). Majority and token minority group relationships: Power acquisition and communication. *Academy of Management Review, 8*, 292–300.

French, J., & Raven, B. (1959). The bases of social power. In D. Cartwright (Ed.), *Studies in social power* (pp. 150–167). Ann Arbor: University of Michigan.

Hunsaker, J., & Hunsaker, P. (1990). *Strategies and skills for managerial women*. Cincinnati, OH: South-Western Publishing.

Ivancevich, J., Szilagyi, A., & Wallace, M. (1977). *Organizational behavior and performance*. Santa Monica, CA: Goodyear Publishing.

Kanter, R. (1977). *Men and women of the corporation*. New York: Basic Books.

Kennedy, M. (1989, Jan./Feb.). Corporate politics can be dangerous and dirty: Here's how to come out alive—and thrive. *Executive Female*, pp. 23–25, 63.

Laws, J. (1975). The psychology of tokenism: An analysis. *Sex Roles, 1*, 51–67.

Morgan, P., & Baker, H. (1985, Aug.) Building a professional image: Learning assertiveness. *Supervisory Management*, pp. 15–20.

Ott, E. (1989). Effects of the male-female ratio at work: Policewomen and male nurses. *Psychology of Women Quarterly, 13*, 41–58.

Ray, E. (1988). The concrete ceiling. *Executive Female, 11*(6), 34–38, 41–58.

Reece, B., & Brandt, R. (1990). *Effective human relations in organizations* (4th ed.). Geneva, IL: Houghton Mifflin.

Rogers, L. (1989, Sept.). Getting heard: How to communicate with power. *New Woman*, p. 102.

Yoder, J. (1991). Rethinking tokenism: Looking beyond numbers. *Gender & Society, 5*(2), 178–192.

Yoder, J., Adams, J., & Prince, H. (1983). The price of a token. *Journal of Political and Military Sociology, 11*, 325–337.

CHAPTER 12

Text References

Allen, V., Wilder, D., & Atkinson, M. (1983). Multiple group membership and social identity. In T. Sarbin & K. Scheibe (Eds.), *Studies in social identity* (pp. 92–115). New York: Praeger.

Baron, A. (1984). Career and family: Can they mix? *Business Quarterly, 14*(1), 128–132.

Baron, A. (1987, Sept./Oct.). Working partners: Career-committed mothers and their husbands. *Business Horizons,* pp. 45–50.

Baruch, G., & Barnett, R. (1986). Role quality, multiple role involvement, and psychological well-being in midlife women. *Journal of Personality and Social Psychology, 51*(3), 578–585.

Bem, D. (1987, Fall). A consumer's guide to dual-career marriages. *ILR Report,* pp. 10–12.

Collie, H. (1989, Sept.). Two salaries, one relocation: What's a company to do? *Personnel Administrator,* pp. 54–57.

Connelly, J. (1990, Sept. 24). How dual income couples cope. *Fortune,* pp. 129–136.

Dahl, J. (1985, June 24). As long distance marriages rise, some couples actually prefer it. *The Wall Street Journal,* p. 17.

Friedman, D. E. (1990). Work and family: The new strategic plan. *Human Resource Planning, 13*(2), 79–89.

Gray, J. (1983). The married professional woman: An examination of her role conflicts and coping strategies. *Psychology of Women Quarterly, 7,* 243–253.

Gutman, H. (1976). *The black family in slavery and freedom.* New York: Pantheon.

Hall, D. (1990, Winter). *Promoting work/family balance: An organization change approach, 18,* 4–18.

Hall, D., & Richter, J. (1988). Balancing work life and home life: What can organizations do to help? *Academy of Management Executive, 2,* 213–223.

Hochschild, A., & Machung, A. (1989). *The second shift.* New York: Viking.

Lee, N. (1981, Jan.). The dual career couple: Benefits and pitfalls. *Management Review,* pp. 46–51.

Lobel, S. (1991). Allocation of investment in work and family roles: Alternative theories and implications for research. *The Academy of Management Review, 16,* 507–521.

Mullings, L. (1986). Uneven development: Class, race, and gender in the United States before 1900. In E. Leacock & H. Safa (Eds.), *Women's work: Development and the division of labor by gender* (pp. 41–57). South Hadley, MA: Bergin & Garvey.

Newgren, K., Kellogg, C., & Gardner, W. (1987, Autumn). Corporate policies affecting dual-career couples. *SAM Advanced Management Journal,* pp. 4–8.

O'Brien, T., Gupta, U., & Marsh, B. (1993, Feb. 8). Most small businesses appear prepared to cope with new family-leave rules. *The Wall Street Journal,* p. B1–B2.

Rapoport, R., & Rapoport, R. (1976). *Dual career families re-examined.* New York: Harper and Row.

Reynolds, C., & Bennett, R. (1991, Mar.). The career couple challenge. *Personnel Journal*, pp. 46–48.

Stoner, C., & Hartman, R. (1990, May/June). Family responsibilities and career progress: The good, the bad, and the ugly. *Business Horizons*, pp. 7–14.

When the mother-to-be is an executive. (1983, Apr. 11). *Business Week*, pp. 128, 132.

Wilson, M., Tolson, T., Hinton, I., & Kiernan, M. (1990). Flexibility and sharing of childcare duties in black families. *Sex Roles, 22*, 408–423.

References, Dana E. Friedman, "Work and Family: The New Strategic Plan"

Administration on Aging and Elder Services of the Merrimack Valley, Inc. Elder Care Project for Dependent Elderly Relatives of Wang Employees. (Lowell, MA: 1987).

Berkeley Planning Associates. Small Business Options for Child Care. Report to the Small Business Administration. (Washington, DC: 1988).

Bohen, H., and Viveros-Long, A. *Balancing Jobs and Family* (Philadelphia, PA: Temple University Press, 1981).

Bureau of National Affairs. *Work and Family: A Changing Dynamic.* (Washington, DC: BNA Special Report, 1986).

Catalyst. Maternity and Parental Leaves of Absence. (New York: Catalyst, 1983).

Child Care Employee Project. The National Staffing Study. Child Care Employee Project. (Berkeley, CA: 1989).

Christensen, K. E. *Impacts of Computer-Mediated Home-Based Work on Women and their Families.* (Washington, DC: Office of Technology Assessment, U.S. Congress, 1985).

Christensen, K. E. *Flexible Staffing and Scheduling.* (New York: The Conference Board, 1989).

Coolsen, P., Seligson, M., and Garbarino, J. *When School's Out and Nobody's Home.* (Chicago, IL: National Committee for the Prevention of Child Abuse, 1986).

Freedman, A. *Human Resources Outlook 1989.* (New York: The Conference Board, 1989).

Friedman, D. E. *Encouraging Employer Supports to Working Parents.* (New York: Center for Public Advocacy Research, 1983).

Friedman, D. E. *Corporate Financial Assistance for Child Care.* (New York: The Conference Board, 1985).

Friedman, D. E. "Elder Care: The Benefit of the 1990's?" *Across the Board*, June, 1986.

Friedman, D. E. Productivity Effects of Family Problems and Programs. (New York: The Conference Board, 1990a).

Friedman D. E. *Update on Employer-Supported Child Care.* (New York: Families and Work Institute, 1990b).

Friedman, D. E., and Kolben, N. *A Report of a Survey of Resource and Referral*

Agencies. (Rochester, MN: National Association of Child Care Resource and Referal Agencies, 1990).

Herzberg, F. *Work and the Nature of Man.* (Cleveland, World Publishing, 1966).

Hofferth, S. L. What is the Demand for and Supply of Child Care in the U.S.? Testimony presented before the House Committee on Education and Labor. (Washington DC: The Urban Institute, 1989).

Krug, D. N., Palmour, V. E., and Ballassai, M. C. *Evaluation of Office of Economic Development Child Development Center.* (Rockville, MD: Westat, Inc., 1972).

Levin, R. *Long-Term Care.* (Washington, DC: Washington Business Group on Health, 1988).

Olmsted, B., and Smith, S. *The Job Sharing Handbook.* (New York: Penguin Books, 1983).

Pierce, J. L., Newstrom, J. W., Dunham, R. B., and Barber, A. E. *Alternative Work Schedules.* (Boston, MA: Allyn and Bacon, Inc., 1989).

Stone, R., Cafferata, G. L., and Sangl, J. *Caregivers of the Frail Elderly: A National Profile.* (Washington, DC: U.S. Department of Human Services, 1986).

The Travelers Companies. The Travelers Employee Caregiver Survey. (Hartford, CT: 1985).

Warshaw, L. J., and Staff. *Employer Support for Employee Caregivers.* (New York: New York Business Group on Health, 1986).

Winnett, R. A., and Neale, M. S. "Results of an Experimental Study on Flextime and Family Life." *Monthly Labor Review,* November, 1985, 29–32.

CHAPTER 13

Barnett, R., & Baruch, G. (1987). Social roles, gender, and psychological distress. In R. Barnett, L. Biener & G. Baruch (Eds.), *Gender and Stress,* pp. 122–141. New York: The Free Press.

Braicker, H. (1988, Aug.). Does superwoman have it the worst? *Working Woman,* p. 65.

Carr-Ruffino, N. (1985). *The promotable woman.* Belmont, CA: Wadsworth.

Colligan, M., Smith, M., & Hurrell, J. (1977). Occupational incidence rates of mental health disorders. *Journal of Human Stress, 3*(3), 34–39.

Cooper, C., & Marshall, J. (1978). *Understanding executive stress.* New York: Petrocelli Books.

Craeger, E. (1991, Oct. 8.). Women and stress. *Wisconsin State Journal,* p. 1C.

Cranwell-Ward, J. (1990). *Thriving on stress.* London: Routledge.

Duke, C., & Sitterly, B. (1988). *A woman's place: Management.* Englewood Cliffs, NJ: Prentice-Hall.

Dunham, R. (1980). Stress. In L. Cummings and R. Dunham (Eds.), *Introduction to organizational behavior: Text and readings* (pp. 593–594). Homewood, IL: Richard D. Irwin.

French, J., & Caplan, R. (1970). Psychosocial factors in coronary heart disease. *Industrial Medicine, 39,* 383–397.

French, J., & Caplan, R. (1972). Organizational stress and individual strain. In A. Marrow (Ed.), *The failure of success.* New York: AMACOM.

Greenberg, J. (1987). *Comprehensive stress management* (2nd ed.). Dubuque, IA: Wm. C. Brown.

Holmes, T., & Rahe, R. (1967). The social readjustment rating scale. *Journal of Psychosomatic Research, 11,* 213–218.

Jick, T., & Mitz, L. (1985). Sex differences in work stress. *Academy of Management Review, 10*(3), 408–420.

Kornhauser, A. (1965). *Mental health of the industrial worker.* New York: Wiley.

McGuigan, F. (1986, Apr.). Alleviating stress in the workplace. *Production,* pp. 33–34.

Nelson, D., & Quick, J. (1985). Professional women: Are distress and disease inevitable? *Academy of Management Review, 10*(2), 206–218.

Schaefer, C., Coyne, J., & Lazarus, R. (1981). The health-related functions of social support. *Journal of Behavioral Medicine, 4*(4), 381–406.

Shaw, M. (1976). *Group dynamics: The psychology of small group behavior* (2nd ed.). New York: McGraw-Hill.

Wardwell, W., Hyman, H., & Bahusen, C. (1964). Stress and coronary disease in three studies. *Journal of Chronic Disease, 17,* 73–84.

Whetton, D., & Cameron, K. (1991). *Developing management skills* (2nd ed.). New York: HarperCollins.

CHAPTER 14

Felker Kaufman, C., Lane, P., & Lindquist, J. (1991). Time congruity in the organization: A proposed quality of life framework. *Journal of Business and Psychology, 6*(1), 79–106.

Mackenzie, A. (1990). *The time trap.* New York: AMACOM.

Odiorne, G. (1975). *Management and the activity trap.* New York: Harper and Row.

Oncken, W., & Wass, D. (1974, Nov.). Management time: Who's got the monkey. *Harvard Business Review,* pp. 75–80.

Schwartz, E., & Mackenzie, A. (1977, Autumn). Time management strategy for dual-career women. *Business Quarterly,* pp. 32–41.

Zuker, E. (no date). *Master your future.* National Association of Female Executives.

CHAPTER 15

Text References

Adler, N., & Izraeli, D. (1988). *Women in management worldwide.* Armonk, NY: M. E. Sharpe.

Jelinek, M., and Adler, N. (1988). Women: World-class managers for global competition. *Academy of Management Executive, 2*(1), 11–19.

Kraar, L. (1988, Mar. 28). The new powers of Asia. *Fortune,* pp. 126–132.

Griffin, R. (1990). *Management* (3rd ed.). Geneva, IL: Houghton Mifflin.

Rossman, M. (1990). *The international businesswoman of the 1990s.* New York: Praeger.

Endnotes, Mariann Jelinek and Nancy J. Adler, "Women: World-Class Managers for Global Competition"

1. Discussions of competition are widespread in the business press and current management literature. See, for instance, Thomas J. Peters, "Competition and Compassion," *California Management Review*, 28(4), Summer 1986, 11–26. Several sources for comparison figures on the U.S. economy and those of our trading partners can be found in Lester Thurow's *The Zero Sum Solution*, New York: Simon and Schuster, 1985; and Bruce Merrifield, U.S. Department of Labor, cited in Lester Thurow's "Why We Can't Have a Wholly Service Economy," *Technology Review*, March 1985.

For a thought provoking look at some of the changes, see also Thomas J. Peters, "A World Turned Upside Down," *Academy of Management Executive*, 1(3), Aug. 1987, 231–242.

2. Carol Gilligan, *In a Different Voice*, Cambridge, MA: Harvard University Press, 1982.

3. See Jeff Hearn and P. Wendy Parkin, "Women, Men and Leadership: A Critical Review of Assumptions, Practices and Change in the Industrialized Nations," *International Studies of Management & Organization*, 16, Fall-Winter 1986, 33–60, for a useful discussion from a thoughtfully international perspective.

4. Melvin Konner, *The Tangled Wing: Biological Constraints on the Human Spirit*, New York: HarperCollins, 1982.

5. Gary N. Powell and D. Anthony Butterfield, "The 'Good Manager': Masculine or Androgynous?" *Academy of Management Journal*, 22(2), 1979, 395–403.

6. U.S. Department of Labor, 1982.

7. A. Trafford, R. Avery, J. Thornton, J. Carey, J. Galloway, and A. Sanoff, "She's Come a Long Way—Or Has She?" *U.S. News and World Report*, Aug. 6, 1984, 44–51.

8. Nancy J. Adler, "Women in International Management: Where Are They?" *California Management Review*, 26(4), Summer 1984, 78–89.

9. See Note 8 above.

10. See Nancy J. Adler's "Do MBAs Want International Careers?" *International Journal of Intercultural Relations*, 10(3), 1986, 277–300; and "Women Do Not Want International Careers and Other Myths About International Management," *Organizational Dynamics*, 13(2), Autumn 1984, 66–79.

11. Nancy J. Adler, "Expecting International Success: Female Managers Overseas," *Columbia Journal of World Business*, 19(2), Autumn 1984, 66–79.

12. N. Thal and P. Cateora, "Opportunities for Women in International Business," *Business Horizons*, 22(6), December 1979, 21–27.

13. There are a number of useful resources for information on women in Japanese management, including the following: Tracy Dahlby, "In Japan, Women Don't Climb the Corporate Ladder," *New York Times*, Sept. 18, 1977; M. M. Osako, "Dilemmas of Japanese Professional Women," *Social Problems*, 26, 1978, 15–25; Marguerite Kaminski and Judith Paiz, "Japanese Women in Management: Where Are They?" *Human Resource Management*, 23(3), Fall 1984, 277–292; and Patricia G. Stinhoff and Kazuko Tanaka, "Women Managers in Japan," *International Studies of Management and Organization*, Fall/Winter 1987, 108–132, reprinted in Nancy

J. Adler and Dafna N. Izraeli (Eds.), *Women in Management Worldwide*, Armonk, NY: M. E. Sharpe, 1988.

14. Blas F. Ople, "Working Managers, Elites," *The Human Spectrum of Development*, Manila, Philippines: Institute for Labor and Management, 1981.

15. Audrey Chan, "Woman Managers in Singapore: Citizens for Tomorrow's Economy," in Nancy J. Adler and Dafna N. Izraeli (Eds.), *Women in Management Worldwide*, Armonk, NY: M. E. Sharpe, 1988.

16. Special issue of *International Studies of Management and Organization*, 17(3–4), Fall-Winter 1987; and Nancy J. Adler and Dafna N. Izraeli (Eds.), *Women in Management Worldwide*, Armonk, NY: M. E. Sharpe, 1988.

17. Nancy J. Adler, "Pacific Basin Managers: A Gaijin, Not a Woman," *Human Resource Management*, 26(2), Summer 1987, 169–192.

18. Eric Morgenthaler, "Women of the World: More U.S. Firms Put Females in Key Posts in Foreign Countries," *Wall Street Journal*, Mar. 16, 1978, 1, 27.

19. Edward T. Hall and Mildred Reed Hall, *Hidden Differences: Doing Business with the Japanese*, Garden City, NY: Anchor Press/Doubleday, 1987.

20. See Note 12.

21. See Note 15.

22. See Note 16.

23. See Note 16.

24. Mark Zimmerman, *How to Do Business with the Japanese*, New York: Random House, 1985.

CHAPTER 16

Nullis, C. (1991, June 15). Swiss women strike in job-bias protest. *Wisconsin State Journal*, p. 5A.

Index

About the Author

MARGARET FOEGEN KARSTEN is an Assistant Professor in the Department of Business Administration at the University of Wisconsin-Platteville. She has had case studies published in *Applications in Personnel/Human Resource Management: Cases, Exercises, and Skill Builders* and in *Cases and Exercises in Personnel/Human Resource Management*. Her articles dealing with extracurricular activities as predictors of later business success for women and men have appeared in the *Central State Business Review*.